A Brief History of the Verb *To Be*

A Brief History of the Verb *To Be*

Andrea Moro
Translated by Bonnie McClellan-Broussard

The MIT Press
Cambridge, Massachusetts
London, England

The translation of this book has been funded by SEPS—Segretariato Europeo per le Pubblicazioni Scientifiche.
Via Val d'Aposa 7—40123 Bologna
seps@seps.it
www.seps.it

© 2017 Massachusetts Institute of Technology

Published by arrangement with The Italian Literary Agency.

All rights reserved. No part of this book may be reproduced in any form by any electronic or mechanical means (including photocopying, recording, or information storage and retrieval) without permission in writing from the publisher.

This book was set in Times LT Std by Toppan Best-set Premedia Limited.

Library of Congress Cataloging-in-Publication Data

Names: Moro, Andrea, author. | McClellan-Broussard, Bonnie, translator.
Title: A brief history of the verb to be / Andrea Moro ; translated by Bonnie McClellan-Broussard.
Description: Cambridge, MA : The MIT Press, [2017] | Includes bibliographical references and index.
Identifiers: LCCN 2017014934 | ISBN 9780262037129 (hardcover : acid-free paper), 9780262552059 (paperback)
Subjects: LCSH: English language--Verb phrase. | English language--Grammar, Historical. | Phraseology.
Classification: LCC PE1319 .M6713 2017 | DDC 415/.6--dc23 LC record available at https://lccn.loc.gov/2017014934

Encore.

This book is dedicated to all the beautiful things that come to an end because they prove to me that I am looking for one that does not.

Such a vain presumption of understanding everything can have no other origin than never having understood anything because, when others have experienced but once the perfect understanding of a single thing and truly tasted what knowledge is, they would know that, of the infinity of other conclusions, they understand nothing.
—Galileo Galilei, *Dialogue Concerning the Two Chief World Systems*, first day

... extensive, which is to say: regarding the multitude of understandable things, which is infinite, human understanding is as nothing, for while one may well understand a thousand propositions, a thousand in the face of infinity is like zero; but given intensive understanding, where this term means intensively, which is perfectly, of some propositions, I say that human intellect understands some things perfectly, and has such absolute certainty as does nature itself.
—Galileo Galilei, *Dialogue Concerning the Two Chief World Systems*, second day

In my opinion the distinctive faculty of an active or intelligent being is the ability to give a meaning to this word: is.
—Jean-Jacques Rousseau, *Emile*

Contents

Only One Passion   ix
Acknowledgments   xi
Prologue   xiii

1   *To Be*—and Not "Being"—or, The Names of the Verb   1
    1.1 The Name of Tense   7
    1.2 The Name of Affirmation   29
    1.3 The Name of Identity   44

2   Anatomy of a Sentence   69
    2.1 The Calm before the Storm   81
    2.2 Molecules of Words   85
    2.3 The Anomaly of the Copula: The Asymmetry That Isn't There   121

3   The Strange Case of Verbs without Subjects   127
    3.1 The Quasi-Copula   129
    3.2 *Is* and *There Is*   142
    3.3 "Non-Euclidean" Grammars: Concerning the Rise and Fall of the Subject Postulate   152
    3.4 The Unified Theory of Copular Sentences   161
    3.5 *There Is*, or "And Yet It Moves"   171

4 Epilogues between Language and Necessity 193
4.1 The Form of Grammar: Between Linearity and Hierarchy 195
4.2 Language in the Brain 205
4.3 Losing and Acquiring the Copula 220

Afterword 233
Notes 235
Bibliography 263
Index 281

Only One Passion

There is a God-shaped void in the heart of every person and it can never be filled by anything.
—Blaise Pascal, apocryphal quote

One can become passionate about anything: there are those who forever pursue never-before-heard music, those who hunt for an ideal form, those who design a perfect recipe, others who plunge into a parallel universe in the attempt to understand a mathematical formula. I know people who do whatever they do, looking through the lens of a passion, like a polarized filter. Sometimes, pursuing a passion, one can follow roads that would otherwise never have been traveled, explore places inhabited by reason and imagination; one can glimpse the form of questions that would otherwise never have been posed.

I am passionate about a verb: the verb *to be*. Certainly it's only one passion, but it's passion that reawakens true demands, the demands of the truth. What you're about to read is the history, as I tell it, of the analysis of the verb *to be* and of the discovery of a formula that responds to some crucial questions about this verb. Like all histories, this one is partial, subjective, and limited, but perhaps only by being partial, subjective, and limited can a history be comprehensible. Why read this history? Because I'm convinced that only by knowing the histories behind formulas can we come to understand them fully, and because, above all, by telling you about my passion, the desire to discover new formulas will arise in you.

* * *

The story of the notion of the copula told here is a development of the appendix of a volume dedicated to the structure of copular phrases (Moro 1997), in turn based on an article (Moro 1988) that takes up the theme of my dissertation (Moro 1987). The need for a history of the term was justified in that technical volume by the need to orient the reader in an intricate bibliography built up over the centuries by authors who were not always aware of the existence of approaches that were different and sometimes incompatible with each other. Since Moro 1997 (which contains a detailed discussion full of bibliographic citations), other works dealing with the subject have been published, and updated a bit at a time, but they preserve the same basic intuition that I will present here. The most succinct version is my essay "Copular Sentences" that, along with many pertinent essays by other authors, may be found in *The Blackwell Companion to Syntax* (Moro 2006a; see also Moro in press a, in press b).

Acknowledgments

Except the Lord build the house, they labor in vain that build it.
—Psalm 127

I was twenty-three years old when my teacher Giorgio Graffi handed me problem of the verb *to be*; it was only many years later that I understood that a teacher's job, in addition to transmitting a passion, is to direct students toward issues that aren't so difficult that they can't be solved, but not so easy that the students aren't allowed to express their own ideas. Since that day, I've never abandoned the theory of sentences with the verb *to be*, and I always return to it with new reflections. Many people have accompanied me along this path in addition to Giorgio Graffi: Luigi Burzio, Stefano Cappa, Ersilia Cattaneo, Gennaro Chierchia, Noam Chomsky, Guglielmo Cinque, Marcel den Dikken, Robert Frank, Morris Halle, Richard Kayne, Giuseppe Longobardi, Luigi Rizzi, Alessandra Tomaselli, and Raffaella Zanuttini. A man is defined within the context of the encounters he experiences and, though I've done nothing to deserve it, I've had the privilege of meeting these people.

I'm also indebted to friends who've had the patience to read this layperson's version of my research on the verb *to be* and to Maurizio Bruno and Remigio Allegri of Adelphi Publishing, who, with great competence and critical ability, not only ferreted out errors of all kinds, but also gave me valuable advice on how to improve this book, touching on issues I would have never been aware of on my own. Writing for interested nonspecialists is a mysterious undertaking, which follows no preestablished paths, and Maurizio's and Remigio's suggestions have been invaluable for the Italian edition; as for the English one, I can't say if I'm more grateful for or impressed by the inventive and critical spirit that Bonnie McClellan-Broussard and Anne Mark put into translating and copyediting the original text, respectively. Also, my special gratitude goes to Marc Lowenthal at MIT Press for fostering these ideas on language and for sharing the passion for tantalizing efforts to understand reality. I would like to thank Silvia Albertini, Valentina Bambini, Robert Berwick, Franco Bottoni, Stefano Cappa, Gennaro Chierchia, Noam Chomsky, Denis Delfitto, Michele Di Francesco, Alberto Ferrari, Robert Frank, Giorgio Graffi, Ciro Greco, Richard Kayne, Umberto Manfredini, Giovanni Nava, Andrew Nevins, Henk van Riemsdijk, Marco Riva, Luigi Rizzi, Rosella Testera, Marco Tettamanti, Roberto Tintinelli, Alessandra Tomaselli, Raffaella Zanuttini, and Marco Vigevani, my Italian literary agent and friend, who gave me a great deal of encouragement to write this book and get it translated. Without the support of all these people, their critical ability, and—miraculously—their affection, I wouldn't have been able to complete the project. A final thank-you to my grandma "Nonna P," who gave me the gift of a method for studying: without that night that I spent as a boy with you and *Richard the Lionheart*, none of this would have been possible.

Prologue

For I see a man must either resolve to put out nothing new or to become a slave to defend it.
—Isaac Newton

London 1918. As an inmate of an overcrowded Brixton prison, someone writes, "It is a disgrace to the human race that it has chosen to employ the same word 'is' for these two entirely different ideas." Who could inveigh against a verb while World War I was raging outside? That man was Bertrand Russell, one of the twentieth century's most influential intellectuals; Russell had been imprisoned just that year for his pacifist activities against the United Kingdom's participation in the war. During his imprisonment, based on a series of conferences he had held the previous year, the great philosopher wrote this sentence in the pages of his *Introduction to Mathematical Philosophy* (Russell 1919, 172), an important book that he published the next year, once the war was over and with it his imprisonment. To complicate the matter further: what was an invective against the verb *to be* doing in a book about mathematics? And what ideas was Russell writing about?

It's a long story, a story that began at least in the fourth century BC, when Aristotle started to deal with the verb *to be* in his treatises. A story that has never been interrupted: it traversed the duels of medieval logic, it passed through the battles between the great geniuses of the Port-Royal school in the seventeenth century, it influenced the grand nineteenth-century project of mapping the family tree of languages, to finally end up on a mathematician's table at the beginning of the twentieth century. In truth, Russell wasn't the last person to deal with the verb *to be*, and the voyage of this verb doesn't end here: others have discussed it after him, and in fact, the debate is still very much alive.

But what's so special about this verb, one that was able to lead Antoine Arnauld—the much-persecuted Jansenist priest who inspired one of the most important texts in the entire history of linguistics, the *Port-Royal Grammar*—to write that if languages were to have only one verb, it would be the verb *to be*, the only authentic one? This is the story we'll deal with here. We'll try to dismantle Russell's preoccupations, demonstrating that the verb *to be* isn't ambiguous at all and that it is, definitively, not a disgrace to the human race.

But allow me one premise.

It's said that the "Homeric question"—the way in which every culture has proposed and resolved the question of the authorship of the *Iliad* and the *Odyssey*—is something of a common thread throughout civilization. By following it, we can find the key to a culture and extract from it a representative image, a "sample," so to speak, of its essence. The interpretation of the verb *to be* is, in a certain sense, the "Homeric question of linguistics": understanding how each age has interpreted this verb leads to an understanding of how language has been considered in its entirety in the various periods that mark the history of (Western) culture. The parentheses used here are mandatory; we'll soon see why, but it's enough for now to hint at the reason for so much caution by saying that in at least one-third of known languages the verb *to be* doesn't exist. So perhaps the disgraced are fewer than previously thought, but since those of us who *do* speak languages with the verb *to be* and its equivalents are squarely in that category, we might as well determine whether the disgrace is real or merely presumed.

If you're willing to trust a would-be mathematician, I'll also say that sentences with the verb *to be* are in some ways the Fermat's theorem of linguistics: to demonstrate this theorem, mathematicians have had to resort to (almost) all areas of their discipline, as those who have entered the Borges-like labyrinths that lie behind this innocent door know quite well. Sentences that use the verb *to be* also have deep and complex roots, and understanding their structure helps us to understand the nature and the general architecture of human language. So, what I promise you is a journey not only through time but also—so to speak—through the geography of linguistics, through the various areas into which the continent of natural languages is naturally divided. This journey through linguistic time and place will build on classical antiquity, where the problems of the nature and forms of language were first posed. We'll traverse vast and dangerous regions, narrow passages, and daring crossings, but I want to advise you that, at present, I won't give a detailed account; we're only dealing with the notes of a curious tourist who was drawn into an exciting journey by those who preceded him.

... dum taxat rerum magnarum parva potest res exemplare dare et vestigia notitiai.
... so far as it goes, a small phenomenon can offer an image of larger events and a track toward their knowledge.
—Lucretius, *De rerum natura*

1 *To Be*—and Not "Being"—or, The Names of the Verb

"Listen then," as they (the story-tellers) say, "to a very pretty story"; which you, I dare say, will take for a fable, but I regard as a true story: for all that I am about to say I wish to be regarded as true.
—Plato, *Gorgias*

We don't see the light. We only see the effects that it has on objects. We know of its existence only because it's reflected by what it encounters in its path, thus making objects visible that we wouldn't otherwise see. So a nothing, illuminated by another nothing, becomes something. Words work the same way: they don't have content in and of themselves, but if they encounter someone who listens to them, they become something. Analyzing language is like analyzing light. We find ourselves in the same situation: we learn to know that what's scrolling under our eyes right now has a meaning only because our brains are built to comprehend these sentences as instructions to produce meaning, not because meaning resides in the sentences. And what we can hope to decipher, at least for now, is the structure of these instructions: that is, their rules, the primitive elements they are composed of and the laws that govern how these elements are combined, the extent to which these instructions may vary, and maybe eventually, but only eventually, the way in which they are inscribed in our bodies. Certainly, this approach will give short shrift to all that language conveys: for example, emotions, art, and poetry are left out, but we have no reasonable alternatives for moving forward. It's as if we were in the position of someone who, having to describe a caress, gave only the anatomy of a hand: it wouldn't be easy to distinguish a caress from a slap, but if nothing else we'd be able to begin by not confusing it with a kick.

Instead, we often deceive ourselves: we see sense and perfection where neither sense nor perfection exists, at least no more than my eye or my left foot has sense. In our voyage to discover the facts and the mysteries of the verb *to be*, we have to take this into account. But there's no reason to insist on this point at the moment. Only by dirtying our hands with data and concrete cases can we succeed in understanding this aspect of the study of language. Certainly the verb *to be* is not an easy subject, enmeshed as it is in philosophical, metaphysical, theological, and, of course, linguistic ruminations from every era. The verb *to be* is contested by many disciplines, and often—as I hope will be clear at the end of this book—this has clouded the discussion, leading to contradictory conclusions.

The first thing we need to get rid of is the belief that the verb *to be* has an equivalent in every language. Nothing could be further from the truth, and any generalization based on such an assumption is destined to wither miserably when faced with the actual evidence. This is not to say, of course, that all analyses of the verb *to be* that don't consider it as a simple accident—a peculiar characteristic of some of the world's languages—should be thrown out, but it does mean that above all we must know how things stand. We're at a delicate point in our journey: we must have an idea, even if an approximate one, of the degree to which the verb *to be* exists in the world's languages, even if we haven't yet clarified exactly what we're talking about. Unfortunately, we always find ourselves in a similar paradoxical situation every time we talk about the structure of language because, as one of the fathers of modern linguistics, Ferdinand de Saussure, said: in language, *tout se tient*—it's all interconnected. So it's like the map of a city; you can't understand clearly where a street leads if you don't first have an idea of how the city is laid out, and you can't understand the city until you know which streets wind their way through it. Likewise, we can't talk about the verb *to be* unless we first understand its position within language. However, given that we have to begin somewhere, let's begin by surveying the prevalence of the verb *to be* in world languages and by considering what we know about it intuitively as speakers, independently of theoretical reflections and any comparative examination.

If we consult the *World Atlas of Linguistic Structures Online* (*WALS*; Haspelmath et al. 2008), one of the most complete and detailed atlases of contemporary linguistics, we realize immediately how diffuse the verb *to be* and its equivalents are in the world's languages.[1] In a representative sample of 386 languages, where 211 exhibit the verb *to be* or its equivalent, there are a good 175 where not only is there no equivalent verb: there's nothing. To be clear, there are languages in which to say *John is a teacher*, you say something like *John a teacher*. Of course, things are not that simple; reality is much more varied, and obviously, in not all of these languages is a word corresponding to *to be* lacking in the places where we find it in English. At one extreme are languages like Italian and English, where the verb *to be* is always necessary. At the opposite extreme are languages like Sinhala (spoken in Sri Lanka) and Tubu (spoken in Libya) where the verb *to be* doesn't exist (Australia and New Guinea are also home to a striking concentration of languages of this type). Finally, there are, as it were, intermediate cases, where the verb *to be* is absent but only under certain conditions: in Russian and Maltese, for example, the verb *to be* is never used in the present; this is also the case in Hungarian, where the verb *to be* is omitted whenever the sentence has a third person subject.

If we look at the verb *to be*, as a verb, which is to say distinct from the other parts of speech such as adjectives and pronouns, the situation becomes even more complex. In Hebrew, for example, when it is expressed, the grammatical element that has the function of the verb *to be* in English takes the form of a personal pronoun; so, to say that John is a teacher I can say the equivalent of *John a teacher* or *John he a teacher*. Cases of this type—those that can have a pronoun (personal or demonstrative) in the place where English has the verb *to be*—are very frequent in northern and central Asia, North Africa, the Middle East, eastern Indonesia, and Melanesia. Similarly in Turkish, an agglutinative language, the pronoun is fused into a single word with the predicate, and to say *I am Turkish* one simply says *turkum*, where the suffix *-um* expresses the pronoun in its function as the verb *to be*.

And there's more: if we distinguish between sentences that express locative predicates, such as *John is in the garden*, and sentences like *John is a gardener*, the situation is even more intricate. Referring again to the previous sample from *WALS*, of the 386 languages only 117 use the same verb for the two types of sentences. Spanish, for example, has respectively *Juan está en el jardín* and *Juan es un jardinero*; in Irish, to say *He is a teacher* one says *Muinteoir é* (lit., 'is teacher he'), while to say *He is in the room* one says *Ta sé sa tesomra* (lit., 'stays he in the room'); and the same is true for Mokilese (spoken in Oceania) and Waskia (spoken in New Guinea), as it is for many other languages. Not only that, but with respect to locative predicates, there are languages that are called "mixed," like Dutch, where we find more words used like the verb *to be* and more verbs used to express locative predicates.

Let's stop there. Despite its fragmentary nature, this excursus should convince us that to regard the verb *to be* as universal would constitute an embarrassing stretch. That said, we can't deny that the verb *to be*, principally in Ancient Greek and then in modern languages (Romance and Germanic languages in particular), has truly served as a point of accumulation for many thinkers' ideas, guided by the most disparate perspectives. In the following chapters, we'll see the main lines of analysis that have led to a "theory of the verb *to be*"; I will try to show how, in many cases, different and often irreconcilable positions are hidden beneath an apparent unity. After reviewing these lines of analysis, we'll see how, even today, the verb *to be* constitutes a focal point of linguistics and, in some ways, a field of inquiry that opens unexpected doors onto the general architecture of human language. The verb *to be* is a bit like the fruit fly in genetics, the famous *Drosophila melanogaster*: it may appear innocent and secondary but, if properly analyzed, it proves to be a useful model for deciphering much more complex architectures.

Having arrived at this point, it will be useful to make explicit a premise only implied until now. What I'm speaking about must be clearly distinguished from that about which I don't know what to say. I'm dealing with the verb *to be* as an element in a linguistic system, and not with the meaning with which the word *being* is often used in the philosophical tradition: so, *to be*—and not "being"—is all I'll talk about here; as for the rest, I'll gladly remain silent.

To tell the truth, it's no surprise that it was the verb *to be* that became, first in the Greco-Latin tradition and then in the modern tradition, a key term in philosophical thought.[2] To better understand the origins of the philosophical meaning of the verb *to be*, it is perhaps useful to dwell on a different—yet in many ways similar—case, that of the verb *to do*. For convenience, we use a verb that is normally used to express the performing of an action (*do a somersault*, *do your homework*, etc.) to indicate any conceivable action. Used in an absolute manner (i.e., without a complement), the verb *to do* then becomes a sort of abbreviation, a "verbal pronoun," which stands for 'to do something', or rather 'to do anything'. A similar process has led to the use of the verb *to be*, as philosophers interpret it, to mean 'to exist'. Of each entity, abstract or concrete, that exists (is), one should be able to say something. That is, one should be able to assign a predicate to everything and, typically in definitions, this happens through the use of the verb *to be* (*This is a butterfly*, *Seventeen is a prime number*, *Francesca is a physicist*, …). Just as the verb *to do* is used as an abbreviation for all conceivable actions, so the verb *to be* on its own is used as an abbreviation to indicate the application of (at least one among) all conceivable predicates—"to be anything," and therefore, by way of metonymy, to be the subject of a predicate. Nevertheless, on its own, and this is the point, *to be* doesn't express a predicate, and *to do* doesn't express an action (we'll return later to the theme of the verb *to be* as something distinct from predicates). It is then up to the philosophers to distinguish and weigh what the ontological implications related to being able to be subject to predication are. What's important to us here is that not every ontological, or perhaps more generally philosophical, discourse can be based on the claim of linguistic evidence.

So, this is the limit of our research even if, despite this drastic reduction of the field, the flow of exchange to and from philosophy will prove to be anything but trivial.

Before entering into the heart of the current debate on the nature and role of the verb *to be*, in this chapter we'll take a brief look at what have been the most important schools of thought over the centuries. A final note: throughout this introductory discussion I have never used the technical term "copula": such an omission in a book about the verb *to be* cannot be accidental. The fact is that, contrary to what is often thought, this term is more than a little problematic, as much from a philological point of view as from an interpretive one, despite its broad use even in grammar textbooks.

Certainly, in the history of science it's not the only case in which a well-established technical term with a long tradition hides interpretations that are very different, if not incompatible. Let's think about words like *atom*, *gene*, or *energy*: since their introduction they've never been abandoned, yet their meaning has changed profoundly over the centuries. To the ancient Greeks, who introduced the term "atom," it meant 'indivisible', while we all know that one of the principal objectives of contemporary atomic physics is to discover how many and what parts an atom can be broken down into.

Something similar happened to the word "copula": over the centuries, the meaning of this term has undergone transformations and acquired new uses, and sometimes it has also been falsely attributed to thinkers who have never used it—if only because they lived before it was introduced.

Patiently sifting through Western linguistic tradition, almost as if it were a detective story, it's possible to find at least three schools of thought that regarded the verb *to be*, so to speak, as the name of three different concepts closely dependent upon the manner in which their contemporary linguistics interpreted the nature of language in general: as the name of tense, as the name of affirmation, and as the name of identity. Understanding how the verb *to be* has been described in language also means understanding what the general perspective is from which the latter is viewed—a unique opportunity. Let's begin with classical antiquity.

1.1 The Name of Tense

A very simple way to begin to understand how the verb *to be* functions is to reflect upon a series of example sentences such as *A picture of the wall caused the riot, A picture of the wall will cause the riot, A picture of the wall causes the riot*, and so on, and to compare it with another series: *A picture of the wall was the cause of the riot, A picture of the wall will be the cause of the riot, A picture of the wall is the cause of the riot*, and so on. One immediately gathers that these two series are associated with one another. The sentences are practically pairs of synonyms; that is, what varies in one series is the verb *to be*, and in the other the inflection of the verb *to cause*. As a first approximation, therefore, we can say that the verb *to be* is the support for verbal inflection when the sentence contains no verb with which to express it. If we then continue our exploration and focus on the two series of sentences separately, we realize that what varies between the sentences on the level of meaning is only the tense.

It's easy to say the word "time." But it will come as no surprise that the notion of time is in reality anything but simple. It's important to distinguish between grammatical "time" (or tense) and physical "time." In Italian, both of these concepts are expressed with the polysemous word *tempo*. Unlike Italian, languages such as English use two different terms: *tense* for the grammatical concept and *time* for the physical one. Of course, the relationship between the two terms is not causal, but it is interesting to note that both, despite their ease of use, are in fact elusive. Let's start by trying to think about the notion of physical time. How do we know that time exists? Just look at a clock. But what is a clock? Let's look at the simple case of a clock with hands: we're talking about a mechanism that translates the variations of time into regular variations of space (the movement of the hands). Thus, we understand that time passes because our memory makes us compare the two different positions of the clock's hands, and puts them into an order coherent with the laws of space. Can we therefore define time as the perception of the coherent order of different spatial configurations? Doesn't the order in which we place the different images perhaps already admit that we know what time is? Why, for example, do we not "see" the hands go backward? But if we admit that the differences in time are perceived as differences in spatial position, does that mean that when nothing changes in perceivable space, time doesn't pass? Obviously not. Or rather, one might possibly start from here and define time as the only thing that changes *regardless*, even when everything remains (apparently) the same. The question thus becomes a different one and seems to return us to our point of departure: how do we know that something changes regardless? Better if we stop here. It's evident that we're not confronting a simple notion, and I won't even try to address it in a systematic way; I'll limit myself to repeating what St. Augustine says in his *Confessions*: "Therefore what is time? If no one asks me, I know; if I want to explain it to someone who asks me, I don't know" (XI, 14–17).

Yet this notion—intuitive, but difficult to grasp rationally—comes to be encoded in human language in a sophisticated way, so sophisticated that no one has yet managed to develop a theory that describes in detail what grammatical "time" is and how it works.[3]

To complicate the scenario, we add another element that refers in some way to physical time, so-called *aspect*. Aspect, a notion that began to be cultivated and addressed in a systematic way in the grammar of the Stoics, refers not so much to the moment when a certain event occurs with respect to another moment, as to whether it has been completely or incompletely accomplished. It does not appear that the Stoics had a specific term for "aspect" and, truthfully, the very history of the development of this term's technical meaning is quite complex and somewhat circuitous: the starting point is probably the Greek *eídos* 'view, appearance, form, idea', which came to us through its translation into Russian *vid* (also linked to the same Indo-European root of *eídos*), by way of nineteenth-century Slavic linguistics. Certainly it's no coincidence that the Stoics themselves were the ones to grasp the significance of this important characteristic of the grammatical system (Dahl 1994). The refined linguistic thought of the Stoics, which by the intrinsic nature of their philosophy placed language at the center of their contemplation, had enormous influence in later centuries. For instance, the Stoics are responsible for the notion of grammatical case and the canonical classification of cases (nominative, dative, genitive, etc.), as well as much of the terminology that refers to the structural organization of verbs; they also gave rise to etymology and introduced such a precise theory of meaning that it can be seen, in some ways, as a forerunner of modern semiotics. This inestimable cultural heritage certainly came to us through the hands of Dionysius Thrax, an Alexandrian grammarian who lived in the second century BC, who, although neither able to carry through the Stoics' program nor preserve it from some inevitable confusion, wrote what can be considered the first extant grammar known to us—the *Téchne grammatiké*, or *Ars grammatica* in Latin—which in fact became the reference text for thirteen centuries, so much so that a distinguished twentieth-century scholar said that every contemporary grammar book owes some debt to Dionysius Thrax (Forbes 1933, as cited in Robins 1967, 31n58).

But let's return to verbal aspect. A simple example should clarify this interesting property of natural languages. If I say *I crossed the stream*, I have effectively crossed the stream. If instead I say *I was crossing the stream*, I'm still referring to a past event, the crossing of the stream, but that's not to say that I've accomplished it, or that I've reached the other side. This insight becomes evident as soon as we want to complete the two previous sentences by adding *when something prevented me from reaching the other side.* In the first case, the addition is impossible and creates a contradictory sentence: *I crossed the stream when something prevented me from reaching the other side.* In the second, however, the addition makes perfect sense: *I was crossing the stream when something prevented me from reaching the other side.*

The terminology commonly used to refer to verbs is of no help in distinguishing between tense and aspect. The most striking case is the term "imperfect": obviously, it has nothing to do with perfection. This term is a translation from the Latin *imperfectum*, which is simply the negation of *perfectum* (from *perficio*), understood as 'done completely'. The error—so to speak—is therefore in classifying the imperfect as a tense and in comparing it to the simple past tense. They are both in the past—and one is certainly not less worthy of "perfection" than the other. The difference between them is "aspectual": in the first case, the action wasn't fully completed, it's not accomplished; in the second, it is. For simplicity's sake, and above all because this property doesn't specifically pertain to the verb *to be*, we'll continue to focus only on tense and not on aspect, simply accepting the traditional classification.[4]

One of the descriptive systems for tense in natural languages dates back to a German physicist active in the first half of the twentieth century, Hans Reichenbach, who was also involved in the philosophy of science and in particular the structure of space-time in the theory of general relativity. Reichenbach's system (Reichenbach 1947), although not entirely satisfactory, still remains an essential reference for anyone dealing with this subject. Reichenbach introduces a system based on three coordinates: speech time, the moment in which the sentence is spoken (S); event time, the time of the event being talked about (E); and reference time, the moment that the speaker is using as a reference time relative to the event (R). The combinations (direct and indirect) between these three coordinates generate a grid of conceivable temporal relationships. All native speakers of Romance languages who have tried to learn English know from experience how much the grammatical systems that implement temporal relationships in the two languages differ and how difficult it is to equip ourselves with a model that relates the two systems. No wonder then that some linguists, faced with the complexity of the problem, leave the field with a declaration of surrender such as this: "That any overall semantic analysis can be given of the inflections of all the verbs in a language is a naive and unwarrantable assumption" (Robins 1967, 30). Also, in many languages some temporal relationships, understandable and distinct on the semantic level, flow together into the same tense on the grammatical level (think for example of Italian as it's spoken in the north of the country, where the present perfect typically replaces the past absolute in common speech without affecting the communication system). There are also cases where a language doesn't distinguish on the grammatical level some of the forms that are hypothetically possible on a purely combinatorial basis. For example, the English form *I would have been walking* (in Italian literally, *io ausiliare-condizionale avere stato camminante*), which combines unreality (*would*), anteriority (*have*), and continuity (*been...-ing*), can't be directly translated into an Italian verbal form. We need to paraphrase, something like *Sarei stato nella condizione di star camminando*, as the "literal" translation *Sarei stato camminante[5] isn't admissible. To give a simple example of Reichenbach's system of coordinates: if I say *Mary studies*, the three coordinates coincide; if I say *Mary will study*, the coordinate that refers to the event (the fact that Mary studies) differs from the moment of utterance (the moment when I utter the sentence *Mary will study*), in that the event follows the utterance; if I say *Mary would have studied*, things become even more complex because—in one possible reading, one that takes it as a fact that there was a time when Mary actually started studying—not only does the time that refers to the event differ from the time of utterance, but the time that the speaker chose as reference precedes both the time of the utterance and the time of the event itself (i.e., the fact that Mary studies occurs at a time earlier than the utterance and following a period in the past to which I refer).

The situation is becoming vertiginously complex, but it's not necessary for us to enter into the intricate and for the most part still unsolved problems concerning the representation (and the grammaticalization) of temporal references in natural languages; for this topic, see Bertinetto 1986, Hornstein 1990, ter Meulen 1997, Giorgi and Pianesi 1998, Bonomi and Zucchi 2001, Guéron and Lecarme 2004, and the references cited therein. What I want to point out is that the verb *to be* is integrated into this system in an essential way. In fact, recalling the analogy between the verb *to be* and verbal inflection, if I say *A picture of the wall was the cause of the riot* or *A picture of the wall will be the cause of the riot*, the only thing that is modulated is precisely the temporal reference, while everything else is left intact.

The verb *to be*—and its equivalents—is therefore one of the complex mechanisms with which some human languages express tense in their grammatical systems. Expressing tense, however, not only has an important role from the general cognitive point of view; expressing tense also means constructing a complex linguistic object that has special properties, as we'll see in a moment. In fact, this had already been noticed by none other than Aristotle.

Ipse *Non* Dixit: *The Copula in Aristotle*

Ipse dixit: he said it; therefore, it's true. Such was the esteem and good fortune of Aristotle, from classical antiquity down to well beyond the Middle Ages and the Renaissance, that it was enough for a thing to have been said by him for it to be believed undoubtedly true. However, there are cases where words were put into Aristotle's mouth that he never said. One of these involves the copula; we'll soon see why.

Aristotle, observing in his own language phenomena similar to those I've mentioned in regard to pairs of sentences like *A picture of the wall caused the riot* and *A picture of the wall was the cause of the riot*, must have been quite impressed by the particular phenomenon that occurs in the sentences above, to the point that it became a central point in his theory of language. But why did Aristotle deal with language? And why does the verb *to be* hold such an important place in his system? People in the Classical

Greek culture were generally very interested in language, but caution should be exercised in attributing interests and results. First and foremost, language interested them as a communication tool: writing well and speaking well in public were certainly very important (and profitable). As is the case today, those who knew how to write and speak in public had an enormous advantage over the competition, in any field of endeavor. Writing schools, where one learned grammar, and schools of rhetoric, where one learned public speaking, were widespread, not only in the Classical era and the Hellenistic period. In Rome as well, in both the Republican and the Imperial eras, generations of students were shipped to Athens by their families to attend the large schools that flourished there, modeled on that of Isocrates, founded at the beginning of the fourth century BC. There they would learn the art of writing and public speaking in Greek, but also in Latin. The reason why the Greek tradition was especially coveted is obviously neither casual nor exotic, and it was connected to two special circumstances of Greek history.

The first, certainly more contingent fact is that in Greece and *Magna Graecia* several varieties of Greek were spoken, at least three branches corresponding to the Doric, Aeolic, and Ionian colonies. The second is that the Homeric poems, already considered by contemporaries as an essential foundation of culture, show evident linguistic contaminations, and the ancient philologists who sought a reconstruction faithful to the poems' original form felt the need to clean up the text—which in turn led to new contaminations. So when Alexander the Great decided to collect together all of the Greek writings of his time, there was the problem of how to choose among the various versions. This mammoth undertaking—no less ambitious than the construction of the Museum, the edifice dedicated to the muses that Alexander wanted built in the city founded by him—amassed such a concentration of knowledge that it established grammar in a virtually definitive way. One of the fascinating traces of the Greeks' method of linguistic analysis, in addition to the taxonomic and descriptive ones that were manifested in the canonization of grammar, is clearly visible in the two antithetical ways of seeing what makes human language a "meaningful" system, traditionally labeled as the polemic between *anomalists* and *analogists* (see Colson 1919 and the references cited therein, in particular the classic works of Heymann Steinthal (Steinthal 1863)).[6] The anomalist sees language as something that is generated on the basis of a totally symmetrical and monotonous system, where everything is aligned in rigid and predictable proportions, like an immense crystalline lattice; meaning lies in the unforeseen breaking of this lattice: the anomaly. On the other hand, the analogist thinks that language arises from an amorphous mass of elements, where meaning can only emerge from the manifestation of systematic correspondences that organize the formless, irregular magma: analogies. These two positions, so antithetical as to be obviously irreconcilable, had a huge practical effect on the cataloguing of written material and were radicalized into two different schools and the two schools into two people: Aristarchus of Samothrace, sixth director of the library of Alexandria, for the analogists, and for the anomalists, Crates of Mallus, head of the school of Pergamum, a flourishing Greek city on the coast of what is today Turkey. This tension between those who were seeking hidden regularity in the sea of differences and those who instead focused on cases that stood out in a network of similarities has never been completely resolved and may well be regarded as an archetype of all modes of observing phenomenal reality. Not only in antiquity—renowned on this issue are both the surviving passages of Varro's *De lingua latina* and the fragments of *De analogia* dedicated to Cicero by Julius Caesar, who, according to Suetonius, wrote it as he crossed the Alps with his army—but even today, in almost all fields of knowledge, although this is almost never explicitly admitted, this polarization distinguishes two paradigms of how to look at the world. Italo Calvino, in his *Lezioni americane* (published in English as *Six Memos for the Next Millennium*), reports a quote from Massimo Piattelli-Palmarini, in turn influenced by Henri Atlan (Atlan 1979), which I think well represents this opposition in modern science:

> Among the scientific books into which I poke my nose in search of stimulus for the imagination, I recently happened to read that the models for the process of formation of living beings 'are best visualized by the *crystal* on one side (invariance of specific structures) and the *flame* on the other (constancy of external forms in spite of relentless internal agitation).' ... The contrasting images of flame and crystal are used to make visible the alternatives offered to biology, and from this pass on to theories of language and the ability to learn. (Calvino 1988, 70–71)[7]

So, from language to biology and back: the history of ideas is encyclopedic in the etymological sense.

But we must stop here: surely, the Alexandrian (and more generally the Hellenistic) era was a formidable one, destined to lay the foundations of our entire civilization. Practically in the same era, geometry was also canonized due to the work of Euclid, and it's truly amazing how geometry and grammar—which have remained substantially unchanged from that time to this—have been and still are the basis for the education of new generations of schoolchildren throughout the West, and indeed almost all over the world. This fact alone justifies taking an interest in how grammar functions. But it's not the only one, and perhaps not even the most important.

Along with this philological interest, evidently not by chance, philosophical reflection on language in all its various facets has always played an active role in Greek thought—in fact, the Greeks first developed it—and by "philosophical reflection" I mean not so much the description of the grammatical system as the analysis of the nature and the function of language. Plato—for example, in the famous dialogue *Cratylus* (but also in *Theaetetus* and the

Sophist)—had already touched on two key points of the philosophy of language when he asked if language originated from convention (*nómos*) or nature (*phýsis*) and what mechanisms hold the words of a sentence together. In regard to the second issue, that of the mysterious glue that unites nouns and verbs, Plato makes use of a musical metaphor; in fact, he uses the verb *harmóttein* 'harmonize', 'to fit well within a composition', the same metaphor that we use today when, confronted with a sentence like *John run, we say that the subject and the predicate don't "agree" (*si accorda* in Italian, which—in the nonreflexive form *accordare*—can mean 'to tune', as a musical instrument). Of course, not all reflection on language ends with Plato, but it's not entirely out of place to reiterate, in this area as well, Alfred North Whitehead's famous assertion that all of Western philosophy would develop as "footnotes" to the Platonic dialogues.

Aristotle, Plato's student, inherited from the master this centrality of language in his philosophical work. His interest in language isn't so much that of the grammarian or rhetorician—someone who wants to teach writing and public speaking—as that of one who understands that it's the primary path to accessing the logical structures of reasoning. It is in this scenario that Aristotle's reflections on the verb *to be* develop in many of his writings, but in particular in his essays *Categories* and *De interpretatione* (On Interpretation), and in the *Poetics*.

The first, fundamental thing to observe is that Aristotle does not use specific technical terms to talk about the verb *to be*. And here we immediately encounter one of the big misunderstandings born around the term "copula." Attributing to Aristotle the use of this term for the verb *to be* is a glaring anachronism—as we'll see in the next section, it wasn't introduced until the Middle Ages—an anachronism, though so firmly established that it is often taken for granted and as a given, even in authoritative critical texts such as that of John Ackrill (Ackrill 1963), well known in the Anglo-Saxon world where it is perhaps the most cited.[8] Aristotle, when speaking of the verb *to be*, simply used the third person present indicative form, or the infinitive, preceded by a neutral article: *tó estí(n)* 'the it is' or *tó eînai* 'the *to be*'. The only alternative technical term used by Aristotle, even if rarely, is *sýndesmos*: but *sýndesmos* means 'conjunction' and is also used to talk about the word *kaí*, which in Greek is used for the conjunction *and*. But what a difference between saying *Paul is Francesca* and saying *Paul and Francesca*—although by mere coincidence exactly the same vowel is used for both in Italian (*è* /ɛ/ for *is* and *e* /e/ for *and*, one open and the other closed).

So, we'll proceed step by step, reconstructing the theory of the verb *to be* according to Aristotle directly from his own words. Let's start by saying that Aristotle narrows his focus to the types of language objects that are of greatest interest to those concerned with logic: the so-called "declarative" sentences (apofantic). But what is a sentence? If we faced this question seriously, the book you have in hand would weigh at least three times as much. Giorgio Graffi, one of the most authoritative contemporary scholars of the history of linguistics, building on the calculations of John Ries (1931) and Eugen Seidel (1935), has estimated the number of existing definitions of *sentence* in the middle of the last century at more than three hundred (Graffi 2001). It's curious that there's such difficulty in finding a common definition of a concept that's so central, especially if we consider that even children use the word "sentence" casually without having taken any general linguistics courses. It's certainly not the first and only case: just think of the term "word," whose meaning seems simple but isn't at all. As in mathematics or in physics, it also happens in linguistics that, in order to develop a line of reasoning, it's not always necessary to have complete definitions of the elements involved. For example, it's possible to perform complex calculations or to study functions without having a definition of *number*, or to describe a model of motion in space without having defined what is meant by *space*.

Usually, when someone asks what a sentence is, the first answer is that we're talking about a sequence of words with meaning. The definition given by Priscian, a Latin grammarian who lived in Byzantium in the fifth century, is famous: "ordinatio dictionum congrua sententiam perfectam demonstrans" (*Institutiones grammaticae*, II, 4.15), which means 'a coherent arrangement of words that demonstrates a complete sense'. By adopting this definition, we discard combinations like *branch Como that of the of lake*; but it's not hard to understand that we're dealing with a sieve that is too restrictive on the one hand and too loose on the other. In fact, we would include sequences like *that branch of Lake Como* in the group considered sentences—while we know intuitively that this sequence is not a sentence—and we would discard single words such as the Italian *arrivarono* 'they arrived', which certainly can be considered a sentence in Italian even though it is not made up of a (coherent) arrangement of words. In order to come to an acceptable definition of *sentence*, following Aristotle we must arrive at a compromise: instead of defining all kinds of sentences, we'll focus on only one kind. In fact, if we throw out the sentences that are prayers, orders, questions, and invectives, and those that are subordinate to others, there remains virtually only one type of sentence: declarative (affirmative or negative, active or passive), the type that asserts the state of things like *Your heart beats*, *The pizza is already cooked*, or *The centurion doesn't find the body*. The declarative sentence, of course, plays a central role for those working with logic (and others), because it is precisely with this type of sentence that the concept of truth (value) is introduced.

Aristotle was certainly thinking about the subject of truth when he wrote that "not all sentences are declarative, but only those in which there is truth or falsity. There is not truth or falsity in all sentences: a prayer is a sentence, but is neither true nor false" (*De int.*, 4, 17a, 2–4). In this way, Aristotle is able to better qualify in which cases a sequence of words with meaning constitutes a sentence: the possibility of saying whether the meaning expressed by the sequence is true or false is thus the defining characteristic of a declarative sentence.[9] Starting from this premise, if I say *their invasion of Rome*, I haven't uttered a sentence because it makes no sense to ask whether *their invasion of Rome* is true or false, but if I say *They invaded Rome*, I've uttered a sentence because I can say whether it's true that they invaded Rome or not, as is quite clear because the first expression can't be negated, while the second one can.

Aristotle also takes care to define the ingredients that make up truth or falsehood: "for falsity and truth have to do with combination and separation" (*De int.*, 1, 16a, 12–13). Combination and separation of what? The idea in this case is that the two items combined are a property and an entity able to enjoy this property. To render the idea of this exceedingly complex and in some ways intuitively emerging concept, the Greek philosophers used a metaphor: that which gathers together all the properties came to be seen as the thing that "stands underneath" or that "is subjected to" all of its properties. It's a bit like asking what happens to Napoleon if he takes off his hat, or if his curl is cut off, or if his name is changed, and so on. It's certainly not easy to see at what point one can stop, certain of having arrived at what underlies it all—the "napoleon-ness." This subject takes up a large part of Western philosophy and has justified the emancipation of ontology—and in this case also mereology—as an autonomous discipline. In any case, the idea that truth and falsity depend on the combination of a property with a substance and the separation of a property from a substance has remained a winning model. We find traces of it everywhere, certainly in reflections on language. It is in fact for this reason that the element to which it is said that a certain property is attributed, which in Greek is known by the technical term *hypokeímenon*, was translated for the first time into Latin by a great medieval philosopher of the sixth century, Boethius, as *subjectum* 'that which stays under', 'that was thrown under', or, more precisely, the subject.[10] To indicate the property attributed to a subject, Aristotle instead makes use of a common Greek verb indicating someone who is speaking in front of an audience, or accusing someone: *kategoréo*—hence the noun *kategoroúmenon*, rendered in Latin by Boethius as *praedicatum* 'predicate' (consider the term "category," which means 'type of predicate'), as if to say that the predicate is what is said to submit to something else that *stays under* (underlies) the properties, namely, a *substance*. Subject and predicate are the two main pillars of Western linguistic and logical thought, two columns that have withstood cultural earthquakes and erosion for well over two millennia of our civilization's history. Even today we still talk about the subject and the predicate without ever having contradicted Aristotle's definition, although we are trying to find ways to reduce these notions to something else (and we'll come back to this) and to formulate them in ever different and, at least on the surface, more sophisticated ways. Subject and predicate thus constitute the structure of the sentence, the conditions without which its nature is not even expressible. Aristotle, in order to support this, his vision of things, begins a sort of autopsy of sentence structure in order to isolate the vital organs; in this process, the verb *to be* plays a decisive role. Let's proceed step by step: it's a bumpy path.

Elsewhere in his writings, in which he examines the components of the sentence, Aristotle writes, "Every statement-making sentence must contain a *rhêma* or the inflection of a *rhêma*" (*De int.*, 5, 17a, 9–10). As we see, here Aristotle does not use the term *kategoroúmenon* 'predicate'; he prefers to use a different term, *rhêma*. Traditionally, *rhêma* has been translated as 'verb', transposed directly from the Latin *verbum*, a term that came antonomastically to mean 'word', although in reality, this last term in Greek is not actually *rhêma* but *lógos*.[11]

The problem, as you'll notice immediately from these few lines, isn't a minor one. We know that perfect consistency can't be expected in the writings of Aristotle that have survived: unlike Plato's, Aristotle's surviving writings are those intended for circulation within the Lyceum, the school he founded in Athens in 336 BC in response to the Academy that Plato had opened, also in Athens, some fifty years earlier. These writings, known as "esoteric," contrast with the "exoteric" ones, of which only meager fragments remain and which are of a more popular nature as they were composed for an external public. Interpreting Aristotle, therefore, is particularly difficult precisely because of the nature of the material we have, which obliges us to dig into the text, hunting for clues often neither explicit nor obvious. The case of the oscillation between "predicate" and "verb" is one of these. But the passage from *kategoroúmenon* to *rhêma* is not inconsistent. If *kategoroúmenon* is a counterpoint to *hypokeímenon*, as *predicate* is to *subject*, then *rhêma* is a counterpoint to *ónoma*, as *verb* is to *noun*. We talk about subject and predicate when speaking of logical functions, and we talk about noun and verb when speaking of grammatical categories: in the sentence *Francesca wins*, *Francesca* is subject and noun, *wins* is predicate and verb. In this sense, *rhêma* seems completely interchangeable with *predicate*. This conclusion seems to be confirmed by another point in Aristotle's writings, where he says that "[*rhêma*] is a sign of what is true, that which is true for a subject" (*De int.*, 3, 16b, 9–10). So, is there no difference between *kategoroúmenon* 'predicate' and *rhêma* 'verb'? There is a difference, and it's enormous; but to see it, we need a clear-cut case, one that allows us to grasp with the naked eye how things stand. This case will be provided by the verb *to be*, which in Greek, as in so many Indo-European languages, can be used in the construction of a sentence.

To Be—and Not "Being"—or, The Names of the Verb

There are two different types of analysis involving the verb *to be* in Aristotle: some explicit, others implicit. We'll follow the two paths in order. Aristotle tells us that one of the fundamental characteristics of a *rhêma* is also true of a verb: "A verb is that which in addition signifies time" (*De int.*, 3, 16b, 6). Adapting an example from his notes, we'll say that *comb* is the common name/noun referring to an object and *combs* is a verb, because *combs* means that someone is performing the action of "to comb now"; changing the verb's inflection can in fact change the time/tense, so *combed* means that someone performed the action of "to comb" in the past. In Italian, only verbs have this ability, not nouns; one cannot change a noun, assigning it to a moment in time (except perhaps by using the prefix *ex* in cases such as *ex-president*). But we must be careful in reading the definition of *verb* given by Aristotle: "[A] verb is that which in addition signifies time." Why does he say "in addition"—in addition to what? The following example supplies the answer: "[T]here is no difference in saying that *a man walks* and that *a man is walking*" (*De int.*, 12, 21b, 910). No doubt the phrase doesn't sound great in Italian—one wouldn't say *Un uomo è camminante* 'A man is walking' instead of *Un uomo cammina* 'A man walks'—but in Ancient Greek, as in English, both of these sentences were perfectly admissible. So, for Aristotle, *is walking* and *walks* are de facto equivalents and since a *rhêma*, a verb, "in addition signifies time," what remains if I take away the time indicator, which in the first sentence is evidently expressed by the verb *to be*, is the predicate, *walking*. It follows that the verb *to be* is not a predicate. Aristotle repeats this conclusion explicitly in another passage: "When the verb *is* does not fit, as in *enjoys health, walks*, the verbs have the same effect, which applied when *is* was added" (*De int.*, 10, 20a, 3–5). So, for Aristotle the verb *to be* is not a predicate, but expresses tense when the predicate does not consist of a verb.

Let's summarize. In deciphering the scaffolding of the affirmative sentence, we've distinguished two fundamental pillars (the subject and the predicate) and another additional component (tense) usually expressed syncretically on the predicate, when the predicate is a verb, or by an autonomous verb, the verb *to be*, when the predicate is expressed not by a verb but, for example, by a noun. In every case, the verb *to be* is not a predicate; it's "only" a verb. In this scenario, the verb *to be* appears, in a certain sense, as secondary compared to the two fundamental pillars: the subject and the predicate. This is not surprising, given that the defining property of the sentence is seen as the possibility of affirming whether a certain sequence of words expresses a truth or not, and considering that the possibility of expressing a truth derives, in the final analysis, from the attribution (or negation of attribution) of a predicate to a subject and not from tense. Aristotle is certainly explicit about the secondary nature of the verb *to be*—indeed, on closer inspection a "tertiary" nature, since it comes after the subject and the predicate: "For example, in *a man is just*, I say that *is* is the third component" (*De int.*, 10, 19b, 20–22).

We arrive at this conclusion—namely, that the verb *to be* is not a predicate but only a support for tense—not only through explicit admissions by Aristotle, but also by a careful reading of some of his other passages, decidedly less explicit, almost cryptic, and in some ways surprising. An interesting case is a passage that is often translated this way: "If nouns and verbs are transposed, they mean the same thing, for example, *a man is white* and *white is a man*" (*De int.*, 10, 20b, 1–2). In this case, Aristotle's examples translated into Italian or English don't sound great, but they were perfect in Ancient Greek. What matters here, however, is a fact that, if we're not careful, escapes as if it were an irrelevant detail in a puzzle. What's the only word that doesn't change position in the two examples? The verb *to be*. So, seeing that in the sentence the only thing that doesn't change places is the verb *to be*, the translation is wrong; it should be 'if nouns and predicates are transposed', keeping the translation of *ónoma* as 'noun' and using "mixed" terminology, or even interpreting Aristotle's statement to mean 'if subjects and predicates are transposed'. In any case, the examples above confirm indirectly that the verb *to be* is not a predicate, fully consistently with what has been said before.

Another very interesting case, highlighted a few decades ago by Italian linguists, consists of an example in the nature of a paradox (De Mauro and Thornton 1985, Graffi 1986). There is a phrase in Aristotle's writings that can be made into a slogan, thus: "Without *rhêma*, neither affirmation nor negation" (*De int.*, 10, 19b, 12). How is *rhêma* to be translated in this case? Two very famous translations, especially in the Anglo-Saxon world, state it as follows: "Without a verb there will be no affirmation or negation" (Ackrill 1963, 54) and "Unless there is also a verb, there is no affirmation or denial" (Cooke 1938, 141). One of the most famous Italian versions, in the *Organon* edited and translated by Giorgio Colli, also sounds similar: "Without the verb neither affirmation nor negation" (Colli 2003, 70). So what is the problem? The problem is that the sentence in question is certainly an affirmation, but in Greek it doesn't contain even the shadow of a verb. So, by definition—and it's exactly the definition of an affirmation that Aristotle is giving here—this sentence cannot be an affirmation: this is the paradox. The error that generates the paradox should be very evident by now: it was translating *rhêma* as 'verb' rather than 'predicate'. The sentence in question certainly contains a predicate and a subject, even if it doesn't contain a verb, so it has the green light to be an affirmation: what is lacking, if anything, is tense, but in definitions tense certainly isn't the essential part. The fact that the "missing" verb is clearly *to be* indirectly reinforces the hypothesis that the verb *to be* is not a predicate, and therefore makes the current translations wrong. Among other things, in Ancient Greek, sentences without the verb *to be* were quite frequent, much more frequent than in a language like Italian, where they are basically reduced to expressing prohibitions: for example, *Vietato dar da bere ai cicisbei* 'Giving dandies drink forbidden' or *Minigonne non ammesse negli spazi della biblioteca* 'Miniskirts not allowed in the library area'.

Before I conclude this brief portrait of the verb *to be* in Aristotle, an example of no small import remains to be discussed. In a passage from *De interpretatione*, Aristotle himself, who has just held that the verb *to be* is the third element of a sentence, offers up a case where he seems to want to say that the verb *to be*, when added to a noun, produces an affirmative statement: "[A]lso the word *goat-stag* means something, but as is, it doesn't [yet mean] anything true or false, if the verb *to be* is not added in the affirmative or negative form, either in the present or in some other tense" (*De int.*, 1, 16a, 17).

How do we reconcile this case with the theory? Over the centuries, it has been suggested that this use of the verb deviates from normal use (see the appendix in Moro 1997), and it has been proposed that the verb *to be* might sometimes *also* have the function of a predicate, the predicate of existence, even though Aristotle himself expresses—if hermetically, not to mention cryptically—the contrary of this hypothesis in *Posterior Analytics* when he states, "[S]ince being is not a genus, it is not the essence of anything" (*Post. Anal.*, B7, 92b, 13–14). Other famous examples of existential usage of the verb *to be* that come to mind are biblical passages like *Dixit Deus ad Moysen: ego sum qui sum* (Exod. 3:14) 'I am who I am' (sometimes also translated as 'I am that I am'). These cases should constitute counterexamples to the theory of the verb *to be* as a third element in the essential scaffolding of a sentence, alongside the subject and the predicate. We have already seen, however, that in reality the verb *to be* is, in this case, the verb that can be followed by all possible predicates, and so stands for all possible predicates, as the verb *to do* stands for all possible actions. It's a bit like saying *I am the one who does*, meaning by this to say that I am the one who does anything, the doer par excellence. As we will see, in the Middle Ages Abelard proposed a "proof by contradiction" that the verb *to be* cannot be a predicate of existence, using the weapons he knew how to wield better than any other: the blades of logic. But for the moment it's worth noting how sentences of this type in Italian, where the verb *to be* appears without a predicate, can be expanded (so to speak) by adding an element with the predicate function, like a pronoun. In addition to *Dio è* 'God is', we can say *Dio c'è* 'God there is', where *ci* 'there' expresses the (abstract) predicate of place that establishes the sphere of God's existence, while this addition of *ci* doesn't work in other, meaningless phrases like **Dio c'è buono* 'God there is good'. This shows that the verb *to be* does not in itself have an existential predicative value; it shows simply that there is an implied predicate, which can be expressed with *ci*. On the other hand, the use of a locative predicate expressing existence shouldn't be surprising. Is it not true that the etymology of the Italian *esistere* 'to exist' contains the Latin verb *sistere*, the causative form of *stare* 'stay/stand'—namely, 'be placed in a location' (*ek-sistere*)?

In the next chapters, we'll extensively discuss the role of this most innocent and insidious pronominal element, *ci*, and its equivalent in other languages. For now, it's enough to have clarified that the philosophical values of *being* should be kept distinctly separate from the verb *to be* and from all related philosophical terms, such as those that derive from the genitive form of the present participle of *to be* in Greek, *óntos*, from which of course the term "ontology"—first used by Jacob Lorhard, Swiss philosopher from the second half of the sixteenth century (Lorhard 1606)—or the science of "being." If we really want to give a name to the science of the verb *to be*, rather than *ontology* we might venture to try *einaiologia*, from the infinitive of the verb *to be* in Greek, *eînai*, used as an alternative to *estí(n)* 'is' by Aristotle as a way to indicate the verb *to be*.

We've completed the first leg of the journey: the theory of the verb *to be* in Aristotle. The verb *to be* is not a predicate; it is the support for grammatical tense in sentences where tense cannot be expressed by the predicate. This theory has been enormously successful, as have many of Aristotle's other insights in the fields of logic and linguistics. Practically no one has been able to avoid making reference, explicitly or implicitly, to this theory. However, it's worth noting that many have attributed the meaning 'copula' to the "name of tense" identified by Aristotle, although this term never appears in Aristotle, a fact that has at times complicated the interpretation of his texts.

The Good Luck of the Aristotelian Version

The "good luck" of Aristotle's analysis of the verb *to be*—which is, as the philologists say, the spread of this analysis through times and cultures—has been impressive and has continued almost uninterrupted since its formulation. Traces of this theory are to be found in every Western grammatical treatise. In the *Critique of Pure Reason*, Kant says, "*Being* is obviously not a real predicate; that is, it is not a concept of something that could be added to the concept of a thing" (Kant 1787 [1929, 504]).[12] Even though he continues by grafting onto his treatise the seventeenth-century vision of the verb *to be* (which we will address in the next section), the Aristotelian matrix is unmistakable (see also the quote from *Posterior Analytics* given above as a possible archetype of this meaning of the verb *to be*). In the last century, even when linguistics was already emancipated as an autonomous science relative to rhetoric and philology, and based on the solid foundation of comparative analysis of Indo-European languages, the problem of the origin of sentences with the verb *to be* was raised and the answers that came about doubtless reflect the Aristotelian theoretical framework. Let's hear what Joseph Vendryes, French linguist and scholar of Celtic languages, said: "The introduction of the copula into the noun phrase is easily explained. There is a notion that a simple juxtaposition of subject and predicate cannot express: it is the notion of tense" (Vendryes 1921, 146). And in this Vendryes showed that he developed the notion of the "noun phrase," which his master, Antoine Meillet (also French, a linguist, and a famous scholar of Greek) defined as follows: "If the predicate, which is the essential element of the phrase, is a noun, it is called nominal; if the predicate is a verb, or a verb other than the verb *to be* or a copula, it is called verbal" (Meillet 1934, 356). Therefore, in the words of these two authoritative leaders of twentieth-century comparative linguistics, the Aristotelian theory of the origin of the verb *to be* as a "sign of tense" is now virtually taken for granted: neither Vendryes nor Meillet, nor many contemporaneous works up to the grammars used in our schools today would be understandable were it not taken into account.

But to complicate the story, other analyses of the verb *to be* have been developed; often these infiltrate the tradition without being detected, creating great confusion around the theory of this verb. Two moments in which a different view of the verb *to be* emerged were the Middle Ages and the century of great geniuses, the seventeenth century. We'll discuss them in the next section.

1.2 The Name of Affirmation

The verb *to be* expresses tense; by now there are few doubts about this. Is this the only way to consider the role of the verb *to be* in language? Aristotle—as we have just seen—thought that it was the third ingredient in the sentence, in order of importance after the subject and the predicate. But it's then emancipated from this costarring role: the necessity of the verb *to be* in the construction of a sentence has resulted in its becoming synonymous with affirmation, to use a not-so-daring linguistic synecdoche. Fundamentally, when examined, the verb *to be* is the only thing that doesn't change when we exchange the subject and the predicate. But that's not all: we also see how the verb *to be* becomes indispensable to understanding a mechanism that is at the heart of deductive logic, the syllogism. In this section, we'll essentially deal with two historic moments of Western philosophical thought and language: the period of medieval linguistics—namely, Scholasticism, which continued the difficult work on the anatomy of rational thought that began with Aristotle's *Organon*—and the period of Cartesian linguistics, when rationalism began to take the shape that would later provide the support so essential to the growth of the empirical sciences on the one hand, and would lead to the inexorable and embarrassing divorce between mind and body on the other. The analysis of the verb *to be* in these two periods is well represented by these two statements. Let's start with the Middle Ages.

The Truth Machine: The Copula in Syllogisms

Few eras have been as luminous as the Middle Ages. In the Middle Ages, the intelligence and culture of intellectuals expressed itself at the highest levels in many fields, certainly in the fields of logic and reflections on language, not to mention art and politics. All of this was not coincidental; rather, it was linked to the new cultural climate that flourished during those years, especially beginning in the thirteenth century. Perhaps only in the Middle Ages has the West experienced educational planning that was so uniform and so effective. The *scholae*, from which medieval philosophy took the name *Scholastic* and which would be immensely influential in the entire history of the Western world and beyond, were organized throughout Europe according to a common, rational pattern: that of the Liberal Arts, divided into the trivium (grammar, rhetoric, and logic) and quadrivium (arithmetic, geometry, astronomy, and music). A schema that Charlemagne adopted for the foundation of the first school—the *Schola Palatina* in Aachen—directed by Martianus Capella, a Carthaginian lawyer of Late Antiquity who lived around the fourth or fifth century AD. In this tumultuous cultural environment, attention to method became erratic; method as a guarantee of effectiveness in research was at the heart of the discussions of intellectuals of every stripe; and, of course, at the heart of method is logic, the mechanism by which thought progresses and discovers new things or confirms known concepts. So it's not surprising that language, so intimately linked to thought, would be subjected to such precise and subtle dissection during this historical period. But another fact renders the Middle Ages distinctive in regard to reflections on language: in this period, Latin became the lingua franca for all European cultures. In the universities, not only were works not published in the various local languages—as often happens now, as well—but people were thinking, arguing, and writing together in the same language. In a certain sense, the spread of Latin was comparable to (if not greater than) that of Greek (i.e., the so-called *koiné* or common language) in the Alexandrian era—that is, between the end of the fourth century BC and the beginning of the fourth century AD. Latin thus became the cultural equivalent of buttresses in Gothic cathedrals, which flourished everywhere in those same years as the dominant and innovative architectural model. Like buttresses, Latin supported the central structure, bolstering the sustaining column and favoring momentum toward new horizons in a huge concerted effort. Without buttresses and without Latin, perhaps we'd still be only dwarves standing on the shoulders of dwarves.

In this atmosphere of unity and cultural vitality, where religious thought and the Church were undoubtedly fundamental driving forces, although not without ambiguity and violent influences, the first great attempt to acknowledge, explain, and justify the substantial unity of human language was born, within the central current of the so-called "Modistae" philosophers. The grandiose (and ambitious) project of the Modistae (Modists) was to explain the structure of the world, of language, and of logic as the consequence of a cosmic order guaranteed by God. In this sense, the *modes* in which we speak (*modi significandi*), the *modes* in which physical reality is organized (*modi essendi*), and the *modes* in which we understand (*modi intelligendi*) must necessarily be able to correspond with each other. This project, among other things, had a dual effect, which is relevant here: on the one hand, it reinforced the idea that in order to know logic—the mode with which we think—it was fundamental to have a good knowledge of the structure of language; on the other, it suggested that all languages are in fact one, since they reflect the physical structure of the world and the world has a single physical structure for everyone. An irrefutable trace of this intuition is found in the often-cited words of Roger Bacon: "Grammatica una et eadem est secundum substantiam in omnibus linguis, licet accidentaliter varietur" ('In its substance, grammar is one and the same in all languages, even if it accidentally varies'; Wallerand 1913, 43). It would take another seven centuries of linguistics for the substantial unity of human languages to be reconfirmed, this time on a biological and not a theological basis, thanks to the intuition and work of an American linguist, Noam Chomsky, whom we will discuss extensively in the next chapters.

In the great undertaking of the Modistae, which to define as simply "cultural" would be an understatement, the verb *to be* was once again an important link between grammar and logic for its role in the "truth machine" constructed from words: a syllogism. The syllogism (from the Greek, *syllogízesthai* 'to gather together', 'to calculate together', and so 'to conclude', 'to infer') is a seemingly simple logical-verbal mechanism; however, its effects are not yet fully understood. We shouldn't be surprised by the fact that the theory of the syllogism was inaugurated by Aristotle in the *Prior*

Analytics (*Anal. prior.*, A, 24b, 18–20). Let's start with an example, bearing in mind that we must necessarily keep the discourse on a simple level. If I say *Gertrude is a poet, A poet is a woman, Therefore Gertrude is a woman*, I've constructed a syllogism. That is, I've gathered together three sentences that indicate a cogent deductive argument: a major premise (*Gertrude is a poet*), a minor premise (*A poet is a woman*), and a conclusion (*Gertrude is a woman*). The structure of the syllogism was explored by the Modistae in detail in order to illustrate which combinations of major and minor premises can lead to a valid conclusion. For example, although in the previous case the major and minor premises are affirmative, negative premises are also possible: *Gertrude is a poet, A poet is not a rose, Therefore Gertrude is not a rose*. Or the first premise can be general and the second premise specific: *All poets are a gift of nature, A gift of nature is a rarity, Therefore all poets are a rarity*. And so on; combining affirmative, negative, general, and specific, we have all we need to construct all possible types of syllogisms. To aid in memorizing the structure, imaginative mnemonic schemes were also invented, like those taught in school to help students remember taxonomic order in biology (*King Phillip Came Over From Great Spain: King*dom, *P*hylum, *C*lass, *O*rder, *F*amily, *G*enus, *Sp*ecies) or the Great Lakes (*HOMES: H*uron, *O*ntario, *M*ichigan, *E*rie, *S*uperior). The trick, in the case of syllogisms, was to associate a vowel with each type premise—*A* with affirmative general, *E* with negative general, *I* with affirmative specific, and *O* with negative specific—and to build a simple mnemonic in which the order of the vowels in the words repeated the type of syllogism structure: *Barbara Celarent Darii Ferio Cesare Camestres Festino Baroco Darapti Disamis Datisi Felapton Bocardo Ferison Bramantip Camenes Dimaris Fesapo Fresison*. In this way, from among all the possible logical combinations (256 unless we take into account the order of the two premises) one could discard the illicit ones and be confident of having constructed a valid syllogism.

The evaluation of the function of syllogisms could take us too far off track; the literature in this field is immense and the debate on this topic still alive and vibrant (see, for example, Kneale and Kneale 1962, and especially for the Middle Ages, Pinborg 1972 and the references cited therein). It could lead us to ask ourselves, for example, if a syllogism really increases our knowledge of the world or if it's not just a baroque paraphrase of what we already know (a kind of analytic survey, in Kantian terms); it could lead us to talk about the difference between deductive and inductive logic and the role of intellectual giants such as Francis Bacon, Kant, and Frege. So why are we talking about the syllogism here? Certainly the answer will be obvious at this point: because the linguistic element that allows for the expression of a syllogism in Latin and in most of the Romance and Germanic languages is the verb *to be*. The verb *to be* is an indispensable element of the machine—it is, so to speak, *the linchpin* of the syllogism—and this was noticed by the great Abelard, a French monk, logician, and Scholastic theologian who died in the mid-twelfth century. There are two reasons why Abelard must be associated with the history of the verb *to be*: on the one hand, he was interested in the role of the verb *to be* in the syllogism; on the other, in a more specifically linguistic sense not unrelated to the first, he had to resolve the anomalous case of the verb *to be* when it was accompanied by only one noun. As Kneale and Kneale (1962, 206) observe, "It is clear that for his [Aristotle's] theory of syllogism he assumes in every general proposition two terms of the same kind, that is to say, each capable of being a subject and each capable of being a predicate." For example, let's take "Barbara" (*AAA*: that is, major premise affirmative general; minor premise affirmative general; conclusion affirmative general): *Every spider is a furry animal, A furry animal is affectionate, Therefore every spider is affectionate.* In this syllogism, the role of the verb *to be* is quite evident: it allows *a furry animal* to function as a predicate in the major premise and as a subject in the minor one, automatically spitting out the final deduction, like a well-oiled machine. It is the verb *to be* that holds the parts of the truth machine together, producing the final effect—and what matters to us here is that no other verb could have the same effect. Abelard was among the first to talk about the verb *to be* in this case as a "copula"—the act that, by uniting, generates a new entity. Certainly the spread of the term "copula" is linked to the name of Abelard—Aristotle, as I've already noted, didn't use any equivalent term to indicate the verb *to be*; he limited himself to calling it *tó estí(n)* 'the *it is*' or *tó eînai* 'the *to be*'—but there is evidence of its previous use, at least in the "Dialectic" of Garlandus Compotista, a philosopher of the school of Liege active in the eleventh century, about whom not much is known. Therefore, it was Abelard who spread the use of the term; it has been shown that at least a century earlier it was being used as a technical term in Scholasticism and Garlandus Compotista's early use raises historiographical questions of no small import about this term.[13] At any rate, with Abelard the term "copula" is now widely attested and, what's most important to us here, it is uncoupled in a significant way from the theory of the verb *to be* as an expression of time/tense, the cornerstone of the Aristotelian theory. Attention to its role as mediator between subject and predicate is now prevalent, and this will allow for evolution to the next stage.

As I noted earlier, discussion of the copula in Abelard's work wouldn't be complete if we didn't recall that he also took positions explicitly against the hypothesis that this verb could be a predicate (in contrast to—I mention it again for clarity—all other verbs). In particular, Abelard never accepted the idea that the copula could be a predicate of existence, so as not to shatter the foundations of the syllogistic mechanism. A direct mark of his concern about this issue, and the attempt to remove any residual suspicion about the predication capacity of the copula, is found in his *Dialectica* (Abelard 1956, 161–2) and takes the form of a *reductio ad absurdum* or reduction to absurdity, typical of mathematicians and logicians; once again, in the medieval manner, the strength of reason is fully revealed. In essence, Abelard says this: if, when I say *Socrates is* and with *is* I express an implied predicate of existence, then I should be able to substitute *is existing* for *is* and say *Socrates is existing*; but, if this were so, which is to say that the copula could express a predicate of existence, what would keep me from repeating the operation, substituting *is existing* for the *is* in the last sentence? I would thus have *Socrates is existing existing*, and then *Socrates is existing existing existing*, and so on to infinity, without ever reaching a stopping point to interpret the sentence, which is in fact extremely interpretable.

The first step in the move away from Aristotle is complete. The verb *to be* is no longer considered only as a support for tense; it is *also* the linguistic element that fuses, or *couples*, the subject with the predicate, and generates truth. It is, as I've said, the linchpin of the truth machine constructed of words that is the syllogism. This distancing is obviously not total; indeed, in some ways it confirms Aristotle's theory in the sense that, as in Aristotle, the verb *to be* is never treated as a predicate, nor as a predicate of existence. But the idea of the verb *to be* as a copula, as a fusing element, has by now caught on and is grafted onto the Western tradition as one of the principal currents in the history of this verb's interpretation—a strong current that will be reinforced over the centuries until it arrives in our classrooms.

However, the path is still rocky and some important sections still remain to be explored. One of these is the development of linguistic thought in the so-called era of the great geniuses: the seventeenth century.

Grammar as a Mirror of the Mind: The Copula in the Era of the Great Geniuses

Human language is, after all, the great scandal of nature: human language forces us to acknowledge an unprovoked and sudden discontinuity between living beings; its structure interrupts the evolutionary scale—as an unexpected singularity—and reveals the mind's framework as perhaps nothing else can. And not because human language enables representations of the world, which moreover can be transmitted from one individual to another—even a whale or, as far as we know, a dragonfly exhibits these properties—but because the *structure* of this code is not shared with any other animal nor is it present in them in either an "embryonic" or a perfected form, unlike other cognitive functions—such as the sense of orientation, vision—or physical structures such as the circulatory system. This doesn't make us any better than whales or dragonflies—who could ever tolerate such an idea?—but it certainly makes us special compared with all other living species. But in what sense is the structure of this code not shared with any other animal? Only by leaving the realm of anecdotal approximation and relying on rigorous formal proofs will we succeed in understanding this question, and it's even more necessary if we want to provide a response. Linguistics has the disadvantage of often being polluted by the fact that many, solely because they're able to speak, feel entitled to have a theory about language, as if by merely having a cold, one could have one's own theory about the immune system. It's not like that. We'll see it clearly in the section dedicated to the twentieth century; linguistics is a science, like the others, and its nature is revealed only by conducting experiments, formulating theories, and selecting the questions and the data that are increasingly considered central. But now let's focus on the seventeenth century, when this state of affairs regarding the architecture of human language begins to be fully grasped, at least on an intuitive level.

The first to systematically investigate the nucleus of formal properties that are distinctive to human language were the intellectuals of the Port-Royal school. The history of this institution is troubled and complex. The Cistercian Abbey of Port-Royal was founded at the start of the fourteenth century in the Chevreuse Valley, southwest of Paris. At the start of the seventeenth century, it became famous when it came under the patronage of the influential Arnauld family, and a succession of Arnauld family abbesses took charge of directing it. A community of highly prominent intellectuals flourished near the abbey—including figures such as Blaise Pascal and Jean Racine. Perhaps their prominence was all too evident: those who participated in this cultural enterprise sided with the gloomy Jansenists, against the Jesuits, and were defeated in the religious dispute between these groups. The charge of heresy was not long in coming: in 1708 a papal bull issued by Clement XI suppressed the abbey, and the iconoclastic fury escalated to the point that it was physically destroyed two years later. What is the verb *to be* doing in such a tragic story? Its role is linked precisely to the peculiar nature of human language. We'll see how the verb *to be* was considered by Port-Royalists as a unique opportunity to highlight the special framework of human grammars and ultimately the human mind. But first we must grasp, at least in an approximate way, what was scandalous about the nature of human language (for a seventeenth-century intellectual).

The Port-Royal school is inextricably linked to Cartesian thought. René Descartes is listed in encyclopedias as a philosopher and a mathematician. His specific contributions in these fields are enormous, but his intellectual stature and influence in Western culture are so impressive that they can't be easily reduced to fit in a specific pigeonhole. One of the cornerstones of Cartesian thought was the certainty that everything that we perceive in the physical world can be explained by a mechanical model, a model where the primitive elements come into physical and local contact. This would lead to overwhelming scientific and technological development: just think of how heat can be understood as the effect of disorderly movement of particles. Of course, the mechanistic vision didn't always lead to valid theories: for example, Descartes would interpret the gravitational force between celestial bodies as the effect of swirling vortices filled with cosmic matter (the ether) within which the bodies themselves were trapped, like debris in a whirlpool. We know today how much Newton suffered when he noticed that gravitational pull could only be described as action at a distance, when he realized that he had to give up a theory of physical and local contact between elements and content himself with a mathematical description of phenomena: Cartesian mechanistic thought, absolutely dominant in the culture of the time, was the farthest thing from his theory that it was possible to imagine. Even Leibniz acted against this danger, thundering his dissent to Newton's theory of gravitation in the preface to the first book of his *New Essays on Human Understanding*; the danger, according to Leibniz, was regressing to a pre-Cartesian stage with a devastating drift into heresy. For Leibniz, to accept Newton's theory of gravitation was "in reality to return to the occult, or what is worse, inexplicable qualities" (Leibniz 1765 [1896, 59]; on this topic, see Pérez de Laborda 1980 and Maglo 2003). Thankfully, the love of truth overcame the fear of being accused of (intellectual) heresy, to say nothing of witchcraft, and the history of science was changed forever. Ironically, today, when we know very well (following Michelson and Morley's experiments) that the ether doesn't exist, searching for a particle that mediates the gravitational pull in a manner consistent with Einstein's theory of general relativity is still a central problem of physics, almost as if the ghost of Descartes, cast out of the realm of psychology, wanted to regain possession of the cosmos.

But what did Descartes think about the psyche? What mechanism could ever be capable of explaining it? The fact is that

Descartes couldn't fail to notice that there are more things in heaven and earth that go beyond simple mechanical contact, above all in our heads. And among these things, for Descartes, there was the human mind. To Descartes, in fact, the human mind did not seem reducible to a mechanical contact and, what's worse, its behavior could not be predicted from other principles. For Descartes, the human mind is essentially creative and its creativity is manifested in humanity's inexhaustible capacity to produce and comprehend sentences that have never been heard before. Therefore, language is scandalous (also) because it's impossible to describe it according to a scheme of mechanical contacts; it's not something *measurable*. Descartes radicalized this dichotomy to such an extent as to propose two immensely famous and opposing expressions: the "thing that occupies space" (*res extensa*), thus measurable, and the "thing that thinks" (*res cogitans*). There are no intermediate spaces between the two nor is there any possible reconciliation, at least for Descartes. To tell the truth, with a bold neurophysiological interpretation he attempted to prove the "material" connection between the soul and the body through the famous hypothesis that the point of contact between these two worlds, otherwise mutually invisible, was seated in the epiphysis or pineal gland. It's curious to note how, within the context of a bold empiricist program, Descartes in fact based his hypothesis on a deductive principle that assimilated the pineal gland to the soul: both are unique (as compared with, for example, the amygdala, a similar organelle of which the brain has a pair) and indivisible. Descartes was never satisfied with this hypothesis, to which, he explicitly confessed, he had devoted too little time; nor did his contemporaries gave much weight to this proposal, which in fact was quickly abandoned (see Lokhorst and Kaitaro 2001). Descartes's seed was to bear fruit in other fields. However, despite the failure of a unified program, the importance of the study of the mind as distinct from mechanics remained, along with what most interests us here: the central role of language (and logic) in this research program. Language and logic, two sides of the same "thing that thinks," were absolutely central to the Port-Royal school: their study was seen not as *a* road, but as *the* main road to making the regularities of the human mind evident. But the impact of Descartes's thought on the Port-Royal school is even more important and includes another, methodological aspect of his philosophy.

One of the cornerstones of the Cartesian method is to conceive the complex as a result of the interaction of simple elements. This methodological precept becomes almost a dogma in modern science. In the words of Jean-Baptiste Perrin, winner of the 1926 Nobel Prize for Physics, the final task of the scientist is to "explain what is visible and complicated by means of what is simple and invisible" (Perrin 1913). On this point there is also perfect coherence with the investigation of language by the Port-Royal school and, of course, the verb *to be* plays a fundamental role. We'll hear from Antoine Arnauld in his own words how a sentence should be viewed. The quote is taken from a book that would become extraordinarily famous; it would be reprinted from 1660 up until the second half of the nineteenth century, and not as an antiquarian curiosity but as a functional textbook. The title says it all: *Grammaire générale et raisonnée: Contenant les fondemens de l'art de parler, expliqués d'une manière claire et naturelle* ('General and Rational Grammar, Containing the Fundamentals of the Art of Speaking, Explained in a Clear and Natural Manner'). It's a "rational" grammar, because it's through the use of reason that the apparently chaotic structure of language can be comprehended. We cannot fail to notice that this attempt at rational analysis of language recalls another great moment, the linguistics of the Modistae, but with entirely different aims, methods, and horizons. First of all, the subject of the Port-Royalists' investigation of grammar is no longer a kind of rarefied language, Latin, but a specific language, French, although the universalist pretension never ceases to be a constant in their research as well: rational analysis of French is only accidentally different from rational analysis of any other language. A typical example of a reduction from complex to simple is seen in analyzing a sentence like *Invisible God has created the visible world* (see H. E. Brekle's translation of the *Grammaire*: Brekle 1966, 68), which comes to be viewed as the composition of three distinct sentences, the first "principal and essential" and the others dependent, respectively: *God has created the world*, *God is invisible*, and *The world is visible*. It is certainly no coincidence that Noam Chomsky dedicated an entire essay to this period in the history of linguistics, focusing on the Port-Royal grammar and asserting, "In many respects, it seems to me quite accurate, then, to regard the theory of transformational generative grammar, as it is developing in current work, as essentially a modern and more explicit version of the Port-Royal theory" (Chomsky 1966, 83).

We'll return to these issues when we consider how the verb *to be* is dealt with from the perspective on language that is rooted in Chomsky's thought; for now, we'll look at another example of reduction from complex to simple, quoted in the Port-Royal grammar, which is indicative of the degree to which Aristotelian theory was still active. The example refers to analyzing the predicate of a sentence:

In fact, given that men are naturally inclined to abbreviate their expressions, they have almost always joined to the affirmation some other meanings in the same word. They have joined to it that of some attribute, so that in such a case the two words constitute a proposition, as when I say *Petrus vivit—Peter lives*—in that the word *vivit* includes the affirmation and, in addition, the attribute of being alive; so, it is the same thing to say *Peter lives* as it is to say *Peter is living*. (*Grammaire*, 96)

As this passage indicates, the "true" structure of a sentence is viewed as the breakdown of subject and verbal predicate into subject, copula, and nominal predicate.

We're certainly not looking at a historical or etymological reconstruction of the verb *to be*: it's simply that, once again, the Aristotelian tripartite division of sentence architecture inexorably emerges. But this time not without criticism—we're now quite a long way from the unwieldy *ipse dixit*:

> The variety of these meanings joined in the same word [i.e., predication, affirmation, and tense as in *vivit*] is what has impeded many people, otherwise quite gifted, from clearly understanding the nature of the verb, in that they considered it not according to what is essential to it, namely affirmation, but rather according to these other relationships that, in that it is a verb, are accidental to it. Thus Aristotle, stopping himself at the third type of meaning added to that which is essential to the verb, defined it as *vox significant cum tempore,* a word which signifies together with time. (*Grammaire*, 98)

If on the one hand Arnauld confirms the tripartite structure and the essential underlying architecture of sentences including the verb *to be*, on the other hand he sharply distances himself from Aristotle. For Arnauld, the verb *to be* is not only a simple temporal expression, it's the name of an affirmation. Indeed, Arnauld goes so far with this copula-centric vision as to state:

> It can be said that the verb in itself should have no other use than to indicate the link that we make in our minds between the two terms of a proposition, but it is only the verb *to be*, which we call substantive, which has remained in this simple state. ... [I]n each language only a single verb would have been necessary, that is[,] the one we call substantive. (*Grammaire*, 96–97)

So, the verb *to be* is even seen as the only verb in its own right. This verb qualifies as a central clue in the investigation leading to the identification of the load-bearing elements of the sentence's scaffolding. And the sentence's scaffolding, in turn, as a foreshadowing of the typical human cognitive process:

> The judgments that we make about things (as when I say, *the earth is round*) necessarily include two terms, one called the subject, the other the

attribute [which in English we call "predicate"] which is that which is affirmed, like *round*; and, further, includes the link between these two terms, which is properly the action of our minds which affirms the attribute of the subject. ... And the verb is exactly that, a word whose principal use is that of signifying the affirmation. (*Grammaire*, 94–95)

So, in the Port-Royal grammar, the copula is to be found at the intersection of the trajectories that make up a complete vision of the human mind: it is seen as the catalyst, the linchpin (sometimes, for brevity's sake, hidden in a verb) around which nothing other than the structure of human judgment turns and takes on substance.

Therefore, we have concluded the second stage of the history of the verb *to be* through the centuries: alongside the vision of the verb *to be* as a support of tense, we place that of the verb *to be* as the name of affirmation and as the "copula," the element of creative fusion between two independent concepts embodied in words that result in a judgment. We must also take these currents into account in order to understand the importance of copular sentence analysis in the twentieth century, but a new controversy is lurking; it insinuates itself into linguistics through the misgivings of mathematicians and logicians. Let's make a leap forward in time, moving from seventeenth-century France to nineteenth-century England.

1.3 The Name of Identity

A story that appeared in the collection *Plato and a Platypus Walk into a Bar ... : Understanding Philosophy through Jokes* is about a man who asks another man what the earth is resting on; it proceeds as follows:

Dimitri: If Atlas holds up the world, what holds up Atlas?

Tasso: Atlas stands on the back of a turtle.

Dimitri: But what does the turtle stand on?

To Be—and Not "Being"—or, The Names of the Verb

Tasso: Another turtle.

Dimitri: And what does *that* turtle stand on?

Tasso: My dear Dimitri, *it's turtles all the way down!*

(Cathcart and Klein 2007, 1)

For those who, between the end of the nineteenth and the end of the twentieth centuries, tried to give mathematics a firm, earthly footing, the sensation of vertigo must have been much the same. A footing that is both logical and elementary, by which I mean one firmly rooted in a small number of clear, definable elements. But the more these scholars shook things up, at least beginning with the great Gottlob Frege, the more their footing sank in the quicksand of paradoxes and contradictions. The culprit responsible for this was recognized by almost everyone that mattered who was working in the field of natural language philosophy: if humankind had not been given such an imprecise tool—they thought—there would have been no misconceptions and, in the end, logic and therefore mathematics would have been grounded not in quicksand but on the bedrock of formulas, with no space for redundancies and misconceptions. It was necessary to find a remedy for all of this, and the most merciless diagnoses seemed clear as soon as one analyzed the verb *to be*. Once again, this verb came to be at the epicenter of one of the most devastating earthquakes that had ever struck philosophy and logic. I have chosen to tell this piece of history by presenting two champions of opposing ways of viewing language who, precisely in regard to the verb *to be*, expressed conflicting opinions in the first half of the twentieth century: Bertrand Russell, the philosopher, logician, and mathematician whom we already encountered in the prologue, and Otto Jespersen, a major Danish linguist, certainly less well known than Russell, but whose contribution to the history of reflections on language is equally impressive.

A Gigantic Misconception: Russell and Identity

We've already seen Russell's reaction in the face of the damage that he thought the verb *to be* was causing: "It is a disgrace to the human race that it has chosen to employ the same word 'is' for two entirely different ideas." But why would a philosopher, logician, and mathematician be so perturbed by the verb *to be*? What damage could this verb ever cause to the logical scaffolding upon which all of mathematics was founded? For once, before reporting the diagnosis, it's worthwhile to anticipate the therapy. Russell continues his tirade: "a disgrace which a symbolic logical language *of course* remedies" (Russell 1919, 192; emphasis mine). The disgrace thus finds in the verb *to be* a precise symptom, but in Russell's eyes the disease is much more extensive: the sick patient is all of language, an imperfect instrument, the cause of so many and such great pitfalls that all of philosophy should start from there, in a sense, if it is to rebuild. This is precisely one of the central points of the school of thought known as "analytic philosophy": an enormous mass of work and effort by scholars such as Gottlob Frege and Ludwig Wittgenstein, to name two, who focused on assessing the weight of language in the philosophical image of the world. But again, for us it's only important to clarify what connotations (implicit and explicit) accumulated around the verb *to be* in this historical phase of Western thought.

A good way to fully understand Russell's concern is to start with the entirety of this passage, too often ignored. Just before launching into his invective, Russell prepares the terrain by writing, "The proposition *Socrates is a man* is no doubt 'equivalent' to *Socrates is human*, but it is not the very same proposition. The *is* of *Socrates is human* expresses the relation of subject and predicate; the *is* of *Socrates is a man* expresses identity" (Russell 1919, 172).[14] On the whole, this is a very dense quote but not so dense that we can't catch a glimpse of the true question through the trees. At the heart of the scandal was a radical, irreconcilable, and dangerous ambiguity in the verb *to be*.

First a preliminary and general note: it's clear that Russell is not expressing the thought of a linguist. To say that *Socrates is human* expresses a relationship of predication while *Socrates is a man* expresses an identity means shuffling the cards around on the table, in the sense that the relationship of identity is always mediated in natural language by a relationship of predication, since we're still dealing with a sentence. Even if one were to use an explicit predicate of identity, such as *to be identical to*, one would still have a relationship of predication, even in the presence of an explicit expression of an identity relationship; therefore, identity and predication are not antagonists from a linguistic point of view. But the question is much more complex and important. Russell's distance from linguistics becomes even more evident when he speaks about the verb *to be* followed by an adjective. Had he adhered to the linguistic tradition up to that time, and of which an intellectual of his caliber must certainly have been aware, he would have had to say either that *is* is the manifestation of time and the true predicate is the adjective *human* (had he been an Aristotelian), or that *is* is the manifestation of affirmation and that the predicate is nevertheless *human* (had he been a Port-Royalist). Evidently, Russell was neither an Aristotelian nor a Port-Royalist, and in this case he deviates radically from tradition by asserting that the verb *to be* is a predicate. The most delicate point, however, is this: why does Russell refuse to admit that *a man* can also be a predicate on a par with *human*, so that he is forced to admit instead that it's the verb *to be* that plays the role of the predicate? In a certain way, he builds with his own two hands the very ambiguity against which he immediately and vehemently lashes out.

This idea that the verb *to be* is a predicate of identity was moreover not one that Russell invented from scratch: the credit goes to his illustrious predecessor, also not a linguist, the great logician Gottlob Frege, who with the famous example *The evening star is the morning star* intended to create an indisputable case in which the verb *to be* produces an identity.[15] We'll deal with the two stars in a minute; now let's get back to the sentence *Socrates is a man*. No contemporary linguist would say that the sentence *Socrates is a man* is always, and I emphasize "always," an identity statement. However, there's no need for a linguist; an attentive scholar would do. There are many ways to prove it, some banal, others less so. We'll start with the first. In Italian and in many other Romance languages, nouns may be replaced by pronouns of a type called "clitic"—which are supported by other words because they are unstressed—and in most cases they agree in gender and number with the nouns they refer to: for example, in place of *Paolo conobbe Francesca* 'Paul knew Francesca' one can say *Paolo la conobbe* 'Paul *la* [her] knew', where the Italian pronoun *la* 'she' is feminine and singular like *Francesca*. In the "majority" of cases, I say, because it's well known—and it's taught in elementary schools—that things change with the verb *to be*. Let's take for example two sentences like *Cleopatra incontrò una regina* 'Cleopatra met a queen' and *Cleopatra era una regina* 'Cleopatra was a queen'. In the (Italian) version with the clitic pronoun, the two sentences are different: *Cleopatra la incontrò* 'Cleopatra *la* [her] met' but *Cleopatra lo era* 'Cleopatra *lo* [so] was'. The same thing happens with a plural noun: *I ragazzi incontrarono i responsabili* 'The kids met the managers', which becomes *I ragazzi li incontrarono* 'The kids *li* [them] met', while *I ragazzi sono i responsabili* 'The kids are the managers' is rendered instead as *I ragazzi lo sono* 'The kids *lo* [so] are'. With the verb *to be*, therefore, the clitic is never inflected: it always occurs in the neutral form *lo*. Certainly in the case of *Socrates is a man*, the clitic version isn't much help, but only because it happens that in Italian the neutral clitic pronoun is homophonous with the third person singular masculine pronoun, as in *Socrate lo è* 'Socrates *lo* [so] is' and *Socrate lo incontra* 'Socrates *lo* [him] meets' (from *Socrate incontra un uomo* 'Socrates meets a man'). But if Russell had used an example with a female name—for instance, that of Socrates's wife, Xanthippe—in Italian the clitic form of the sentence *Santippe è una donna* 'Xanthippe is a woman' would have been *Santippe lo è* 'Xanthippe *lo* [so] is' and not *Santippe la è* 'Xanthippe *la* [she] is', which demonstrates that *una donna* 'a woman' functions as a predicate. Obviously, there's no reason to think that *un uomo* 'a man' functions any differently. We conclude that, at least in the linguistic realm, the sentence *Socrates is a man* can't *always* be analyzed as a sentence where *a man* doesn't perform the function of a predicate.

Another, less direct proof that the verb *to be* is not a predicate of identity is based on the domain of grammar that has produced very interesting theoretical and empirical results, namely, the theory of pronoun interpretation (*binding theory*). This is—it's true—a less direct proof, but one that seems to me to decisively corroborate the hypothesis that the equivalent of *a man* in the sentence quoted by Russell can *never* be analyzed if not analyzed as a predicate. Let's return for a moment to our two stars, focusing on a surprising property of the verb *to be*—surprising but so simple that it often escapes attention. It's easy to explain with an example. If I say *Mary is her admirer*,[16] *her* can't refer to Mary; with any other verb, things change. If instead I say *Mary knows her admirer*, *her* can continue to refer to someone else but this time it can also just as well refer to Mary. This special property of the verb *to be* has been the subject of many studies, and it seems to be invariable—mutatis mutandis—in the languages of the world. One way it has been described—not without disputes, as evidenced by Chomsky 1986, Giorgi and Longobardi 1991, and Moro 1997, among others—is this: if a group of words that revolve around a noun like *admirer*, technically called a "noun phrase" (such as *that smart admirer, her admirer*, etc.), has a so-called "referential" capacity—where by "referential" I mean in the intuitive sense the opposite of predication—then a pronoun that is contained in that phrase (such as *her* in the previous examples) can refer to the subject, otherwise not.

Now let's return to our two stars in the sentence *The evening star is the morning star*. This sentence, so famous as to be almost proverbially accepted to indicate an expression of identity, is based on the fact that in the northern latitudes the last star that disappears in the morning, or the planet Venus, is also the first that appears in the evening. The impression of seeing two different "stars" is evocative, but in reality it is a kind of cognitive mirage. If we could continue our observation of the star for the entire time (assuming that it never set), we would see that we were dealing with exactly the same celestial body; therefore, we can say that the evening star is the morning star. But the mirage is not only cognitive: I suggest that it's also linguistic in the sense that, if we're dealing with identity, the verb *to be* is of no import whatsoever. I mean to say that this sentence with the verb *to be* still combines a noun (or a noun phrase) used referentially with a noun (or a noun phrase) used nonreferentially, which is to say with a predicate. How can we prove this hypothesis? The solution is simple and is based on a lexical stratagem, so to speak. It involves using an explicit identity predicate—that is, an identity predicate that is not open to question, such as *identical to*—and seeing if there are differences in the behavior of pronouns that we place as detectors within the two noun phrases denoting the two entities constituting the identity. This is less difficult than it sounds; it's enough to build our sentence in the right context. Let's imagine for a moment that instead of the two expressions *the evening star* and *the morning star*, we have *the evening star* and *its associate in the firmament*; namely, let's imagine that we have available a catalogue of stars each of which is paired with another and we are to consider "the morning star" the associate of the evening star. Now let's compare these two sentences: *The evening star is its associate in the firmament* and *The evening star is identical to its associate in the firmament*. Any native speaker of English will immediately recognize that the pronoun *its* functions differently in the two cases, in fact, in a symmetrically opposite way: when an identity predicate is present (*identical to*), the pronoun can refer to the subject *the evening star*; but when only the verb *to be* is present, that simply can't happen, which makes us conclude without a shadow of a doubt that in that sentence *its associate* is a predicate, not a referential expression. In other words, this experiment proves that the verb *to be* is not a predicate of identity. This, of course, doesn't mean that we can't call the proposition in question an "identity proposition," but it implies that the role of the verb *to be* needs to be well defined and that, if anything, identity needs to be explained independently of it—starting, for example, from the interpretation and from the structure of the noun phrase involved in the sentence.

At this point, it becomes indispensable to clarify the question about the interpretation of the notion of "identity." The road diverges here: on the one hand, we must understand to what degree it's legitimate to admit that a sentence like *Socrates is a man* is an identity statement; on the other, we must understand why, in this specific case, Russell couldn't accept any other analysis. The first path is the more delicate. To say that *Socrates is a man* is an identity statement means admitting that in the world, I am referring to Socrates and to a certain man and I say that they are the same individual. This interpretation may also be paraphrased by saying that both *Socrates* and *a man* have referential value. Even this interpretation is not without its critics. In a famous essay on the notion of referentiality, Peter Geach—an English philosopher and historian of philosophy of great acumen who was born in the early twentieth century—argued against exactly this interpretation, saying that it makes no sense to ask what man Socrates is in the sentence *Socrates is a man* (see Geach 1962). Geach makes this insight the diagnostic foundation for detecting the occurrence of a predicate in a sentence: calling this principle "Buridan's law" in tribute to the great medieval philosopher Buridan, he writes, "[T]he reference of an expression can never depend on whether the proposition it occurs in is true or false" (Geach 1962, 52) This implies that *a man* in the sentence *Socrates is a man* has no referential ability but is instead a predicate, confirming the argument based on the interpretation of pronouns that we have just considered. So, for Geach, a sentence like *Socrates is a man* can never be an identity statement. Not all philosophers, logicians, and linguists of the twentieth century follow Geach—indeed, to tell the truth, almost no one does. Also worth mentioning, among those who *don't* follow him, is Willard Van Orman Quine, who unconditionally accepts Russell's ambiguity hypothesis, with tremendous consequences for his philosophical system (see, for example, the entry *copula* in Quine 1987).

The problem, as far as we're concerned, is that the supposed identity relationship expressed in the sentence *Socrates is a man* is not affected at all by the presence of the verb *to be*, as is clearly seen in a sentence like *Xanthippe considers Socrates a man*. Here the verb *to be* doesn't appear, but the relationship between *Socrates* and *a man* remains the same as it is in *Socrates is a man*; therefore, if the relationship between *Socrates* and *a man* is one of identity, it remains one of identity, regardless of whether the verb *to be* occurs or not.[17] At this point, however, the road isn't very interesting, at least for the goal we've chosen: if the identity relationship isn't tied to the verb *to be* but only depends on the quality of the other elements—if, for example, the verb *to be* is followed by an adjective or a noun—we don't have to worry about it here. If anything, a legitimate question is whether or not the noun phrase that follows the verb *to be* in these cases should *always* have predicative value or whether it can *also* have a referential function. We're faced with a central question for the subject of this book, and we'll see how the proposed solution reconciles these two seemingly incompatible positions. However, before moving on to Jespersen's reaction to this hypothesis, we still need to understand why Russell was so annoyed by the fact that, in the offending sentence, *a man* can be a predicate of *Socrates*. And the mystery of why his invective is found in a book on the philosophy of mathematics will finally be resolved.

Among the many cultural activities that Russell engaged in during this period of his life, certainly a central one was the rebuilding of mathematics (logic) in an attempt to eliminate those paradoxes that he had discovered and that had wrecked the dream of the giant, Frege. Although 24 years his junior, Russell was able to come into contact with Frege on several occasions. One of the most dramatic moments in this relationship took place in June 1903, when Russell sent a letter to Frege as the latter was preparing the second volume of one of his most ambitious works, *Grundgesetze der Aritmetik*, or *The Foundations of Arithmetic*—with which the author proposed to establish the *entire* edifice of arithmetic on the basis of set theory. Russell, who was 31 years old and had for a few of those years been working on the notion of infinite sets, had noticed that there was a flaw in this colossal system: it contained a paradox that could bring everything down, like a sand castle in a hurricane. The paradox—which then became known as the "Russell antinomy"—consists in the possibility of defining a set R that is made up of sets that do not contain themselves. Now we'll take R: if R contains itself, R is not a set of sets that don't contain themselves and therefore I was wrong to call them that; if instead R doesn't contain itself, now it must be included in R, because of how I have just defined R, and once again I'm wrong in saying that R doesn't contain itself. So, we truly don't know what to make of R. Other, more or less picturesque formulations of the paradox have been given. A typical example is the sign in the shop window of a village's only barber, which reads, "Here is one who shaves all those, and only those, who do not shave themselves." The question is, Who shaves the barber? If the barber shaves himself, then the sign is false because it's not true that he shaves only those who don't shave themselves; if he doesn't shave himself, the sign is still false because everyone who doesn't shave himself has to be shaved by the barber. I could construct many more examples like this, but I don't want to lose sight of the real reason for this digression. In the end, I'd be happy to deal less with barbers and stars, but I have to reveal the mystery behind Russell's invective against the verb *to be*.

Once Russell had voiced this antinomy, many tried to resolve it, including Frege himself—who was regrettably unable to do it. It occupied great minds such as Ernst Zermelo, who proposed an axiomatic theory of sets, and Wittgenstein, and of course even Russell himself tried. Russell's solution, presented in his monumental three-volume work *Principia Mathematica,* written together with Alfred North Whitehead and published between 1910 and 1913, was called "type theory." It's a complex theory, which has given rise to many currents in research, including so-called "Montague grammar," a formal system for inferring the semantics of propositions based on a simple idea: that of building increasingly complex objects (the types) by progressively combining "atomic" elements, that is, those that can't be further broken down into primitive elements. One of the axioms of type theory is that a type can only be combined with a different type (of the appropriate type, but still different); from this follows as a corollary that an item of one type can't be combined with an element of the *same* type. For example, the "verb" type *flies* can be combined with the "noun" type *Icarus*, giving rise to the phrase *Icarus flies*, translating into practice the idea that predicates are combined with subjects; but the "noun" type *Icarus* can't be combined with an item of the same type like *Sinatra* because the result would be meaningless, **Icarus Sinatra*. In this way, Russell's antinomy can't occur, because it's impossible to define a set that belongs to itself. The scaffolding of arithmetical logic was saved, but at a high price.

How relevant is the verb *to be* in all this? It's important, very important, because if we admit that words—simplifying a bit—are assigned different types, when I say *Socrates is a man* I must be careful not to admit that *a man*—which of course belongs to the same type as *Socrates*, which is a noun phrase—can be a predicate of *Socrates*. In other words, I must at all costs avoid a noun's (or a noun phrase's) being the predicate of another noun (or noun phrase); this would reintroduce the antinomy and we'd be back where we started. So, for Russell the only alternative to keep from demolishing type theory was to admit that the verb *to be* was necessarily a predicate of identity when followed by a noun (or noun phrase), or that the two nouns (or noun phrases) that precede and follow the verb *to be* are both referential—which is to say neither of the two is a predicate—exactly as it is with any other transitive verb, that is, those involving two nouns or two noun phrases. Since, however, a sentence like *Socrates is human* displays no conflict between elements of the same type—because *human* is an adjective and therefore doesn't belong to the same type as *Socrates*—there is no longer any need (or possibility, since adjectives can't be referential) to admit that the verb *to be* is an identity predicate. The predicate is *human*, and for Russell, the verb *to be* simply accompanies the predicate relationship, not unlike the way the Port-Royalists intended when they thought of the verb *to be* as a sign of affirmation. Recognizing that this ambiguity in the function of the verb *to be* was irreducible, indeed—we could say—constrained to admit the existence of *two* different verbs *to be*, Russell gave up and launched his famous invective against the verb *to be* as being a "disgrace to the human race."

I will argue against this analysis in the next chapter, returning to what we've already seen regarding pronouns; what is certain is that Russell's inauspicious announcement was immediately taken up by the community of logicians and linguists. As I've already mentioned, this idea that the verb *to be* ambiguously expresses identity one minute and predication the next has now, in fact, taken hold everywhere—strengthened by the partial quoting of the passage in which Russell expressed his thought, that is, omitting the part with the examples—or even so thoroughly taken for granted that it's not even quoted at all. In addition to Quine (1987), among the philosophers I must mention at least Donald Davidson (2005) and Jerrold Katz (1990); among linguists certainly Chomsky (1986b)—to cite perhaps his most explicit work on this issue—and, in its wake, virtually all of the generativists (with the exception of Giuseppe Longobardi); then Émile Benveniste (1966), M. A. K. Halliday (1967, 1968), functionalists like Simon C. Dik (1987), typologists like Bernard Comrie (1997), and many authoritative descriptive grammars of modern languages, among them Randolph Quirk and Sidney Greenbaum's (1973) for English, Maurice Grevisse's (2007) for French, and Lorenzo Renzi, Giampaolo Salvi, and Anna Cardinaletti's (1988/1991/1995) for Italian.

Finally, I mention another highly influential founder of modern linguistics, Richard Montague (1973), and his pupil, Barbara Partee (1986), who played a major role in introducing the methods of mathematical logic into formal linguistics. Montague grammar deserves special consideration, having greatly contributed to spreading the theory of the ambiguity of the verb *to be* in contemporary formal linguistics. It should be noted, among other things, that this theoretical model adapted naturally to the style and methodological presuppositions of the research current inaugurated by Chomsky; today, the fruits of this union perhaps represent the most promising field of research in formal linguistics (see the brilliant synthesis presented in Chierchia and McConnell-Ginet 1990).[18] Montague grammar is itself a generative grammar, a formal system that describes the semantics of propositions in natural languages, combining type theory with other logical tools, such as the American mathematician Alonzo Church's lambda calculus and the notion of truth defined by Alfred Tarski. In addition to Montague's original formulation of the theory, very important work on these themes has been done by David Dowty, Robert Wall, and Stanley Peters (1981) and by Partee (1986). The verb *to be* receives a particular treatment in all of the works developed within this paradigm of formal research: it is analyzed as an element able to interact in different ways according to the type of the elements with which it is combined, unlike any other verb. It's quite interesting to note that the complex Montagovian formula that was associated with the verb *to be* ($\lambda P\lambda x P\{^\wedge \lambda y\ [x=y]\}$) indisputably assumes and integrates Russell's dichotomous vision. In fact, once applied to linguistic expressions, depending on whether it is combined with a noun or an adjective, this formula is able to generate both a formula that represents an identity and one with a relationship of predication, exactly reconstituting Russell's analysis, although in advanced formal terms.

Clearly, in the early twentieth century the history of the verb *to be* is already complicated enough: in addition to the sign of tense and the sign of affirmation, there is now the idea—certainly not devoid of aspects that are obscure and frankly muddled—that the verb *to be* is also an expression of identity, not to mention that some see in this verb a predicate of *existence*. We are now quite a long way from the purity of the Aristotelian system that, as I have pointed out, has never been abandoned. In chapter 3, I will try to argue in a systematic way against this polysemantic vision of the verb *to be*, but right now it's worth remembering the resistance, however isolated, that opposed Russell's interpretation: that of the great Danish linguist, Otto Jespersen.

The Great Exorcism Failure: Jespersen and the Revenge of Language

In 1909, Otto Jespersen—Danish linguist and professor at Copenhagen University between 1893 and 1925—wrote a monumental, seven-volume description of English, *A Modern English Grammar on Historical Principles*. Earlier, he had written an analysis of the development and structure of English created for speakers of other languages, first published in 1905 and still in print a century later, *Growth and Structure of the English Language*. Among his most interesting writings are his *Analytic Syntax* from 1937, a decidedly hermetic *summa* of his linguistic thought, and *The Philosophy of Grammar* from 1924, a fascinating text that even today holds many surprises; we will return to these works in chapter 3. Jespersen was passionate about language the way an entomologist is passionate about insects: he wasn't hunting for the perfect butterfly, he simply sought to take into account all possible insects, primarily to arrive at a full description of how they really function. It was inconceivable for him to think of "remedying the disgrace generated by language"—to paraphrase Russell—just as it would be inconceivable for an entomologist to think about "remedying a butterfly with transparent wings": either it's there and is to be described, or it isn't and it shouldn't be assumed. All without asking for help from other sciences. This attitude is very clear in how Jespersen talks about the verb *to be*—but a premise is necessary.

One of the driving forces of Jespersen's scientific thought, and in some ways also its limitation, is the idea that linguistic facts should not be explained through the use of extralinguistic categories: grammar cannot be reduced to something else; it has its primitive elements, its rules, and its complex objects that in no way resemble objects in other domains. This methodological assumption had enormous repercussions on his scientific production. On the one hand, it excludes the possible use of tools borrowed, for example, from formal logic or mathematics in order to understand language; on the other—when entering into the merits of a particular linguistic structure—one is obliged to find in linguistic facts an "internal" diagnostic that keeps metaphorical and anecdotal discourse, all too typical in linguistics, at a distance.

An important example of the consequences of this autarchic program lies in the problem of identifying a sentence's subject. For Jespersen, as for almost all linguists starting with Plato and Aristotle, the problem of how to identify the subject and the predicate is a central point of linguistics. Jespersen understood immediately that there were indirect ways to identify these elements and that meaning could not be of any help. We all remember when, as beginners at logical analysis, we were taught that to identify the subject, one must recognize who performs the action. We surely know that there are at least two mistakes in this strategy (although it can be useful for beginners). First, not all subjects perform an action. For example, if I say *Cain suffers*, Cain doesn't perform any actions; if anything, there is a condition in which Cain finds himself. Second, if I say *Cain kills Abel*, it's quite true that *Cain* is the subject, but it's no longer the subject when I say *Abel was killed by Cain* even though *Cain* is the name of the one who performed the action.[19] Jespersen wanted to find a way to define the subject that was "internal" to language, a way that used the phenomena of language to understand how to identify this element. Nor can the fact that a language contains a system of "cases" be helpful in this regard. In some languages, as I've mentioned, the nouns not only are inflected in the singular and the plural, but also are modified according to their grammatical role within the sentence: for example, as the direct object (like *John* in *I see John*) or as the indirect object (like *John* in *I give a book to John*). In Latin, for example, the proper name *Johannes* becomes *Johannem* when it's used as a direct object and *Johanni* when it's used as an indirect object. In many modern European languages, the case system is active only in pronouns. In Italian, *gli* and *lo* are the two inflections of the third person singular pronouns *egli* and *lui*, so I say *Gli presento Francesca* 'I introduce Francesca to him' or *Lo presento a Francesca* 'I introduce him to Francesca', depending on whether the pronoun stands for the person who introduces someone or for the person who is introduced to someone. We see the same thing in languages such as English, where the third person pronoun *he* is inflected as *him* when it acts as a direct object (*John saw him*). According to a traditional terminology, *he* is said to be in the nominative case while *him* is in the accusative. This state of affairs has often led to a certain degree of confusion, suggesting that the nominative case is the distinctive mark of the subject. In reality, simple examples are enough to understand that this isn't true. Let's imagine a sentence like *He has killed him.* Certainly the subject is in the nominative case (*he*) and the direct object is in the accusative case (*him*). However, it can happen that one sentence becomes dependent on another, as in *Peter believed him to have killed him*. In this example, the subject of *to kill* is the first *him*—that is, a pronoun inflected in the accusative case, the same one that in the first English sentence (*He has killed him*) was in the nominative case (*he*). Therefore, at least if we limit ourselves to cases, it seems that language does not give clear indications of how to identify the subject.

Jespersen, however, didn't give up. He thought that language in itself could contain the litmus test that would allow one to identify the subject apart from logical (or ontological) considerations, and he determined this litmus test to be agreement: the phenomenon according to which two (or more) words share characteristics of a predetermined paradigm. A simple example is agreement in number (*a thorn*, not **a thorns*) or, in Italian, in number and gender (*il vento* 'the wind: singular masculine definite article + singular masculine noun', not **i vento* 'the wind: plural masculine definite article + singular masculine noun'). In this case, to simplify a great deal, *number* means simply whether a thing is present singularly (only one thorn, only one wind) or in a plurality of instances (more thorns, more winds). By crossing this obvious fact with another equally obvious one—the distinction between verb and noun—Jespersen proposed an elegant strategy for defining a subject: the subject is the noun (or, as I mentioned earlier, the group of words that gravitate around a noun technically called a "noun phrase" or "NP") that agrees with the verb. So, the subject in the sentence *Cain kills Abel* is *Cain*, while it's *Abel* in *Abel is killed by Cain*; similarly, it's *brother* in *The brother of these pirates kills the groundhog*. Jespersen says, "The grammatical subject cannot be defined by means of such words as 'active' or 'agent', ...[T]he subject as a grammatical term can thus be defined only in connection with the rest of the sentence in *its actual form*" (Jespersen 1937, def. 34.1, emphasis mine). Spoiling the party in this seemingly elegant system, as might be expected, is the verb *to be*; let's see why.[20]

Let's start with a concrete example provided by Jespersen himself in *The Philosophy of Grammar* from 1924: *The prettiest girl at the ball was Miss Castlewood*. This type of sentence presents a special case of the use of the verb *to be*, which we have already encountered in Russell: it is a sentence in which the verb *to be* is accompanied by an NP in the sequence NP V NP. However, this case is, so to speak, even more special because if we exchange the order of the two noun phrases, to a first approximation the sentence does not appear to change in meaning: *Miss Castlewood was the prettiest girl at the ball*. Jespersen did not consider these sentences a marginal problem; in fact, he returned to these anomalous cases in 1937, using the example sentence *The only man who knew the secret was Thomas*. Here also—as in the preceding case—the two noun phrases can change position, giving *Thomas was the only man who knew the secret*. This type of "symmetric" sentence will be at the center of the discussion in the next two chapters, and it's certainly not appropriate to anticipate that discussion here; what's important now, and it's very important, is to note that in this case the agreement isn't helpful in identifying the subject because the verb *to be* agrees in the same way with both the first and the second noun phrase. Naturally—it could be argued—the same issue would occur with *The prettiest girl at the ball knows Miss Castlewood*. But in this case it would be very easy to find a way to identify the subject. It would be enough to make both the preverbal and the postverbal noun phrases plural and see how the verb behaves. It's easy to see that the verb is only sensitive to the number of the preverbal noun phrase: so, *The prettiest girl at the ball and her sister know Miss Castlewood* but *The prettiest girl at the ball knows Miss Castlewood and her sister*. With the verb *to be*, this isn't possible because, for some reason, in sentences with *to be* the two noun phrases must have the same number: either they're both plural or they're both singular, and consequently the verb agrees.[21] How do we escape this impasse? Obviously, we can't admit two subjects; the sentence would lack a predicate, given that for Jespersen, as for Aristotle and the Port-Royalists, the verb *to be* is not a predicate, as we'll see in a moment. In this case, the diagnostic technique based on agreement seems to be a spectacular failure.

Obviously, there would be an immediate way to put things to rights: interpret the verb *to be* as a predicate of identity. But let's hear how Jespersen reacts to the idea of accepting this proposal, the legacy of Frege and Russell: "The linguistic copula *is* does not mean or imply identity but subsumption in the sense of the old Aristotelian logic" (Jespersen 1924, 153). And again: "In the mathematical formula $A = B$ we should not take the sign $=$ as a copula and B as predicative, but insert the copula *is* before the predicative *equal to B*" (Jespersen 1924, 154; see also Jespersen 1937, 133). Jespersen utterly rejected the mere idea of importing from mathematical logic the notion and notation of identity, a rejection that could only end in an act of surrender: "The two terms connected by *is* ... may change places as subject and predicative" (Jespersen 1924, 153). An embarrassing white flag that even ten years later would be flown in a way that left no room for justifications. In trying to reduce the notion of subject and predicate to the notion of "extension," which is the plurality of the sets denoted by noun phrases, Jespersen says, "There are cases in which the extension is equal [as in *Beauty is truth* and *Truth is beauty*]; this means that we cannot decide which is the subject and which is the predicate" (1924, 136). In other words, the verb *to be* actually prevents the complete implementation of the autarchic program that Jespersen had desired for linguistics, creating a "flaw" in the system, a singularity that leaves things indeterminate and indeterminable. Certainly, Jespersen knew that there were simpler cases: "If one of the substantives is perfectly definite, and the other not, the former is the subject; this is the case with a proper name [as in *Socrates is a man*]" (1924, 150). But that matters little; the fact is that there is an entire class of sentences—which we can call "symmetric" copular sentences,[22] that is, those where the noun phrases can switch positions around the verb *to be*—where the subject does not seem to be able to be identified, and this flaw is enough to give the impression that the great exorcism of logic from the body of linguistics was a grand fiasco, at least if we stop at the formal tools that Jespersen had available to him.[23]

Above all, unlike Russell, Jespersen definitely had a keener sensibility for linguistic data—nor was language, to be honest, Russell's central concern. This sensibility was manifested in the attention that Jespersen dedicated to another class of delicate phrases that needed to be accommodated in the overall scheme for diagnosing the subject. I'm talking about sentences like *There is a problem* and its Italian equivalent *C'è un problema*, sentences that are usually technically called "existential sentences" (we'll discuss these sentences at length in the following chapters). In this case, what does the verb *to be* combine with? Does a sentence like *There is a problem* perhaps have a structure equivalent to that of a sentence like *This is a problem*? Once again, this verb doesn't allow itself to be easily pigeonholed. Meanwhile, the verb *to be* seems to agree with the noun phrase that follows it. In fact, we say *There are many problems* and in Italian *Ci sono molti problemi*; therefore, if we follow Jespersen's agreement-based diagnostics to the letter, the subject would be the noun phrase that follows the verb. But this solution doesn't seem to work generally. In fact, in English, the subject can never come after the verb in a simple affirmative sentence; that is, I can't say *ature *Runs a man*. How are the pieces of this fragmented mosaic to be combined? Jespersen's solution is not without ambiguity: "In some respects (place in the sentence, etc.) this *there* behaves as an ordinary subject, and many grammarians therefore class it as a kind of subject" (Jespersen 1937, 129). Jespersen was thus constrained to invent a spurious category, the "lesser subject," which is found in an "inferior position" (Jespersen 1924, 154)—essentially an anomalous construction where "the verb precedes the subject and the latter is hardly treated grammatically like a real subject" (Jespersen 1924, 153).

It's interesting to note that, among other things, this analysis of existential sentences based on the hypothesis of a "lesser subject"—which for convenience we could call "Jespersen's generalization"—was also extended to other cases, usually called "existential sentences," which we will revisit: "This analysis is extended to cases involving verbs other than the copula such as *exist, stand, lie, come*" (Jespersen 1937, 130). Regarding existential sentences, Jespersen reprises, at least implicitly, Abelard's refusal to consider the verb *to be* as a predicate of existence: "When philosophers form sentences like *God is*, this is felt as a rather unnatural transference from the normal use of *is* as 'copula'. ... If we answer the question: *Is he dead?* by saying: *Yes, he is*, does that mean 'he exists' or 'his death exists'?" (Jespersen 1937, 133). In a certain way, Jespersen gives us the sense of having simply returned to the point of departure, to have returned to Aristotle's theory, which considered the verb *to be* as an unambiguous and nonpredicative element—except

To Be—and Not "Being"—or, The Names of the Verb

that between Aristotle and Jespersen more than two millennia had passed, and meanwhile a lot of new data and many new theories had formed, developed, and sometimes fallen out of use. For Jespersen to then offer a simple exhumation of Aristotle's theory is anachronistic, to say the least.

There is no need—I believe—to add any more in order to convincingly say that the analysis of the verb *to be* in the first decades of the twentieth century is anything but resolved; what's worse, it has become encrusted with three different traditions that deceptively tangle its threads, often leading to confused conclusions. On the one hand, Aristotle's theory, according to which the verb *to be* is definitively the name of tense, has never faded away. On the other hand, there is the analysis of the verb *to be* as a copula—that is, as the element that couples the subject with the predicate and gives birth to an affirmative sentence—that arose in the Middle Ages, continued with new accents from the influential Port-Royal school, and is now attested and followed in modern times even in grammar textbooks. Furthermore, there is the idea, canonized by Russell, that the verb *to be* also expresses identity, which is accepted by virtually all linguists (and philosophers). Finally, in contrast to the authoritative opinions of a philosophical stamp, such as that of Kant, in many quarters the hypothesis persists that this same verb is also a predicate of existence, and with this the putative meanings of the verb *to be* rise to (at least) four. Certainly, it's not that the various theories have simply been deposited like stratified sediment and consolidated without changes. For example, Jespersen, whose linguistic sensibilities couldn't make him accept the rationalist contrivances typical of Port-Royalist and medieval linguistics, accepted Aristotle's theory, but not in its entirety. In fact, he distanced himself from Aristotle—albeit without naming him—and was fully consistent with the autocratic linguistic program when he said, "Logicians are fond of analyzing all sentences into three elements, subject, copula and predicate; *The man walks* is taken to contain the subject *the man*, the copula *is*, and the predicate *walking*. A linguist must find this analysis unsatisfactory, not only from the point of view of English grammar, where *is walking* means something different from *walks*, but also from a general point of view" (Jespersen 1924, 131). And he considered the grand comparative tradition of the nineteenth century unsuitable, and used changes in language as an explanation: "Sentences containing *is* probably have their origin ... from 'nominal sentences' in which two words were ... placed together as subject and predicative; later these were brought under the usual type by the addition of the least substantial verb ..., in much the same way as other sentences were made to conform to the usual type by the addition of the colourless subject *it* (*it rains*, ... , etc.) ... [Q]uestions of supposed original development should not determine our analysis of things as they are in our own day" (Jespersen 1937, 135). As we see, even the term "substantial verb" or "verb that expresses substance" has been turned upside down with respect to the Port-Royalist tradition, raising along with this historiographical questions that still await an answer.

We'll stop here. The more than two-thousand-year history of the analysis of the verb *to be* thus enters the twentieth century freighted with problems, misconceptions, incrustations, controversy, and misunderstandings, explicit but also implicit. At this point, a universally accepted version of a theory about the verb *to be* doesn't exist, and often the different traditions are only visible in vague allusions and sometimes not even noticed. What impact does the verb *to be* have on linguistics in the second half of the twentieth century? We'll talk about this in chapter 3: in the next chapter, we must instead reconstruct the environment in which the verb *to be* will then be understood in a new way. For a while, then, we'll almost abandon the verb *to be*; but if we didn't go through the effort of this reconstruction, we would never come to

To Be—and Not "Being"—or, The Names of the Verb

understand the advantages (and disadvantages) of the theory that will be outlined at the end of this book. In the period we've just discussed, the dream of a linguistics based on logic was shattered and the alternative of an autarchic program that did not make use of ideas from logic seemed to falter; if we must be cast out of the paradise that we've built, at least we must appreciate its architecture first.

2 Anatomy of a Sentence

Language is more like a snowflake than a giraffe's neck. Its specific properties are determined by laws of nature; they have not developed through the accumulation of historical accidents.
—Noam Chomsky[1]

With this chapter, we enter into a new atmosphere. Both because at a certain point we'll leave history behind and try to move ahead toward paths not yet fully traveled, and because linguistics in the second half of the twentieth century enters a new phase, in some ways never before experienced: the phase Giorgio Graffi, in his monumental and authoritative *200 Years of Syntax* (Graffi 2001), defines as linguistics' "era of syntax." For the first time, in fact, this domain assumes the role of the central driving force behind the entire discipline, similar to phonology in the nineteenth century, although obviously drawing on results from other domains of the discipline as well. It's precisely from this "syntax-centric" perspective that the verb *to be* can be studied more thoroughly, clearly highlighting the motive for its controversial starring role over the course of the centuries. In essence, we'll be dealing with this phase in the next chapter.

However, for a moment we need to take a step back to Geneva in the late 1800s, when a young man from a wealthy family—

where scientific culture was an integral part of family life—was interested in linguistics, among an array of passions including puzzles and spiritualism (let's not forget that in that era hypnosis was the focus of what were more or less the salon discussions from which the discovery of the unconscious would later emerge). This young man was named Ferdinand de Saussure, and we're indebted to him for one of the most influential perspective changes in the history of linguistics—if not for the originality of his thinking, then certainly for the impact it would have on contemporary culture. While still very young—he was twenty-one—he achieved well-deserved and widespread fame in linguistic circles with the famous *Mémoire sur le système primitif des voyelles dans les langues indo-européennes* (1879), in which he illustrated the mechanism that accounted for some previously unexplained phenomena of Indo-European languages' vowel systems. But we wouldn't be talking about Saussure here and now if it weren't for the final ten years of his academic life, which this multifaceted scholar devoted to reestablishing linguistic terminology and methodology, with which he was never satisfied. Nor, in truth, must he ever have been satisfied with this work since, as it appears, he destroyed his own notes at the end of each lesson, so that it's only because of the diligence of two of his students—Charles Bally and Albert Sechehaye, who didn't directly participate in the courses—that we know the fundamentals of his linguistic thinking as they're presented in the famous *Cours de linguistique générale* (1916). Not that Saussure was dealing directly with the verb *to be*; on the contrary, perhaps this is one of the few topics that he *didn't* address in a specific way. However, he gave us the chance to view the elements of linguistics in a new way, one that revolutionized not only linguistics but also many other fields of knowledge. We must follow our path through this revolution, and its appendices, in order to understand the role that the verb *to be* plays in formal linguistics' current model.

In fact, with Saussure the notion of "structure" takes mature form, although this term never appears in his *Cours* and instead we find *système*. There are many ways to think about the notion of "structure"—a familiar term, commonly used in many different contexts: an architectural structure, an organizational structure, a mathematical structure, a narrative structure, a psychological structure, a biological structure. What do they have in common? First of all, there's the fact that they're composed of elements that are smaller relative to the whole and dependent on each other in a more or less complex way: for example, in an architectural structure, bricks make up a wall but none of them, taken individually, is the wall.[2] So far, it seems as if there's nothing particularly interesting. The essential innovation of Saussure's definition of structure lies in the fact that every element of a structure, in the sense that he intends, has no *intrinsic* value; it only has value relative to the other elements. We'll say that all the parts of the structure are defined in a "differential" way. The theoretical and empirical significance of this concept isn't quick and easy to understand, but it's precisely the concept of a system of "differential" elements that's the core of structuralism. In his lectures, Saussure compared the elements of a language—its words, its sounds, its meanings—to the pieces on a chessboard: it makes no sense for me to ask what value a certain consonant or word has in a language if I don't know what it stands in counterpoint to, in the same way it doesn't make sense for me to ask whether having a rook in a specific square on the chessboard is good or not until I know how many other pieces are still in play and where they are—in other words, until I know how the position of the rook is differentiated relative to the other elements on the chessboard.

Naturally, as often happens in science, the contribution of an individual acts as a trigger, yes, but revolutions are then always determined by a group of people (often in the same generation; see Feuer 1982) who give impetus to an idea. With regard to the notion of structure this fact is, if possible, even more true. The notion of structure and structuralism spread like wildfire, in the most diverse disciplines: certainly through all areas of linguistics, but also into literary criticism, anthropology, psychoanalysis, sociology, biology, music, art forms in general, and even to mathematics, where the birth of abstract algebra marks perhaps the most absolute form of the structuralist investigation (for this last field, see the work of Nicolas Bourbaki, in particular Bourbaki 1948).

The first practical application of structuralism was in the domain of phonology—the sounds of language. In this sense, Saussure was truly the driving force behind this revolution, but without the contribution of another great linguist, the Russian Roman Jakobson, this entire field would not have reached the level of comprehensiveness and depth that it did. Jakobson, having come into contact with Prague's stimulating linguistic environment (dominated by Prince Nikolai Sergeyevich Trubetzkoy, who made decisive contributions to the structuralist program in phonology), was forced to move to the United States to escape Nazi persecution. There, the impact of his vision of language, which brought the structuralist dream to completion, took canonical form in a famous text written together with one of the cofounders of generative grammar, Morris Halle (Jakobson and Halle 1956). When structuralism arrived in the United States, it was definitively strengthened and assumed different and predominant contours.

As we've just seen, the essential idea of the structuralist vision, the one that sparked the entire revolution, is that the value of an element—its impact on reality—is not intrinsic but lies in its (differential) relationship with other elements. This concept can be pushed to the limit by acknowledging that the only value a certain element has in a structure is its difference relative to the values of the other elements, where by "value" we obviously mean any property relevant to that structure. We can see this central assumption of structuralism in a simple example. Imagine that we have to characterize the members of a rugby team, 15 different individuals in all. There are many ways to distinguish them: we can say which school one attended, his hometown, his parents' names, how much he weighs; what color another one's eyes are, when was the last time he cut his hair, what his favorite movie is, and so on. This method allows us to distinguish individuals in a sufficiently accurate way, by selecting for each one a variable number of characteristic properties; if, for example, there were only one player with albinism, that would be enough to distinguish him from the others. In fact, this is the natural method we use, unconsciously and practically, when we think, for example, of our friends. However, there is also another way to identify elements of that same group: we can choose a number of definable properties for all individuals and say whether that property is present or absent for *each* individual. Of course, this method only makes sense if we're trying to reduce the number of properties to the minimum. For example, with 2 well-chosen properties—let's say A and B—I can identify at least 4 individuals: the one who has property A and property B (conventionally notated [+A, +B]), the one who has property A but not property B (type [+A, −B]), and so on. If there are 3 properties, the possible number of individuals in purely combinatorial terms is 8; with 4 properties, the number is 16; with n properties, it's 2^n. When the number of properties used to define a set of linguistic elements is less than the number of the elements themselves, we say the elements make up a *natural class*. Now let's go back to our rugby team. It's enough to define 4 well-chosen properties in order to distinguish all the players in a homogenous and differential way; in fact, the 4 properties would give 16 possible combinations and so at least one of them could be absent in the group of 15 players. Let's say that the first property is a weight of more or less than 220 lbs.; the second, a height of more or less than 5′3″; the third, whether the player was born in Massachusetts or not; and the fourth, whether or not the player is Catholic. If these properties were well chosen—for example, if not all of the players weigh more than 220 lbs., not all are shorter than 5′3″, not all are Catholics, and not all were born in Massachusetts—by combining them all we could distinguish all of the players. In fact, we would have an extra player who wasn't included in the team and perhaps doesn't even exist, a player created "artificially" as a coherent mix of those same characteristics that we chose.[3]

One of the first cases cited in linguistics as an application of this method—both because it was conceived first historically and because it allows circumscribed cases to be built—is the system of sounds in a language. Take for example the system of vowels in Italian, consisting of 7 sounds (even if there are only 5 different graphic symbols; in fact, Italian has 2 *o* sounds and 2 *e* sounds, each open and closed). To define all of these vowels, we need only 4 well-chosen properties (plus 1 invariant property to distinguish the vowels from the consonants, which we can omit here). One property refers to how we position our lips to pronounce the vowel (rounded lips, as for *o*, or not), and three refer to the position of the tongue relative to possible movement along the vertical axis (high or not, and low or not; for example, the tongue lowers when pronouncing *a* after *e*) and the horizontal axis (retracted or not; for example, the tongue retracts when pronouncing *u* before *i*). Some combinations are impossible; others simply identify vowels that don't exist in Italian but that might exist in another language.[4] In any case, with this system it's possible to deduce that the vowels in themselves aren't entities defined in an independent and qualitatively different way; vowels are nothing but a combination of independent articulatory instructions activated simultaneously. In a certain sense, vowels don't exist, or they exist "after." Or rather, what exists, and what we perceive, are independent configurations of instructions that we don't perceive as such and that result in vowels, just as atoms of strontium and polonium are separable into common elements—protons, electrons, and neutrons—in different arrangements (and quantities). The system of vowels is therefore described as if it were structured in a "periodic table," in some ways similar to that used for the chemical elements.

The structural method is a method that leverages differences. One of the most famous passages in Saussure's *Cours* is a very elegant synthesis of this philosophy behind the research paradigm:

> Everything that has been said up to this point boils down to this: *in language there are only differences*. Even more important: a difference generally implies positive terms between which the difference is set up; but in language there are only differences without positive terms. Whether we take the signifier or the signified,[5] language has neither ideas nor sounds that existed before the linguistic system, but only conceptual and phonic differences that have issued from the system. The idea or phonic substance that a sign contains is of less importance than the other signs that surround it. Proof of this is that the value of a term may be modified without either its meaning or its sound being affected, solely because a neighboring term has been modified. (Saussure 1916 [1959, 120])

What concrete and abstract changes did the notion of structure bring about in linguistics? This is obviously a tough question, but for our purposes it isn't necessary to give a comprehensive answer. Our journey must lead us to an understanding of how the verb *to be* has come to be interpreted in modern linguistics, not to a complete overview of this discipline. All the same, this detour is an obligatory step, without which we would neither understand the true advantage of the structuralist method, nor understand how this method has led to a radically different vision of human language. So, we're talking about a genuine scientific revolution, but one that—for reasons that escape me—remains unknown to most people, while others, such as relativity and natural selection, always seem to be on everyone's lips.

Let's take another look at the discussion, point by point. There are at least three radical changes, conceptually distinct but not completely unrelated, that come into play when we look at language from the structuralist perspective. I'll list them in an arbitrary order, giving each a conventional name, to help us refer to them in the course of our journey. First, if what matters are the relationships, elements that have the same relationships to other elements of the system must be considered equivalent and, in principle, they can be exchanged (the *commutation principle*). Second, given an incompletely filled grid that combines certain properties, if the grid is correct, it will lead to the discovery of new objects that could fill the empty grid spaces (the *retrieval principle*). Third, not all possible combinations of primitive elements are used in every language (the *redundancy principle*). All three properties have analogues in models used in other empirical sciences—the prototypical example is, as I've just mentioned, the periodic table—and there's no need to insist too much on this theme at a theoretical level. Instead, I'll give three simple examples, starting with the last case, the redundancy principle, and again using the sounds of a language as primitive elements.

The redundancy principle is expressed in two different ways. On the one hand, it coincides with a type of overabundance *in absentia*. Let's take, for example, the Italian word *sostenevano* 'they uphold', which contains 11 letters corresponding to sounds (technically, 11 letters corresponding to 7 phonemes, 4 of them used twice).[6] As there are about 30 phonemes overall in standard Italian, this word is part of a galaxy of possible combinations numbering almost 18 million billion words (more precisely 17,714,700 billion), each with 11 phonemes.[7] Obviously, Italian doesn't contain all of these combinations, both because some result in sequences of sounds that are impossible in that language (consider a sequence of 11 identical phonemes, or 11 consonants), and because we simply don't have 18 million billion concepts to express (if we don't consider individual numbers, assuming that each number indicates a concept).

However, the redundancy principle also manifests itself in a structural way that's different from a simple overabundance of combinations, and it's best to keep these two aspects distinct. In this second case, redundancy is manifested *in praesentia* when information in the communication code is repeated when there's no logical need to do so. For example, if I say *quella strana nuova bella simpatica bionda ragazza* 'that strange, new, beautiful, nice blond girl', I repeat the morpheme that expresses the singular feminine in Italian, -*a*, no fewer than seven consecutive times, whereas, in principle, once would be enough to distinguish it from the masculine singular variants. It's often debated whether or not the redundancy phenomenon has a functional origin; certainly, being able to count on the possibility of an overabundance of information facilitates communication, which for various reasons may be disrupted. However, as often happens in naturalistic considerations—assuming that language is to be seen as a natural object (and we'll return to this idea)—it's always best to be careful in attributing functions to structural manifestations.

The second change that structuralism introduces, the retrieval principle, is the guiding theory for discovering new facts, new cases, and sometimes new languages; and it does so when, for reasons of symmetry, it's expected that a certain language has (or doesn't have) a property that exists in another. This can occur within a single language (for example, when trying to decipher an unknown language by reconstructing inflectional paradigms) or among different languages (as when genealogical models are proposed where unidentified "intermediate" languages are hypothesized, which are sometimes later brought to light). A forceful example of the heuristic value of a structural vision, albeit mediated through the formalism of mathematics (which is structural by definition), is the prediction of the existence of positrons by Paul A. M. Dirac in 1930. Dirac, who shared the 1933 Nobel Prize for Physics with Erwin Schrödinger, noticed that the formula describing the wave function of electrons (negatively charged particles) could also be consistent with values that were, so to speak, "symmetric," and he hypothesized the existence of the antielectron (a positively charged electron called a "positron"), which then paved the way for the discovery of antimatter and the development of the theoretical model that is poetically referred to as the "Dirac sea." Had the electron not been conceived as existing in a structural relationship, it wouldn't even have made sense to ask whether an antielectron existed. Other similar examples could be constructed by citing the periodic table, whose progressive completion was directly based on confidence in structural relationships as the founding principle of the system.

Finally, let's return to the third aspect, commutation. Beginning from the theoretical core of structuralism—namely, that an element's value in a structure is only differential, oppositional—commutation resulted in a discovery procedure that had an incalculable empirical and heuristic scope, both for an intrinsic theoretical reason and for a purely accidental empirical necessity. The discovery procedure inaugurated by structuralism is usually called the "commutative method": basically, if two elements can be commuted (exchanged) within a certain structure, they belong to the same class. Obviously, this is valid on every structural level. It's a valid method for, from time to time, distinguishing types of words—listing what we call the "parts of speech" (noun, verb, adjective, adverb, pronoun, preposition, article, conjunction, and interjection); the smaller elements—"morphemes"—that constitute the building blocks of words in terms of meaning (as in *un- event -ful -ness*, which contains four); and items *larger* than a word, the groups of words often called "syntagmas" or "phrases" (such as *her smile*), to which we'll return shortly. With the commutative method, it's relatively easy to construct classes of elements that characterize a language, especially when semantic insights aren't reliable or when dealing with new languages that contain classes of elements different from the known ones.

The latter type of situation was the accidental reason for the commutative method's special relevance. In the early 1900s, American linguistics was confronted with languages that the models developed for Indo-European languages, models with a two-thousand-year tradition, didn't naturally fit. Not even the traditional parts of speech could be easily identified, except perhaps those of noun and verb. So, the commutative method became an ideal heuristic tool. Even if nothing is known about how many and which parts of speech a given language contains, by performing a sufficient number of commutation cycles and interviewing a native speaker to see if the "switching" is successful, one can obtain equivalence classes between the terms and "automatically infer" the structure of the language—at least, that was the hope. In reality, with this system one can at most infer the equivalence classes between words that have the same distribution. For example, let's imagine that English is an unknown language and we're recording two sentences; we ask a native speaker to read, word by word, these two sentences: *The brother of the fisherman says that the river has been illuminated by a star* and *A long line of lizards crossed the desert without even stopping to dream.* Obviously we know that *brother, fisherman, river, desert, star,* and *lizard* are nouns, while *says, crossed,* and *illuminated* are verbs, *the* and *a* are articles, and so on. But, if we didn't know this, we could try to exchange pairs of words in the two sentences (or possibly even within the same sentence). For example, if we switch *desert* with *river*, we get *The brother of the fisherman says that the desert has been illuminated by a star* and *A long line of lizards crossed the river without even stopping to dream.* In this case, the speaker we're interviewing would say that the two sentences still make sense; the commutation test is then successful, and we know that *river* and *desert* belong to the same class. If instead we exchange *fisherman* for *without*, we get *The brother of without says that the river has been illuminated by a star* and *A long line of lizards crossed the desert fisherman even stopping to dream*; the two sentences don't make sense, so *fisherman* and *without* don't belong to the same commutation class. With a sufficiently large number of examples, which among other things go beyond issues related to nonessential aspects—for instance, agreement—for Italian we'll end up with nine commutation classes, nine classes that are none other than the parts of speech (noun, verb, adjective, adverb, pronoun, preposition, article, conjunction, and interjection), using only this system of exchange and a speaker who knows how to tell us whether or not the exchange is acceptable.

The enthusiasm for this system—which was called "distributionalism"—was also motivated by another, deeper question, showing once more the intrinsic link between linguistics and, in general, the exploration of the mind. Distributionalism—the canonical version of which is certainly that featured in Leonard Bloomfield's *Language* (1933)[8]—fit in perfectly with the neopositivist school of psychology known as behaviorism, which used the denial of introspection as a heuristic model, in favor of the stimulus-response model, the manifesto of their program. The typical example of an experiment based on the response to a stimulus is the well-known "Pavlov's dog" experiment—named after the Russian physiologist Ivan Pavlov, recipient of the 1904 Nobel Prize in Medicine or Physiology—which demonstrated that a stimulus that had nothing to do with food (the sound of a bell) was able to induce salivation in animals even in the absence of food, after they had sufficient exposure to the sound of the bell accompanied by food. Doubtless this is a very important achievement, able to highlight how behavioral conditioning can influence the body and therefore the relationship of the latter with the mind. Nonetheless, it gradually became increasingly evident how little this heuristic scheme was suited to understanding the mystery of the structure of language: I stress, the *structure* of language, because obviously there's little doubt about the link between linguistic stimulation and behavior.

Distributionalism and behaviorism went hand in hand in the enterprise dedicated to understanding the structure of language and, ultimately, the general cognitive processes of humankind. As is often (and perhaps always) the case in science, nothing is worse than the conviction of having arrived at the destination; that's when it's usually necessary to start all over again, perhaps alone. This is what happened in linguistics in the first half of the twentieth century. Even within the revolution I'm about to introduce, there are moments that were considered destinations, which instead turned out to be points of departure. Let's consider sentence structure, for example: the crisis, it's hardly necessary to say, will be due to the verb *to be*. I hope the patience required to complete this part of the journey is outweighed by the surprise of how once again a single verb, *this* single verb, can knock down the scaffolding taken by everyone as definitive and give shape to a new model with unexpected properties.

2.1 The Calm before the Storm

It's curious to note that in science, or sometimes in art, just as things seem to be coming to fruition, almost stagnating, the most radical and unexpected revolutions are unleashed. Let's think about physics. At the end of the nineteenth century, in a lecture given in 1894 and partially quoted in *Physics Today* from April 9, 1968, Albert Michelson—winner of the Nobel Prize in Physics in 1907—said about the state of contemporary physics, "[I]t seems probable that most of the grand underlying principles have been firmly established and that further advances are to be sought chiefly in the rigorous application of these principles to all phenomena which come under our notice." We all know that within ten years physics changed radically: not only did relativity (special and general) and quantum mechanics increase, unpredictably and disproportionately, the amount of available data, but our very way of thinking about the physical world was no longer the same as it had been. Nor did the history of linguistics escape these "anti-Cassandras." The celebrated French linguist Antoine Meillet—whom we met earlier when we were talking about Aristotle—announced with pomp and circumstance, "At least in one sense, it seems that we are at an end that is impossible to surpass: there are no languages, attested in recent or ancient times, that can be added to the Indo-European group; nothing can cause us to anticipate the discovery of texts older than the already known dialects" (Meillet 1934, 401). Of course, what Meillet says is basically true, at least with respect to the Indo-European languages; but the vague sense of claustrophobic, sentential finality in his apocalyptic words was hardly suitable to describe what was about to happen in linguistics in the following years. There were two points where a break occurred with respect to the great nineteenth-century system. One I've already mentioned: the need to describe non-Indo-European languages, those of the indigenous peoples of the Americas, which in combination with the fundamental assumptions of structuralism, helped to create totally innovative models such as distributionalism. The other, much more significant, we'll discuss extensively in the following pages. It won't be hard to see that this second break can be considered a (partial) reaction to excessive confidence in the distributionalist method.

One of the cornerstones of distributionalism was in fact the expectation that, with a good method, grammar would emerge naturally from the data—in other words, in a virtually automatic, inductive way. This confidence in the passive transparency of nature combined perfectly with the behaviorist manifesto. Even in this case, confidence placed in the stimulus-response mechanism as the only heuristic device (though it remains a quite legitimate mechanism in experimental practice) was in a sense radicalized, almost as if controversial or at least ambiguous situations never occurred. If transferred to another field of science, such as physics, this attitude could be compared to hoping that it was enough to take a good look at the sun because the heliocentric theory arises spontaneously from the observation of the data: of course one has to look at the sun, but that's not enough. In fact, we all know how far from the truth this is, and how in reality, without experiments, refutations, and new experiments, a theory can't progress.

It would be a short book published in 1957 that would change everything; it was really a distillation of material taken from a much longer doctoral dissertation that would only be published in full twenty years later. The monograph was simply titled *Syntactic Structures* and the author was Noam Chomsky, a linguist on whose fame we needn't waste words here. When he was 29, he was hired at the MIT Research Laboratory of Electronics by Morris Halle, who, along with Roman Jakobson, would give substance to the structuralist dream of representing all possible sounds in languages with binary differences of common properties. With his book, Chomsky managed to simultaneously destroy myths and introduce new concepts: first, that linguistics, unlike other empirical sciences such as physics and biology, didn't need to go through a discovery process that includes experiments and refutations; second, that grammar is a linear concatenation mechanism (as we'll see in the next section, even though we place words one after the other when we speak, a grammar is much more complex than a linear concatenation mechanism and must include a more complex structural apparatus);[9] third, that the notion of a grammar's global simplicity is a decisive element for evaluating whether or not the grammar is a good model on a biological and psychological basis. Why did simplicity become so important in Chomsky's theory of language? Perhaps this wasn't altogether explicit in *Syntactic Structures*, but it is crystal clear in a review that Chomsky wrote shortly thereafter, of a fundamental behaviorist text—*Verbal Behavior* by B. F.

Skinner (1957), a Harvard University psychologist twenty years older than Chomsky—demolishing the behaviorist vision of language structure. Let's hear it in his words: "The fact that all normal children acquire essentially comparable grammars of great complexity with remarkable rapidity suggests that *human beings are somehow specially designed* to do this, with data-handling or 'hypothesis-formulating' ability of unknown character and complexity" (Chomsky 1959, 57; emphasis mine). The leap was made: nineteenth-century linguistics, with its great undertaking aimed at reconstructing the genealogical relationships between languages, was left far behind. Contemporary linguistics was even faced with a new protagonist, one that would never have been mentioned in the major treatises on Indo-European languages: the child—the infant, as one would say etymologically—the one who does not yet speak but, belonging to our species, is naturally predisposed to learn one or more languages in a short time, on the basis of very few and fragmentary data (on this topic, see Berwick and Chomsky 2008).

So, a theory of language also *necessarily* becomes a learnable-language theory, a theory of language that is essentially a theory of the limits of variation in natural languages—as biology is, in a certain sense, the theory of the limits of variation in living forms. This theory assumes the typical characteristics of the natural sciences: it has a specific symbolic system, a kind of "algebra" or "chemistry" of language, and develops by means of theorems, distinctive symbolic representations, and formal deductions. At Chomsky's suggestion, formal linguistics is often called *tout court* "generative grammar,"[10] borrowing this term from mathematics and by "generative" meaning simply 'completely explicit'. Generative grammar (or generative grammars, if we include those other than the one originally proposed by Chomsky, such as Montague grammar) became a new, large, and promising field of research with study centers all over the world, especially in Holland, Italy,

France, Israel, Germany, Spain, Switzerland, and Japan as well as the United States—a field that in fact brought syntax (and semantics) into the realm of the empirical sciences.

What importance does the verb *to be* have in all this? Considerable importance, because it will lead us to significantly deepen our understanding of the most complex linguistic subjects, especially one that's central to human language: the sentence. Structuralism had opened the door to a new exploration of sentences; we'll see whether and to what degree it was liberated from the past and whether and to what degree it has remained a valid approach even in today's most advanced research.

2.2 Molecules of Words

In the years following the revolution sparked by Chomsky's early work, new ideas developed at an exponential rate: the structuralist lesson even infiltrated syntax in new ways and with new emphases. I believe we can only agree with the great linguistic history scholar Giulio Lepschy when he, although with the necessary provisos, considers generative grammar to be within the sphere of structural linguistics (Lepschy 2000, 57). Several notions were established that still survive today; many of them were organized into a classic text that perhaps represents, retrospectively, generative grammar's most sensational theoretical and methodological leap, namely, *Lectures on Government and Binding* (Chomsky 1981). These lectures in a seminar format—also known as the "Pisa Lectures"—were delivered by Chomsky in 1979 during a long stay at the Scuola Normale di Pisa and concluded with a legendary conference of the first international society for generative grammar, GLOW (Generative Linguistics in the Old World), established only two years earlier by Henk van Riemsdijk, leader of formal linguistics in the Netherlands—and published two years later. The presence of many young Italian linguists in the auditorium is certainly one reason why formal theoretical linguistics received a unique impetus from the study of Italian for at least the next 20 years (again, see Graffi 2001).

In this text we find the first, organic version of the theoretical scaffolding that marked generative grammar's Copernican revolution. It is based on two fundamental ideas. The first is that there are no specific rules that apply to a syntactic structure; rather, there are general rules—known as "principles"—which, by interacting in complex ways, as in a multidimensional Rubik's cube made up of words, give rise to various constructions. The second is that, while these principles are invariant in all languages, the syntactic differences among the world's languages are attributable to the combined effect of small, binary, systematic differences—called "parameters"—neither predictable on the basis of the principles nor reducible to them. The parameters appear, so to speak, like points of variation in the crystal of grammar and often have "cascading" effects, causing many structural differences; but we cannot say a priori at which point in the system a parameter becomes apparent or, in general, in which of its two possible states it is found in a given grammar. Also, by definition, neither the linguist nor the child can deduce the effects of parametric variation on an introspective or rational basis; the value assigned to a parameter in a given language and acquired by the child depends solely and exclusively on experience. No one, to date, has a theory about why the parameters exist (we'll return to this topic in chapter 4); it may well be that the existence of the parameters is simply the price the system pays for its stability, the degree of freedom that must be minimally tolerated in order to preserve the system of principles.[11] We'll see a simple example of a parameter in the following paragraph; in any case, the "principles and parameters" model remains the only possible form for the theory of human language, although, as always happens in the empirical sciences, the implementation of the system—in formal terms but also substantive ones—also varied significantly and quickly and there is no agreement on the number or the format of the parameters (on this topic see, among others, the critical reflections in Rizzi 2006 and Longobardi 2003). Moreover, generative grammar originated more or less at the same time as molecular genetics—the first in 1957, the second in 1953 with the famous article by James Watson and Francis Crick. If we compare a modern molecular genetics text with that first article, it seems as if we're holding an antique, so deep were the changes that followed that first document; the same has happened with generative grammar, though often—and wrongly—this phenomenon is identified as a negative aspect of this particular discipline.

The innovative significance of this model and its theoretical consequences, inside and outside of linguistics, have been enormous. For example, all experiments in the neuropsychological sphere regarding the relationship between syntax and the brain assume in some measure the "principles and parameters" model; the results of exploration into children's language acquisition wouldn't even have been thinkable without this model (see Guasti 2017 and the references cited therein); and the same is true for the description of selective pathologies of language, acquired and congenital, about which we still know so very little (Caplan 1992, Miceli 1996, Cappa 2001, Denes 2009).

As often happens, however, a model's innovative significance doesn't blossom by parthenogenesis. Chomsky's debt to the structuralism of direct Saussurean descent is apparent in a passage from the introduction to *Lectures on Government and Binding*:

In early work in generative grammar it was assumed, as in traditional grammar, that there are rules such as "passive," "relativization," "question-formation," etc. ... These "rules" are decomposed into the more fundamental elements of the subsystems of rules and principles. ... This development, largely in work of the past ten years, represents a substantial break from earlier generative grammar, or from the traditional grammar on which it was in part modelled. *It is reminiscent of the move from phonemes to features in the phonology of the Prague school*, though in the present case the "features" ... are considerably more abstract and their properties and interaction much more intricate. The notions "passive," "relativization," etc., can be reconstructed as processes of a more general nature, with a functional role in grammar, but they are not "rules of grammar." (Chomsky 1981, 7; emphasis mine)

The transition from phonemes to features to which Chomsky alludes is what I exemplified earlier by talking about the vowel system: the vowels are no longer "atomic" objects with specific individual properties; rather, they are the result of the simultaneous combination of more abstract properties defined across all elements of the system. In the same way, there are no longer any relative clauses, interrogative clauses, and so on (except of course as convenient taxonomic labels); there are only abstract principles that are combined to result in linguistic variation—a truly epochal leap.

It was this new theoretical model that would provide the empirical basis for the revolution in the study of language acquisition. Until that moment, the commonly accepted hypothesis was that grammar blooms, so to speak, in a child's brain. However, from that point forward a radically different hypothesis began to take root: a grammar doesn't bloom in a child's brain; rather, only one survives after all the others have been pruned away. "Learning by forgetting"—to use Jacques Mehler's (1974) apt expression—is what this process would come to be called and, as often happens in the history of science, it would eventually make linguistics a model for other research domains, especially in the neurophysiological and neuropsychological fields (see, for example, the controversial work of Jean-Pierre Changeux, from 1983). In the next chapter, we'll see a simple example of this reduction of complexity to the interaction of simple elements, because it directly involves the verb *to be*. Now we'll see how the structure of a sentence is analyzed in this model, beginning with a very important caveat.

Anatomy of a Sentence

We've already observed that linguistics, like other sciences, involves some notions that are intuitively evident but difficult to formalize. Let's take the notion of "word." What is a word? We all have an intuitive notion of "word," and yet we have trouble defining it. One of the most typical definitions—and certainly not a trivial one—is that a word is a sequence of meaningful sounds. However, this definition is both too restrictive and too lax. It's too restrictive because even the *-s* in *dogs* has a meaning, but it's not a word (the bricks that have meaning and that are used to compose words, like *dog* and *-s*, are technically called "morphemes"); and it's too lax because *the dog* also satisfies that definition but here we have two words instead of one. Nor can we rely on the white spaces we put between words, thinking that they correspond to pauses. Except in cases of particular emphasis, we don't pause at all between words: when we say *Linda arrives in Pavia*, we actually say *lindarrivesinpavia*. If we really want to find an infinitesimally brief pause, there is one, but it's within the words themselves, when the stop consonants in this sentence are pronounced (the voiceless bilabial consonant at the beginning of the city's name, /p/, and the voiced alveolar consonant in the woman's name, /d/). A more satisfying and certainly less contemporary definition, dating back to Jespersen, is to say that a word is a meaningful sequence of morphemes pronounced in isolation that cannot be interrupted by other morphemes. Limiting ourselves to the second condition, even without adding the white spaces we can then say that *thedog* is not a word because the sequence can be interrupted, for example, with an adjective, as in *theolddog*. And by this definition *dog* is indeed a word, as it can't be interrupted in the same way: *dooldg. On the other hand, if the notion of "word" is difficult to formalize, the notion of "sentence" is even more so. We'll use the same reduction strategy used by Aristotle; we'll concentrate only on active declarative sentences, using simple examples like *Mary has* *studied physics*. But how do we analyze a sentence? Structuralism also shows the way here.

One of structuralism's lessons, passed on in the distributionalist tradition, is that the flow of words in a sentence should be segmented into progressively smaller blocks and that these blocks are identifiable because they can be commuted in different structures. Let's proceed step by step. If we take *A baker has bought a ukulele* and *The brother of this fisherman took the boat*, what do the two sentences have in common? Certainly not the meaning: they convey two completely different images. However, if we exchange *a baker* with *the brother of this fisherman*, we get two structures that are still acceptable: *The brother of this fisherman has bought a ukulele* and *A baker took the boat*. Therefore, *the brother of this fisherman* and *a baker* can commute, which means they belong to the same category, because of the fundamental principle of structuralism that says the role of an element is given only in a differential manner: if there is no difference, the elements are indistinguishable. The same thing could be done with *a ukulele* and *the boat*, or with *the* and *a*. All of this tells us that the sentences are constructed with similar categories. If we use symbols to represent the categories (e.g., N for noun, V for verb, Aux for auxiliary, P for preposition, and Det for "determiner," the mixed category of articles and demonstrative adjectives like *this*), we can assign to the two sentences *A baker took the boat* and *The brother of this fisherman has bought a ukulele* the following two sequences, respectively: $S_1 =$ Det N V Det N and $S_2 =$ Det N P Det N Aux V Det N. These linear sequences of symbols are organized in such a way as to be grouped into pairs, resulting in a hierarchical structure, similar to a construction made with a series of nesting boxes. For example, looking at S_1, let's start with our intuition and take the first sequence starting with the second Det N. The second Det—an article—combines with the N that follows and not with the preceding V: we can represent this link between Det and N with square brackets: [Det N].[12]

This complex element in turn combines with V, resulting in [V [Det N]]. In the same way, the first Det combines with the first N, resulting again in [Det N]. We're then left with [Det N] and [V [Det N]]: these two blocks combine to make [[Det N] [V [Det N]]]. The composition stops there, having run out of elements. At this point, we need only replace the abstract labels with (the morphemes or) the chosen words: in our current example, [[*a baker*] [*took* [*the boat*]]].[13]

How can we be sure that this grouping is really the right one? What about another one—for example, [[Det N] [[V Det] N]], where the second Det is to be grouped with the verb first? The combinations always respect the principle of grouping in pairs. When dealing with our own language, we know immediately and intuitively that we're not on the right path, but what would happen if we examined an unknown language where the meaning of the words was incomprehensible to us? American linguists found themselves in precisely this situation in the first half of the twentieth century when they began investigating the languages of indigenous peoples, which were so different from the Indo-European ones. A number of diagnostic criteria were drafted to verify that the groupings were correct. (Curiously, these investigations of indigenous languages also had a military use: some native speakers of Navajo, as well as Cherokee, Choctaw, and Comanche, were recruited by the U.S. military to transmit encrypted codes in their languages—languages that wouldn't have been understood even had the codes been broken by the Nazis and their allies.)

There are many ways to proceed in examining the structure of unknown languages. One of these is to build, starting from a given sentence, what's called its corresponding "cleft." Perhaps it's best if I give an example. If I start with the sentence *The baker took the boat* and I say *It is* [*the baker*] *who took the boat*, I still have an acceptable sentence; similarly, if I say *It is* [*the boat*] *that the baker took*, I still have an acceptable sentence. But if I say *It is [*took* *the] that the baker boat*, the sentence is unacceptable. Therefore, we can reasonably say that the system of brackets that we used sheds light on the real grouping of the words in the sequence at the end of the paragraph before last, because the cleft [V Det] doesn't give an acceptable sentence. It's important to note that these phenomena aren't dependent on meaning, understood as the ability to refer to real objects, abstract or concrete. If you were to take a sentence constructed with invented lexical roots like *The gulc has goiged the brals*, you would still be able to evaluate the cleft phenomenon. For example, you could say *It is the gulc that has goiged the brals* and not **It is goiged the that has brals*, even if you don't have the vaguest idea what *a gulc* or *a bral* is, or what *to goig* might possibly mean. It's evident that our intuitions about syntax are independent from meaning. In the Middle Ages, this was already clear. For example, if we take a contradictory sentence like *The triangle is circular*, we understand that it is in some sense acceptable or, even if it isn't, it's unacceptable in a way that's different from a sentence like **Triangle the red is*, where the words don't generate contradictions but are simply in an incorrect order. There are, however, ambiguous cases in which meaning can discriminate among competing structures. If I say *I saw the queen with the telescope*, I must distinguish two different groupings, depending on whether the group *with the telescope* refers to the verb *to see* or to the noun *queen*. We see this very clearly with sentences involving restrictions that depend on the structure of the real world: the sentence *I saw a stork flying to Merano* is ambiguous, but if I say *I saw the Dolomites flying to Merano*, it's evident that the ambiguity disappears. This technique, which involves breaking a sentence down into progressively smaller elements and deciphering the geometry that connects them, has been and still is one of the main domains of syntactic theory in modern linguistics, and the debate is far from closed.

Anatomy of a Sentence

In empirical sciences, formalism often produces progressive synthesis and allows us to observe things in such a way as to favor analogies, ultimately leading to new discoveries. The same thing happened in the development of this area of research into syntax. We can get an idea of how the field developed by focusing on a simple case. For example, if we call the group of elements [Det N] a "noun phrase" or NP, and the group of elements [V [Det N]] a "verb phrase" or VP, we can rewrite both of our original sentences, S_1 and S_2, as [NP VP]. In an equivalent tree structure, a simple sentence like *Jane reads a book* is traditionally represented as follows:

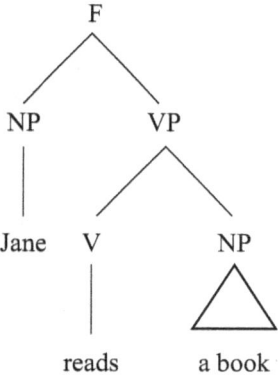

This tree structure (where the triangle simply indicates that the structure underlying NP isn't specified) therefore illustrates the formula that represents the minimum structure of the sentence (in this case with a transitive verb like *to read*). From now on we'll only be dealing with the structure [NP VP], but before I address it, we need to further explore some fundamental characteristics of the syntactic structure of the sentence in a formal way.

We can start with the simple observation that an NP can contain another NP within it. Let's take for example the first NP of our original S_2 (*the brother of this fisherman*). There's no doubt that we're dealing with an NP, because we can construct a cleft sentence like *It is the brother of this fisherman who has bought a ukulele*, but we notice that it contains another NP, *this fisherman*. We can say this with certainty, because this smaller NP is commutable with the larger NP, giving *This fisherman has bought a ukulele*. In formal terms, we can indicate the nesting of these NPs as [$_{NP}$ Det [N [P [$_{NP}$ Det N]]]] and, using only the label NP and ignoring the irrelevant elements, we have [$_{NP}$ ... NP ...]. It's easy to grasp the connection between the production of infinite structures and this structural formula. Simply observe that the symbol NP can contain another NP and that this procedure can, in principle, be repeated infinitely: in fact we can say *the brother of this fisherman*, but also *the brother of that friend of this fisherman, the brother of this sister of that friend of this fisherman*, and so on. This syntactic property, the ability of a structure to contain a structure of the same type, is not limited to the NP. Even a sentence can contain a sentence: for example, if I say [*John says that* [*Andrea knows this thing*]], the sentence [*Andrea knows this thing*] is contained within the larger sentence. Similarly, the sentence within the brackets could be expanded: [*John says that* [*Andrea knows that* [*Frank is coming*]]]; synthetically, ignoring irrelevant elements, I could represent this procedure by progressive bracketing as [$_S$ ... S ...]. I could also expand the sentence in the opposite direction by making the entire initial sentence the complement of another: [*Peter heard that* [*John says that* [*Andrea knows that* [*Frank is coming*]]]].

This property of generating potentially infinite structures by progressively bracketing a certain type of structure within structures of the same type, like Russian nesting dolls, has come to be called "recursion," borrowing a technical term from mathematics, not without forcing it a bit (see Partee, ter Meulen, and Wall 1990, Hopcroft, Motwani, and Ullman 2006). It's essential to recognize that recursion affects all phrases. Not only noun phrases and sentences but also verbs, adjectives, prepositional phrases, and so on, can be composed recursively, given an appropriate choice of words. In formal terms, we can express this generalization with a simple formula, [$_X$ ... X ...], where X stands for any phrase (including, of course, sentences). It's precisely recursion that formally implements the ability of human language to produce potentially infinite structures: to a first approximation, the recursive procedure has no limits, except for the obvious ones due to the limits of memory and the physical ability to produce statements, which an individual can't do infinitely.[14] This feature is extremely important, certainly one of the most important traits of the whole syntactic system, and it's interesting to note that it exists only in the communication code of human beings. We'll return to this feature, but it's worthwhile to be aware of it now. Among other things, this unique capability is also an essential part of the cognitive skills underpinning our ability to count. Although syntactic recursion is something more than the ability to indefinitely extend a sentence by adding new words with a conjunction, in this sense syntax and the ability to count have something in common (just as it's impossible to think of the largest possible number, so it's impossible to think of the longest possible sentence). This is in itself an inspiration to reflect on the specific cognitive abilities of our species in general and the unique architecture of the human mind. Even (tonal) music, particularly in terms of its melodic (as opposed to its harmonic) component, can reasonably be described as a generative mechanism with recursive properties.

Syntax, music, mathematics: it can't be a coincidence that these three abilities are exclusive to our species, even if we're still far from having discovered the common aspects and the generative structure of each one of these—even from a simply descriptive perspective, let alone a neurophysiological one.[15] So, recursion, understood as the capacity to produce potentially infinite structures, combined with the awareness of possessing this capacity, is so important that it could be selected as the distinguishing trait of human cognitive abilities.

A second fundamental property that characterizes sentence structure and the syntax of human language in general—and a surprising property, despite going for the most part unnoticed—is the fact that certain syntactic elements (or entire sequences of elements) can be found in different positions in a structure while maintaining the same grammatical function. For example, in the sentences *They think that Frank will cook this pizza* and *Which pizza do they think Frank will cook?*, the NPs (*this pizza* and *which pizza*) that constitute the direct object of the verb *to cook* are found in two different places: one next to the verb, the other separated, at the start of the sentence. In this second case, the verb phrase (or "constituent")[16] is no longer "connected." This property was first observed by the structuralists—starting at least with Kenneth Pike (1943), as noted by Graffi (2001)—who called such items "discontinuous constituents." This phenomenon of dislocation is now called "(syntactic) movement," and its properties provide one of the most striking proofs of the fact that the complexity of human grammars and language acquisition in children are linked to human neurobiological structure and are not an arbitrary sociocultural convention.[17] The study of syntactic movement has in fact brought to light invariant properties in languages where their existence wasn't even expected, as evidenced by the flourishing of descriptive grammars dedicated to phenomena never studied before (for Italian, see the monumental, three-volume reference work Renzi, Salvi, and Cardinaletti 1988/1991/1995).

The very fact that all languages, even from different families, are subject to the same restrictions on syntactic movement (which we'll come to in the next paragraphs) would be inexplicable if it weren't the consequence of a biologically determined plan, a plan for which, in essence, the acquisition of language is based on a framework that precedes experience—even if, obviously, it's not possible without experience. It's sometimes said that grammar is *innate*: this decidedly unfortunate term utterly obscures the real content of the contemporary linguistic revolution. To say that grammar is innate is equivalent to claiming that an individual's weight is innate. An individual's weight isn't innate. It depends, for example, on the quality and quantity of the person's food intake; these define the limits within which it can vary—if it does—and, to be considered innate, these limits must be determined by those traits of the biological structure that precede experience and that result from the interaction between laws of the physical world and the particular constructive ability of biologically active material (proteins, enzymes, etc.). In the same sense, grammars aren't innate; but the limits on their variation relative to experience are. In fact, all of generative grammar, in essence, is nothing more than a theory of the limits that experience places on the acquisition of language.

Let's return to more technical questions. The intuition underlying syntactic movement is usually explained in a formal way by assuming that the sequence of elements moved (possibly composed of a single element) is introduced into the structure in a base position (which to a first approximation is the one where it appears in affirmative sentences).[18] Then, a copy is constructed in the location where the sequence of elements is actually pronounced; at the same time, the phonetic content of the starting element is deleted (we'll return to this deletion mechanism later in the book). In the case just mentioned, we'll start with an abstract representation like *they think Frank will cook which pizza*, where the direct object relationship is established between the verb *to cook* and the NP *which pizza*. Then the copy of the element to be moved is produced, the NP *which pizza*, generating *which pizza do they think Frank will cook which pizza*. Finally, the phonetic element in the base position is deleted, producing *Which pizza do they think Frank will cook __?* The low dash at the end of the sentence indicates the position from which the NP moved—in this case, direct object position. Even here we're looking at an abstract representation, in the sense that the representation of the sentence *Which pizza do they think Frank will cook?* also contains the symbol "__" which is a piece of information that isn't expressed verbally, just as the labels for the phrases aren't expressed verbally.

It's very important to clarify a fundamental point about the notion of syntactic movement. In using this mechanism, which involves notions such as "copy," "generate," and "delete"—and more generally in using any syntactic representation—we're not referring to an actual, concrete process of progressive composition over time. Every syntactic representation constitutes, so to speak, an "X-ray" of the structure that a speaker interprets when producing or comprehending a sentence: so, this representation works like a "map" to describe the interaction between the elements produced. Syntactic movement isn't actually movement of anything: it's only the representation of two points of a structure that enter into relationship when a linguistic element (be it a morpheme, a word, or a phrase) is interpreted at (at least) two different points. In our example, *Which pizza do they think Frank will cook__?*, the phrase *which pizza* plays the roles of both the direct object of *to cook* and the interrogative element of the sentence containing the verb *to think*. What the actual temporal procedure might be for producing and comprehending these structures is a different empirical problem. This distinction between knowledge of structural relationships and the actual production and comprehension processes they involve is (has been) fundamental in contemporary linguistics. Following the terminology introduced by Chomsky in his works from the 1960s, now definitively part of the canon of contemporary linguistics, a distinction is made between "competence" (the abstract structural relations—precisely, the map—that is in a speaker's mind) and "performance" (a speaker's actual use of these structural relationships in the production and comprehension of statements).[19] Of course, in the best of all possible worlds, performance shouldn't be anything more than competence with the addition of a time variable that takes into account the processes of assembling and filtering possible structures described in terms of competence; however, at the moment no one is able to suggest how abstract relationships of syntax correlate with neuropsychological processes, beyond some major structural properties we'll touch upon briefly in chapter 4 (on this topic, see also Moro 2006b and the references cited therein).

Much has been written about the relationship between competence and performance, and opinions are far from stable (see, for example, Chomsky 2004). The themes developed in this area are quite different. For example, studies on performance often refer to what are called "parsing" mechanisms (sequential analysis; see, in particular, Berwick and Niyogi 1999 and the references cited therein; see also note 14 in this chapter), which shed light on the nature of the processing of syntactic structures. Typical examples used in parsing studies are those in which, once listeners or readers get to the end of the sentence, they're forced to reinterpret the previous words. The famous case in English is *The horse raced past the barn fell*. When listeners or readers come to the word *barn*, they think the sentence ends there. However, they also immediately realize that that must not be the case, since the following word must be accounted for: namely, the verb *fell*, which requires a subject. The only solution is that *the horse* is the subject of *fell* and that *raced past the barn* is a relative clause modifying it (i.e., *The horse [that was] raced past the barn fell*). Sometimes, these types of diagnostic devices are able to highlight the real mechanisms of syntactic processing, but there are neither theories nor practical methods to discover the performance mechanisms.

Another question that has often divided linguists—tangential to the previous one but not completely unrelated—is whether syntactic trees are assembled by composing the parts of the tree in parallel, starting with the smaller blocks (derivational hypothesis), or whether instead they're produced in a single block all at once (representational hypothesis). If we hadn't already seen that time isn't a variable of syntactic competence models, we might ask whether these trees are assembled "progressively" or generated "instantaneously." The problem is typically empirical; it's worth saying that in principle there are no reasons why the syntactic system must proceed in one way or the other. It doesn't seem, at the moment, that there are sufficient facts to tip the balance in favor of either the derivational or the representational hypothesis. This uncertainty is reminiscent in some ways of the situation in physics before the unification of quantum mechanics, when, depending on the particular experiment that was performed, light sometimes appeared to be a particle and sometimes appeared to be a wave. Whether this dispute is resolvable or whether we'll have to think of syntax as having a twofold nature—representational and derivational—is a fascinating problem; however, at the moment it appears that there are no easy solutions (on these topics, see the pioneering works of Luigi Rizzi such as Rizzi 1985, and his more recent reflections in Rizzi 1997). Bearing in mind these theoretical caveats, we'll return to the technical question of syntactic movement.

In the early works of generative grammar, the representation of the sentence that precedes the movements was called "deep structure" and the representation of the sentence that follows the movements "surface structure." The space vacated by the element that moved, designating the category with no phonological content, was indicated with "t" (for "trace" of the element moved) or with "[e]" (for "empty"). The history of these terms in generative grammar might in itself constitute an interesting arena for identifying the driving forces active in this discipline's development. The technical terms "deep structure" and "surface structure," for example, were often misinterpreted. Chomsky himself noticed this in the 1970s:

"Many people have attributed the word *deep* to grammar itself, perhaps identifying 'deep structure' and 'universal grammar.' I have read many criticisms saying how ill-conceived it is to postulate innate deep structures. I never said that, and nothing I have written suggests anything of the sort" (Chomsky 1979, 171). To remedy this misconception, in a second phase the two terms were then changed to "D-structure" and "S-structure," in an effort to connote, in a less misleading way, the two levels of representation (at the same time, Chomsky also began talking about logical form (LF) and phonetic form (PF), as Graffi (2001) notes). Today, references to levels of representation that are not simply the interface with the interpretive semantic component and the articulatory phonological one—the only two really needed for any model of language—are no longer used. This reduction in the levels of representation is one of the most important characteristics of the so-called "minimalist program," which is the most advanced stage of generative grammar (see Chomsky 1995 for the original proposal, the fundamental work Chomsky 2004 for a retrospective criticism, and Moro 1996 for a summary).

Obviously, not all sequences of words can move—otherwise, the sentence *Cain killed Abel* could mean that Abel killed Cain after a movement commuting the subject and object NPs around the verb. More generally, it was immediately evident that movement was in some way subject to restrictions; were this not so, the power of movement transformations would have simply translated the complexity of the phenomena described by previous theories into a different language. A milestone was Joseph Emonds's dissertation, where he proposed the principle of structure preservation, according to which a structure produced by movement can't have a "geometry" different from that of a structure constructed with the rules of phrasal combination (Emonds 1976). For example, the principle of structure preservation prevents a movement that could generate a structure in which the head of a noun phrase has two complements.

This principle dramatically limited the number of possible structures but it still wasn't enough. It was necessary to establish which structures, among those compatible with the rules of phrasal combination, could be generated. This necessity led to a series of discoveries that established the syntactic research agenda during that time. Linguists discovered that a sequence of words that can move in one case might not necessarily move in another, thus identifying what came to be called "locality conditions." An example involving the relative clause construction will quickly clarify the issue. Let's take the two sentences *Mary eats pizza* and *Mary rides a bike* and make each of them the complement of the verb *to know*: *I know that Mary eats pizza* and *I know that Mary rides a bike*. The two final NPs of the two sentences must be moved when they become questions, thus: *Which pizza do I know that Mary eats __?* and *Which bike do I know that Mary rides __?* If instead we start with an example involving a relative clause—that is, a structure in which one sentence is contained within another, like *I know that Mary who rides a bike eats pizza*—one of the two movements is blocked. In fact, the result would be **Which bike do I know that Mary who rides __ eats pizza?* and *Which pizza do I know that Mary who rides a bike eats __?* Once we realize that the two sentences have a relationship of inclusion that generates an asymmetric relationship (the one that has *eats* as a predicate contains the relative one that has *rides* as a predicate), it's not difficult to grasp the generalization that explains this phenomenon. We simply say that an NP cannot move from a relative clause, which is to say from a sentence that modifies an NP contained within another NP. The same is true for verb movement in English. Let's take the sentence *A man who is intelligent is always happy*. Since English interrogative sentences with the verb *to be* are formed by placing the verb *to be* at the start of the sentence, moving the two instances of *is* in our example will give *Is a man who is intelligent __ always happy?*, which is perfectly grammatical, and **Is a man who __ intelligent is always happy?*, which is not. Also in this case, the verb can't be moved from the relative clause. Mutatis mutandis, phenomena of this type are found in all natural languages. To sum up: restrictive generalizations like this are part of "locality theory," which, as I've mentioned, dramatically reduces the number of possible structures (see Manzini 1992 for a critical review of locality theories).

It's important to note that locality restrictions such as those illustrated here involve consequences of extraordinary scope, reaching well beyond purely linguistic questions. First of all, the complexity of the phenomenon and the absence of locality-restriction-violating errors in children's speech during language acquisition is a very strong piece of data in favor of the hypothesis of biologically determined guidance in language acquisition. It's ridiculous to think that a child receives explicit and comprehensive instructions about such mechanisms: the corrections that children are generally given involve simply lexical, phonological, or morphological issues. For example, in terms of morphology, one can point out to a child that we don't say *runned* but *ran* for the verb *to run*, even if we say *punned* and not *pan* for the verb *to pun* (saying *runned* demonstrates among other things that the child is capable of making analogies in the morphological field), but no adults—assuming they're aware of them—would wander into the labyrinths of syntactic locality theory when they correct a child; suffice it to say that no one has yet been able to formulate an acceptable theory covering all known cases of locality restrictions. Also, the fact that there is no rational explanation for the fact that only one of the two structures illustrated in the last paragraph is grammatical—the fact that the restrictions are "unexplained"—suggests that grammar is not driven by communication-maximizing functions or even by the search for some kind of "communicative perfection." In fact, there don't appear to be any reasonable obstacles to imagining an interpretation for a sentence like *Which bike do I know that Mary who rides eats pizza?* Indeed, paradoxically, the language that conveys the most information, with the same vocabulary, would be precisely a language in which *any* combination of words was interpretable—in our case, then, a language without locality or, more generally, a language without any restrictions. A simple example may clarify this point. Let's imagine that Italian and English contain only two words apiece, each word a translation of the other: *Giovanni, John, arriva*, and *arrives*. How many combinations can we make with these words in each language? In English, only one, *John arrives*; the other, **Arrives John*, is ungrammatical. In Italian, we can use both possible combinations: *Giovanni arriva* and *Arriva Giovanni*. The two sentences don't convey exactly the same information: *Giovanni arriva* is the natural response to the question *Cosa fa Giovanni?* '(lit.) what does John', while *Arriva Giovanni* answers the question *Chi arriva?* '(lit.) who arrives'. However, both sentences are completely admissible. In this sense, at least locally, and for this simplified model, Italian conveys more information because it has fewer restrictions. One could at least imagine one "monstrous" language in which all word combinations are associated with different interpretations. But there's no need to rush to the conclusion that restrictions are always and entirely useless, if not harmful.

The undoubted advantage of restrictions is that they drastically reduce the computational load for the child at the spontaneous language acquisition stage (we'll return to this theme in chapter 4; for a critical argument, see Moro 2006b and the references cited therein). The questions raised by localities are a perfect example of how modern linguistics, and generative grammar in particular, offers a perspective on the investigation of language, and more generally of the mind, never adopted in previous centuries: the way that the architecture of language is interwoven with learning becomes clear, and with it the implications for ontogenetic and phylogenetic speculations about language.

Finally, still with regard to locality, it should be added that if the restrictions are invariant in the world's languages, the hypothesis that they are accidental or conventional becomes highly implausible. Even in languages where syntactic movement isn't as evident as it is in Indo-European languages—for example, in Chinese interrogatives, the question-forming element doesn't move to the start of the sentence—exactly the same locality conditions apply (see C.-T. James Huang's (1988) pioneering work). In the 1980s, these facts led to the idea that, at a sufficient level of abstraction, all interrogative elements move, even in languages such as Chinese.[20] In short, it's much more natural that these three aspects—limitations in the types of errors made by children, the unsubstantiated nature of the rules, and invariability of locality principles in the world's languages—can be explained on the basis of biologically determined guidance that precedes experience rather than on the basis of arbitrary, socially shared conventions.

There are obviously many types of locality restrictions; indeed, much of the development of generative grammar from the 1960s to the 1980s consisted precisely in a progressive refining of the theory of locality conditions in at least two distinct avenues of research. While the 1960s fundamentally dealt with surveying and describing all cases in different languages, in the 1970s the various conditions were partially unified under increasingly abstract principles; an important milestone here was John Ross's (1967) doctoral dissertation, published only many years later (Ross 1986). Finally, in the 1980s the attempt to produce a unified theory of *all* locality conditions, encouraged primarily by Chomsky (1986a), came to a halt that doesn't appear to be completely overcome. Whatever the future development of this theory, not only has locality played a central role in our understanding of the architecture of language (indeed, it still does so), but also the stability of the results obtained in this field has resulted in locality violations becoming a canonic diagnostic criterion for highlighting many aspects of structure previously not even described. One of the most stable results of locality theory is tied to sentence structure; this is why we're discussing it now, and what we say will be crucial to discovering one of the mysterious properties of the verb *to be*.

Let's start with the simple sentence structure we looked at earlier: [NP VP], where VP stands for [V NP]. The representation [NP [V NP]] shows that the two NPs are in an asymmetric position relative to the verb V: the NP following V—traditionally called "object"—combines directly with V, [V NP]; the NP preceding V—called "subject"—combines in a second level with the VP, the compound formed from [V NP], to give [NP [V NP]]. The asymmetry of the representation is clear, but what are the empirical data that justify it? As a concrete example, let's take the sentence *They have announced that a picture of the wall revealed the cause of the riot*, which contains a dependent sentence that has the structure NP VP: *a picture of the wall revealed the cause of the riot*. If we try to move elements from inside the dependent sentence's two NPs, we get sentences with varying degrees of acceptability. For example, an extraction from the postverbal NP gives *Which riot have they announced that a picture of the wall revealed the cause of __?*, a sentence that's more acceptable than one with an extraction from the preverbal NP, **Which wall have they announced that a picture of __ revealed the cause of the riot?* This asymmetry between the two NPs that combine with V is traditionally explained by a general locality condition according to which an element can be moved only from an NP that is adjacent to V, which is to say immediately connected with V. In fact, in formal terms the object NP is adjacent to V (i.e., [V NP]), while the subject NP is adjacent to a VP (i.e., [NP VP]). Naturally, as always because we're not dealing with ad hoc conditions that would cause the explanatory value of the theory to be lost, it's necessary to provide independent cases where it's *not* possible to move an element contained in an NP that is at the same time neither a subject nor adjacent to a V. Otherwise, it would be enough to say that an element of a subject NP can't be moved, which would be no more and no less than reproducing with other words what we've already observed. The following sentences are relevant here: *He knows that Guido has given a picture of Andrea* and *He knows that Guido has given a picture of Andrea and a portrait of Frank*. In this case, we have a direct object in the first sentence (*a picture of Andrea*) and two direct objects in the second (*a picture of Andrea* and *a portrait of Frank*) joined by the conjunction *and*. Let's verify what happens when we move elements from within the direct object NP in the two sentences. We get *Whom does he know that Guido has given a picture of __?* in contrast to **Whom does he know that Guido has given a picture of __ and a portrait of Frank?* Clearly, the second sentence is unacceptable. How do we explain this phenomenon, given the principle that items can't be extracted from an NP that isn't adjacent to V? Aren't the instances *of a picture of Andrea* in the two sentences both direct objects and therefore, to a first approximation, adjacent to V? In reality, the generalization holds up very well; we only need to take the presence of the conjunction into account and remember that linguistic elements are grouped in pairs. When the last NP of the sentence is attached with the conjunction, the result is the compound [*and* NP]; the other NP is then added to this compound, resulting in [NP [*and* NP]]: it's the latter that in turn will be compounded with V, resulting in [V [NP [*and* NP]]]. We're therefore able to explain the movement-blocking effect created by the conjunction on the basis of the principle in question. When the conjunction is present, the NP that immediately follows V isn't adjacent to it in structural terms; rather, it is adjacent to a complex phrase that contains the postverbal NP and has the conjunction *and* as its head: namely, ... V [NP ... instead of ... V NP .... So, at least in this case, the locality generalization holds: extraction from the NP immediately following V is impossible because the two aren't adjacent.

Returning to the structure of this sentence, we can conclude that the structural asymmetry between the two NPs (subject and object) is also justified on the basis of locality conditions: only one NP is adjacent to V (the object NP); therefore, extraction is only possible from that NP. Historically, this locality condition that we've seen applied to NP was then generalized to other lexical categories and other phrases. For our investigation of the verb *to be*, it's not necessary to reproduce all of the conditions; it's enough to concentrate on the comparison between extraction from NP and extraction from VP. How is it possible to explain the possibility of extracting from VP in terms of adjacency to V, given that V is contained in VP? One solution, albeit formalized in different ways, was to assume that the locality conditions apply to the NPs that are the arguments of a predicate, but not to the predicates themselves. So, extraction from VP is possible regardless of this locality condition, VP being a predicate. Note once again that this kind of explanation isn't based on arguments of theoretical necessity. Nothing forces us to admit that a predicate isn't subject to the locality conditions. Once again, linguistics proves itself an empirical science: an explanation holds water if it leads to a more concise description of the current facts and to the discovery of new facts. And in this case the choice actually has produced positive results (see, for example, Chomsky 1986, 1995, Manzini 1992).

Another important asymmetry between the two NPs appearing in the sequence NP V NP is due to what's known as "agreement." It's generally said that two words agree if some of their morphological features are the same. For example, one morphological feature is number. If I say *fabric* and *fabric-s*, the two words differ only by the morphological feature of number: one is singular and the other plural. When one of the two words is combined with a demonstrative, the demonstrative and the noun agree; namely, homogeneous features are selected. For example, in *this fabric* both *this* and *fabric* are singular, whereas in *these fabrics* both *these* and *fabrics* are plural. What happens in relation to agreement in an NP V NP sequence? The verb is only sensitive to the number trait of the NP preceding it: *Cain kills Abel, Cain kills Abel and Isaac, Cain and Isaac kill Abel*. Even the agreement expressed by the verb in English is an asymmetric phenomenon:[21] the asymmetry of the representation that combines two NPs in the structure NP VP is thus empirically substantiated on the basis of phenomena of agreement as well as those of locality.

There's still one more step to take before we finish. Looking at an NP, a VP, an AP, or a PP, we note that they're constructed in the same way. In particular, the core consists of an N like *reading*, a V like *to read*, an A like *proud*, or a P like *in*, followed by a phrase that is uniformly defined as "complement (of the head)": for example, [*reading* [*of books*]], [*to read* [*books*]], [*proud* [*of Francesca*]], and [*in* [*this house*]]. It's customary to call V, N, A, or P the "head" of the phrase. In a way, the head functions as the center of gravity for the phrase: it's around the head that the phrase may or may not develop. As we just saw, the head can have a complement to its right. However, it can also accumulate material to the left: [*the* [*reading* [*of books*]]], [*good* [*to read* [*books*]]], [*very* [*proud* [*of Francesca*]]], and [*lots* [*in* [*this house*]]]. The elements that precede the heads are called "specifiers (of the head)." The nature of specifiers is much debated:[22] what is certain is that we can show that a specifier is not necessarily realized by a single word. English provides a simple example. Let's take two NPs: *my father* and *these pictures of Jerusalem*. These two phrases can be combined, resulting in the complex NP *my father's pictures of Jerusalem*, where the NP *my father's* is located to the left of *pictures of Jerusalem*, performing the role of specifier replacing *these*.[23] It's easy to prove that the sequence of elements *my father's pictures of Jerusalem* is an NP. It's enough to take a sentence like *Peter bought my father's pictures of Jerusalem* and verify the acceptability of the corresponding cleft sentence: *It's my father's pictures of Jerusalem that Peter bought.* The sentence is certainly acceptable, whereas if I had built a sentence in which the sequence *my father's pictures of Jerusalem* was interrupted, the result would have been extremely ungrammatical: for example, **It's my father's that Peter bought pictures of Jerusalem.* A complex NP structure like [[*my father's*] [*pictures* [*of Jerusalem*]]] isn't possible in languages such as Italian; nevertheless, we'll see that these languages also display clear cases where a specifier can be realized by a phrase. At any rate, the structure of our current example NP is represented as [[*my father's*] [*pictures* [*of Jerusalem*]]].

To sum up, based on data like these, linguists have come to generalize the structure of *any* phrase, not just noun phrases, representing it in a unified way as [ZP [X YP]], where X, Y, and Z are elements taken from the lexicon that can't be broken down further. For clarity, I'll also show the tree diagram version of this sequence. In this case, the ellipses indicate lexical material that's unspecified as well as free of phonological content, as we'll see later. ZP and YP can consist of one or more words; the head X can consist of at most one word (or even one morpheme if one adopts the smallest unit in the analysis of syntactic structure),

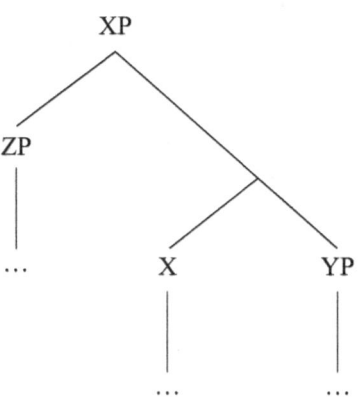

Anatomy of a Sentence

To go into more detail and also explain the structure of ZP and YP: these two phrases have—recursively—the same structure as XP, namely, [$_{XP}$ [$_{ZP}$ QP [Z WP]] [X [$_{KP}$ MP [K NP]]]], where the symbols Q, W, and K indicate any other heads like X, Y, and Z. In tree diagram format, this more detailed structure is as follows:

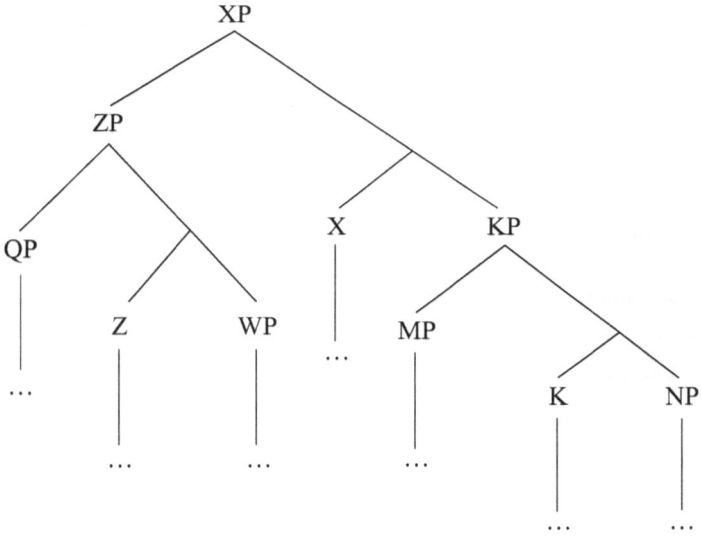

Of course, we could continue to go into detail, but it's clear that the structure [ZP [X YP]] is, so to speak, the "elementary cell" of the syntax of human language, the one into which all the words in a sequence are "inserted." Any phrase in any language can be traced back to a complex interlocking structure of phrases that all have, to a first approximation, a head and possibly a complement and a specifier, as if we were dealing with atoms in a molecule. The resulting geometric representation has interesting properties that are more or less easy to recognize. For example, the structure containing all of the elements has the same form as the elements that make it up, which is to say that it itself is a phrase. This same property of "self-similarity" characterizes, mutatis mutandis, certain geometric objects known as "fractals" (a term coined by Benoît Mandelbrot, who also popularized the concept; see Mandelbrot 1984). Let's look at them briefly.

One of the earliest fractal objects cited in the literature was the Koch curve, named after the Swedish mathematician Helge von Koch, who described its unique properties early in the twentieth century (Koch 1904). This curve can be obtained recursively with elementary geometrical construction: (1) take a line segment and divide it into three equal segments; (2) erase the middle segment, replacing it with two segments of equal length that make up two sides of an equilateral triangle; (3) for each of the current segments, repeat steps (1) and (2). This recursive process can iterate indefinitely. The first four iterations result in the following figure:

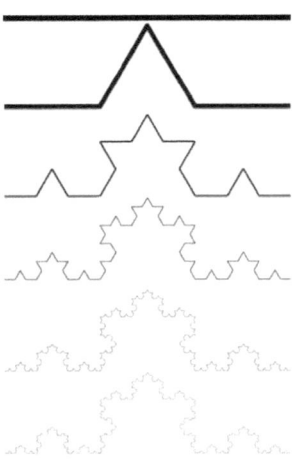

As can be seen with the naked eye from these first iterations, this curve has the property that every small fragment has the same structure as the whole curve (obviously, imagining that we're able to iterate the process infinitely; otherwise, we must specify that the fragment can't be arbitrarily small, lest we again find ourselves with a line segment). Excluding the possibility of continuing the branching indefinitely, phrase structure has a property in some ways similar to that of the Koch curve: namely, part of it has the same structure as the whole. The fundamental difference is that, whereas in the case of the curve we can go down to an infinitely small detail, in the case of phrase structure we can't go below a certain threshold (i.e., below the structure of the smallest phrases contained in the representation). Perhaps we can say that phrase structure enjoys properties of "quasi self-similarity."

Coming back now to natural language, note finally that subphrasal elements—that is, the head, the specifier, and the complement—have different individual properties. The head, in particular, has special properties, as it is the only element that can never be missing in a phrase: for example, an N like *stories* can stand alone (*I've heard stories*) or can be accompanied by a specifier (*I've heard many stories*), a PP complement (*I've heard stories about Rome*), or both (*I've heard many stories about Rome*), but it's impossible for the other elements to appear without the head (**I've heard many about Rome*).[24] In the language of distributionalism, this common property of the phrases NP, VP, AP, and PP—the obligatory presence of the head—is called "endocentricity."

The natural question that arises at this point is, what is the head of the sentence? In fact, our representation of the sentence, [NP VP], has no head. This absence isn't accidental: the distributionalists distinguished the sentence from all other phrases, saying that it is an "exocentric" phrase—that is, a phrase that doesn't contain a head. For a long time, this dichotomy between endocentric and exocentric phrases was accepted in generative grammar. However, beginning with Chomsky's work from the mid-1980s (Chomsky 1986a, 3–4) the representation of the sentence began to be standardized with that of the other constituents, and a head was identified that would also make this phrase endocentric: specifically, the inflectional features associated with the verb—namely, tense, aspect, and subject agreement—were taken to be the head of the clause structure. These features can be expressed syncretically together with the lexical root of the verb itself (as in *cause-s, cause-ing, caus-ed*) or through an auxiliary verb (as in *has caused, was causing, will cause*). From a formal point of view, as a first step the inflectional head was indicated with the letter I (for *inflection*). In keeping with the architecture of all other phrases, the structure of the sentence was represented as IP, that is, [$_{IP}$ NP [I VP]]. Later, toward the end of the 1980s, it was decided to separate the temporal and agreement components of the I head and, by absorbing the features of agreement into other syntactic relationships that we needn't consider here, to view only tense (T) as the head of the sentence. Since then, the structure of the sentence has simply been labeled TP; this innovation, technically called the "split-Infl hypothesis" (see the original proposal in Moro 1988, reprinted and translated in Moro 2013), which has now become the norm, wasn't immediately accepted.[25] However, leaving aside empirical reasons that have compelled the change from IP to TP, it can certainly be said that the analysis whereby the head of the sentence is the inflection component has stabilized to the point that it has become the canonical representation.

Of course, as always, this new theory of the sentence brought with it new issues to be resolved, the price to pay for the advantage of representing all phrases homogeneously. In general, we can identify two different types of problems, one more technical (or, as it's called, "theory-internal") and one with a broader theoretical and empirical scope. Let's look at them briefly. First, how can the inflection be represented with the head T when the tense is expressed not by an auxiliary but by the verb, seeing that the verb V that is contained in VP follows T while in the verb itself the inflection follows V (as in *caus-ed*)? Second, what does it mean to assume that the phrase develops *around* the verbal inflection, or in other words that a sentence is an inflected phrase?

The first problem is solved basically by analogy. First, we note a fact that isn't at all problematic: when the verb isn't inflected directly but appears together with an auxiliary verb, the auxiliary actually precedes the verb; therefore, it makes sense to assume that T precedes the VP as in the representation adopted. The endocentric formula fits (i.e., in a natural way) in sentences like *John has borrowed a book, Frank and Andrea have recorded Mozart's* Requiem. In both of these cases, on the one hand, the nonauxiliary components of the verb (expressed in the past participles *borrow-ed* and *record-ed*) are not inflected, as can be seen from the invariant ending *-ed*, and appear as the head of the VP; on the other hand, the features of tense and of agreement—namely, the inflected component of the verb—occur in the auxiliary (*has* and *have*), which can reasonably be considered, without additional hypotheses, a realization of T. In other words, for these sentences with an auxiliary, the representation of the sentence as TP can be adopted immediately. The tree structure corresponding to a simple example like *John has borrowed a book* will therefore be as follows:[26]

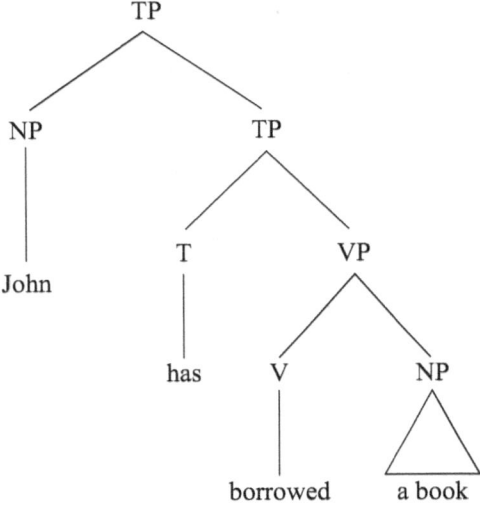

But how can this representation be adapted to a sentence like *Moses carri-ed the tablets*? Applying the formula, in fact, we would instead expect the order of the elements to be **Moses -ed carri the tablets*, given that T precedes V in the tree structure—certainly an unacceptable sentence. To account for this fact, linguists have resorted to hypothesizing that the head *carri* moves to the left of the head T, *-ed*. Technically, the sentence would then have the structure [NP [V-T [__ NP]]], where the low dash as usual denotes the position from which the element has moved, in this case V.

Is this perhaps an ad hoc hypothesis? Are there cases where a head moves toward another head? And when heads move, do they move to the left? These questions are answered by an independent fact that forces us to naturally adopt the hypothesis that one head can move to the left of another. A simple example is the case of the Italian pronoun *ne* (roughly translated as 'of-them'). Let's take the sentence *Alberto ha udito molti racconti su Roma*

'Albert has heard many stories about Rome'. Clearly, this sentence contains the NP [*molti racconti su Roma*] 'many stories about Rome'. It's easy to prove that we're dealing with a phrase; we just need to construct the sentence *Sono molti racconti su Roma che Alberto ha udito* 'There are many stories about Rome that Albert has heard', where *molti racconti su Roma* 'many stories about Rome' behaves as a single chunk. Now, knowing that the head of a phrase can never be absent, how can we represent the sentence *Alberto ne ha uditi molti su Roma* '(lit.) Albert of-them has heard many about Rome'? The natural hypothesis is to assume that *ne* is nothing other than the direct object NP (*racconti* 'stories') that has moved. If indeed, as a counterexample, we put another compatible nominal head between *molti* and *su Roma*, such as *inni* 'hymns', we get an ungrammatical sentence: **Alberto ne ha uditi molti inni su Roma* '(lit.) Albert of-them has heard many hymns about Rome'. So, the sentence is represented as [*Alberto* [*ne-ha* [*uditi* [*molti* __ [*su Roma*]]]]] '[Albert [of-them has [heard [many __ [about Rome]]]]]', or, in formal terms, [NP [N-T [V [Det __ PP]]]], where the head N moves immediately to the left of T. So we have independent proof that the grammar can generate structures in which a head moves from its phrase (leftward) to reach another nearby head.[27] The cases of [V-T] and [N-T] are two particular examples of a general structure: namely, the hypothesis that the verbal head moves leftward to meet the inflectional head isn't ad hoc. It's interesting to note that this idea about the movement of the verbal head, which in a sense "hops" to the left of the inflection—evidently immediately considered the "fixed point" of the architecture of a phrase, the linchpin, so to speak—already appears in *Syntactic Structures*, Chomsky's first book from 1957; the name given to this phenomenon in those years was in fact "affix hopping" (where "affix" means 'verbal inflection'), and the idea was immediately successful, as evidenced by the discussion of it in Lasnik 2000.

The second problem, the one regarding the analysis of the sentence as an inflected phrase, is far deeper. As we've seen, in a sense, the notion of sentence has disappeared in front of our eyes, being broken down into the interaction of simpler structural elements. In other words, in this theoretical framework the sentence doesn't exist as an autonomous element: it's the result of combining an NP with a VP according to the canonical rules of combination mediated by features of tense T. There are no additional special notions that introduce the idea of a sentence as an autonomous element. It's not difficult to recognize in this asymmetric tripartite division Aristotle's original intuition that the sentence is nothing more than the combination of a subject (here, obviously NP) with a predicate (VP) and the addition of tense (T). This analogy isn't just the result of an erudite, a posteriori observation by historians of linguistics. Chomsky himself noted this in 1988 when considering the architecture of the sentence:

One might assume that a transitive verb simply relates two terms, its subject and its object, with no asymmetry of structure [like a two-argument function such as $f(x,y)$]. In fact, that is the assumption made in the construction of formal languages for the purposes of logic and mathematics, and it has often been proposed for human languages as well. Formal languages are constructed in this way for reasons of simplicity and ease in computational operations such as inference. But the evidence indicates that human languages do not adopt the principles familiar in modern logic. Rather, *they adhere to the classical Aristotelian conception* that a sentence has a subject and a predicate, where the predicate may be complex: It may consist of a verb and its object. (Chomsky 1988, 54; emphasis mine)

It is difficult to be clearer: Chomsky explicitly establishes a clean distinction between natural languages and formal languages and, something far from trivial, attributes to the most important structure of natural languages—the sentence—the very structure proposed more than two thousand years earlier by Aristotle.[28]

Naturally, Chomsky doesn't say *only* what Aristotle said. The formal scaffolding, the hypothesis of biologically determined guidance, and the crosslinguistic comparison make Chomsky's theory considerably more complex in its purposes and methods; but basically, at least as far as sentence structure is concerned, the tribute paid to the classical tradition cannot be denied. In particular, the identification of subject and predicate as basic elements of the sentence, associated in this case to precise syntactic configurations, remains one of the fundamental dogmas of syntactic theory: "This idea of defining functional notions in configurational terms has remained a constant in the evolution of Chomsky's concepts, and is one of the important contributions he has made to syntactic theory" (Lepschy 2000, 84). In fact, the subject is defined as the NP that combines with the predicate—which is the VP—through the structural mediation of tense: in this simple observation lies one of modern linguistics' major revolutions, the one that Lepschy calls "one of the important contributions" Chomsky has made to syntactic theory.

Finally, note that this analysis, which unifies the structure of phrases with that of the sentence, has resulted in obtaining in an elegant way a generalization of no small importance—namely, a generalization formulated on the basis of observations developed within linguistic typology—for which see the volume edited by Joseph Greenberg (1963)—and incorporated, so to speak, in the generativist models originating from the work of Giorgio Graffi (1980). Reducing the formal questions to the minimum, a tree structure contains two distinct types of information: one linear (the specifier precedes the head and the head precedes the complement) and one hierarchical (the head and the complement are adjacent; the specifier is adjacent to the compound formed by the head plus the complement). On the basis of very ample empirical observations obtained by comparing significant samples of languages, linguists have noticed that there are some languages where, although the hierarchical order remains valid, the linear order among the elements of a phrase can differ in a systematic and uniform way. For example, in Japanese the head follows the complement, while in languages like Italian and English, as we have seen, the head precedes the complement. The fundamental fact is that this difference affects *all* phrases. Therefore, in Japanese, where for example the equivalent of *after dinner* is *yuusyoku go* '(lit.) dinner after', the equivalent of the phrase *Mary eats the pear* is *Mary wa nashi o taberu* '(lit.) Mary-nominative pear-accusative eats'. More explicitly, in Italian and in English the complements of the preposition and the verb follow the heads to which they are linked, while in Japanese it's exactly the opposite. This fact is not only a strong proof in favor of the hypothesis of quasi self-similarity of syntactic structures, but also a concrete illustration of the notion of parameter, which we've already discussed. The framework of the grammar of human languages is actually composed of a network of universal principles with minimal points of variation—parameters—that may even conspicuously change the surface structure of sentences so much that speakers find the substantial similarity between the structures unrecognizable. One of these parameters is thought to be, in fact, the linear order of the head relative to the complement.[29] Indeed, as occurs in biological systems or in crystals, even small variations in the complex system of syntax also give rise to pervasive differences and to spectacular results on a macroscopic level. The requirement that is obviously imposed on the parameters is that they be easy to identify, seeing that they constitute the trigger point of crosslinguistic differentiation to which children must spontaneously have access.

This is, albeit in a simplified way, the state of the art in terms of sentence structure, accepted by virtually all linguists. Of course, the story doesn't end here; once again the verb *to be* gets in the way, throwing up difficult and interesting theoretical and empirical obstacles that we'll deal with now.[30]

2.3 The Anomaly of the Copula: The Asymmetry That Isn't There

Finally we get back to the verb *to be*. I certainly wouldn't have suggested this long, dense, and—I'm afraid—not so easy excursus if it hadn't been necessary in order to understand what we're now going to confirm: that the verb *to be* shatters the scaffolding of the sentence, as it has been accepted up to the current canonical model, inside and outside the confines of generative grammar. But now the path is downhill. First of all, let's jump back to the first paragraphs of this book, when we were taking a hard look at two series of sentences that were similar except for a single element. The two series were *A picture of the wall caused the riot*, *A picture of the wall will cause the riot*, *A picture of the wall causes the riot*, *A picture of the wall has caused the riot*, and so on, and *A picture of the wall was the cause of the riot*, *A picture of the wall will be the cause of the riot*, *A picture of the wall is the cause of the riot*, *A picture of the wall has been the cause of the riot*, and so on.

Here we must deal with a surprising constellation of data that emerges from these two series of sentences as soon as we analyze them systematically. However, first it's worth noting how relatively little sentences with the verb *to be* have been discussed in contemporary linguistics, especially within generative grammar. This certainly isn't by chance. For example, if we scroll through the bibliographies or the indexes of doctoral dissertations from MIT and other primary centers where generative grammar was researched over the first thirty years of its development—or, more generally, linguistic monographs in the generativist mold, even nontransformational—we see not only that "copula" is largely absent, but also that related entries such as "predicate nominative" and "predicate noun," which are also notions so traditional that they're studied in elementary school, are extremely rare.[31] The fact is that research in those years was aimed at understanding certain locality phenomena for which copular sentences didn't appear, in and of themselves, to constitute a particularly relevant case compared to sentences constructed with other verbs. In reality, as I've noted elsewhere (see, for example, Moro 1997), copular sentences would have undermined many of the generalizations that were being discerned in those years; I believe it was also for this reason that sentences with the verb *to be* were (momentarily) set aside.

An example of how thoroughly this type of sentence would call the current theory into question is one we looked at earlier, using contrasting examples like *Mary is her admirer* and *Mary knows her admirer*, where it's clear that in the first case the pronoun can't refer to Mary, even though the NPs involved are the same. Another interesting case involves extraction of the Italian clitic *ne* from the postverbal NP. Generally, in Italian it's possible to pair a sentence like *Francesca conosce uno studioso di Bach* 'Francesca knows a Bach scholar') with a sentence like *Di studiosi di Bach, Francesca ne conosce uno* '(lit.) of scholars of Bach Francesca of-them knows one'; but, starting from a sentence like *Francesca è uno studioso di Bach* 'Francesca is a Bach scholar', we can't derive **Di studiosi di Bach, Francesca ne è uno* '(lit. of scholars of Bach Francesca of-them is one', which is definitely ungrammatical. At the time when the locality conditions that explain these sentences were being developed, it wasn't immediately possible to account for these data (see Moro 1997 for a detailed explanation). The fact that a set of embarrassing data was ignored is hardly a scandal: in order to move a research agenda forward, often it can be completely reasonable to set certain data aside to try to account for others. The problem, if anything, is whether, once the theoretical and empirical framework is formulated to a first approximation, temporarily discarded data are persistently ignored.

In any case, the empirical framework dealing with sentences containing the verb *to be* is particularly difficult and intricate. We won't take into account all of the data regarding these sentences;

nevertheless, we'll look at selected facts, enough to help us appreciate the debate. First of all, we'll deal with the data. Let's take any sentence from the second series: for example, *A picture of the wall was the cause of the riot*. There's no apparent reason why this sentence, given that it results in the sequence NP V NP, shouldn't be represented according to the usual asymmetric geometry: [NP [T [V NP]]]. In fact, if we try for example to move elements from inside the postverbal NP, as in *Which riot was a picture of the wall the cause of __?*, we discover, not surprisingly, that movement gives a grammatical result—not surprisingly, as only the second NP is adjacent to V, which is a necessary condition for extraction of material. In other words, this sentence with the verb *to be* behaves just like its equivalent with a different transitive verb: *A picture of the wall caused the riot*. If we were to look only at these data, there would be nothing to add; this book would end here and the sentences with the verb *to be* would simply be considered part of the normal sentence schema involving any other transitive verb. But instead, with a minimum extension of the data, something completely surprising happens. What we're about to see is the breaking point of the system, the anomaly of copular sentences.

Let's take the sentence that we just subjected to the extraction test, and exchange the order of the two NPs; we get *The cause of the riot was a picture of the wall*. We obviously still have a sequence of type NP V NP. Now let's focus on the NP that follows the verb. We would expect, of course, to be able to extract material from this NP, as we can in all sequences of the type NP V NP. However, surprisingly, the sentence becomes ungrammatical: **Which wall was the cause of the riot a picture of __?* The result is clear: the NP that follows the verb *to be* in this case doesn't behave at all like a direct object, since the extraction is impossible; if anything, it behaves like a preverbal subject NP. The asymmetry we typically see in the structure of the sentence disappears in this case: the two NPs behave equivalently, in the sense that both block extraction. How is this possible? Obviously, the anomaly can't depend on the verb that we used. If instead of the verb *to be* we used another verb, like *to reveal*, the result would be quite acceptable: *Which wall did the cause of the riot reveal a picture of __?* Nor can the malfunction be imputed to the verb *to be* per se: if the absence of asymmetry between the two NPs accompanying the verb were generalized—that is, if in *all* sentences with the verb *to be* it was *always* impossible to extract material from the NP that follows the verb—we could certainly admit, simply, that the verb *to be* has idiosyncratic properties and at least record this fact as an exception, even if doing so certainly doesn't constitute an explanation. Linguistics, after all, is one of the paradigmatic cases where the idea of "exceptions" has been applied—an idea that has often been used in a strategically profitable way. Admitting an exception is equivalent to deciding that a certain model, although incomplete, is currently too useful or elegant to be abandoned and that it's preferable to set aside the (few) recalcitrant bits of data, building a list of phenomena that—at least at that stage—one decides not to explain. But in this case, what should be noted is that not even the "exception" strategy applies to the anomaly of copular sentences. The reason is clear: not *all* sentences with the verb *to be* of the type NP V NP exhibit this property; instead, of those pairs of sentences that remain grammatical even if the two NPs are permuted, *only one* exhibits it! The situation becomes really intricate: on the one hand, there's no reason to abandon the asymmetric structure of the sentence that was laboriously developed during the various stages of syntactic theory for sentences with verbs other than *to be*; on the other, this structure doesn't work for *to be*. Still, there seems to be neither a reason to abandon it nor an immediate way to adapt it to the new data, since *sometimes* it works even for the verb *to be*. So what's so special about *half* of the sequences of the NP V NP type when V is the verb *to be*? Why do the pairs of sentences not all behave alike despite being sequences of the same type, namely,

NP V NP? This, in a nutshell, is the problem of sentences with the verb *to be*: this is the anomaly that undermines the foundations of the asymmetric scaffolding that supports the structure of the sentence.

As I mentioned, studies of this type of sentence within generative grammar have been few, but they are certainly not entirely absent. Milestones in this passionate pursuit of the formula that explains sentences with the verb *to be* in a unified way have been, in my opinion at least, the works of Roger Higgins (1979), Nicolas Ruwet (1975), and Giuseppe Longobardi (1985). These scholars, carrying out (partially) independent research, were more able than others to focus on the distinctive aspects of this question and to suggest different ways to categorize the various anomalies that occur in languages with respect to the syntax of sentences with the verb *to be*. Higgins produced a taxonomy of copular phrases that reduced all cases to *four* basic types, above all on a semantic basis (especially grounded in Peter Geach's theory of referentiality; see Geach 1962). Ruwet focused instead on phenomena of clitic extraction and on the interpretation of pronouns in sentences with the verb *to be* that involve permutation of the two NPs, highlighting many differences with transitive sentences. Finally, Longobardi decisively showed that, in Italian, the syntactic properties of the NP that follows the verb *to be* in anomalous cases coincide with those of a normal, preverbal subject, providing valuable data for research over the following years. These are milestones that, together with the development of general concepts such as "raising," which we will look at shortly, have led to a proposed unified theory of sentences with the verb *to be*. In the next chapter, I'll present a possible solution that is capable of causing one of the fundamental dogmas of sentence structure, as it was developed over the first thirty years of work in formal linguistics, to fall by the wayside.

3 The Strange Case of Verbs without Subjects

> If we are called on to simplify things that seem to us to be complicated, we are never called on to complicate things that are simple.
> —Madeleine Delbrêl, *The Joy of Believing*

After having dwelt so insistently on the tripartite structure of the sentence—and especially on the fact that a sentence needs a subject and a predicate in a particular configuration—now we'll look at a case that seems to completely contradict everything we've seen so far. We'll closely analyze some special verbs, which is to say those verbs that don't have a subject.[1] The idea that there are verbs without a subject isn't a quirk of contemporary grammars: traditional grammars—for example, those used in schools—talk about impersonal verbs, which are in fact a class of verbs without a subject. Typical examples of these oddities are the so-called "weather" verbs: when we say *It's raining*, we don't imagine a subject that performs or undergoes an action. If it rains, I'm only thinking about a certain weather condition; certainly I can say *The stellar debris rains down from the sky*, but there's no doubt that here we're dealing with a metaphor where the verb *rain* has nothing to do with the weather. We're not going to investigate these cases; instead, we'll be looking at different, far more problematic constructions. It was from detailed and systematic exploration of these constructions that the unified theory of sentences with the verb *to be* was born, and we'll also be looking at why this theory not only resolves the anomaly mentioned above but also obliges us to review the entire structure of the sentence, giving those with the verb *to be* a new, unexpected centrality.

The most innovative aspect of this theory's development—completed over the course of a decade, in the 1980s—is that the formal apparatus plays a leading role in the research, exemplifying the retrieval principle that we noted when we were talking about the fundamentals of structuralism. This isn't an unusual occurrence in other empirical sciences; there are numerous examples showing how a formal theory often leads to the discovery of new facts and new explanations. I've already mentioned Dirac's discovery of the positron, but I could cite many other cases as well. Certainly linguistics is far from having a formal apparatus as potent as that of physics; however, in linguistics we also find examples where the identification of a certain property or a certain linguistic object follows "logically" from theory. It's precisely in situations like this that theorists realize that their discipline has become not only a descriptive system but also a real key to discovering properties of the world. Theoretical linguistics doesn't escape this kind of research; indeed, in some ways it offers unexpected paradigms that make it a valuable model.

This chapter is divided into three sections. In section 3.1, we'll look at a central structural property of natural languages, involving a special type of syntactic movement called "raising." In section 3.2, we'll specifically analyze the verb *to be* and examine the main stages that led to the canonical theory of the 1980s. Finally, in section 3.3 we'll see how letting go of a sentence theory axiom allows us to resolve the anomaly of sentences with the verb *to be*, leading to a unified theory of copular sentences and ultimately to new questions about the general architecture of syntax in natural languages.

The Strange Case of Verbs without Subjects

In this chapter, I won't be using a discursive technique and I won't have to introduce the basic technical apparatus; instead, I'll take advantage of the fact that linguistics is based on a formal system and therefore the argument can take a more compact form (even if perhaps it makes for less easy reading). The use of formal deductive reasoning will also give you, the reader, a way to physically touch, albeit sketchily, how one proceeds in researching the principles of natural languages. Let's start with raising.

3.1 The Quasi-Copula

Sentence structure provides that there is a subject for every predicate and therefore, by definition, a subject for every verb. This is summed up in our sentence formula by the presence of an NP (the subject) and a VP (the predicate) plus of course the representation of tense (T): [NP [T VP]]. However, there are cases such as Italian where this structure—in terms of the order of the elements—isn't always intuitively evident. In fact, alongside the sentence *Giovanni ha telefonato* 'John has telephoned', which immediately conforms to the formula, we can find the sentence *Ha telefonato Giovanni* '(lit.) has telephoned John', where the subject follows the verb, or even simply the sentence *Ha telefonato* '(lit.) has telephoned', where the subject—as traditional grammars say—is understood. The adaptation of the structure [NP [T VP]] in languages other than English, and particularly the variability of the position of the subject in languages like Italian, has been at the heart of linguistic debate for many years and is still a current topic of discussion (see, among others, Chomsky 1981, Rizzi 1982, Rizzi 1990, and, for a critical version of the development of this theme, Graffi 2001 and the references cited therein). Keeping the discourse on a formal level is essential, and we can briefly put forward a solution that will allow us to keep the given formula invariable. Let's take a look at the problematic cases.

We'll start with the sentence *Ha telefonato* '(lit.) has telephoned'. This case is relatively simple: in fact, its structure complies fully with [NP [T VP]], assuming the position of the NP subject is occupied by a pronominal NP that's not pronounced (usually represented by the abbreviation *pro*), also traditionally called—at least in the above-mentioned works by Chomsky and Rizzi—"null subject" or "phonetically unexpressed subject." The structure of the sentence *Ha telefonato* will therefore be represented as [*pro* [*ha telefonato*]]. Let's take another simple example, which also includes a direct object: *Ha letto un libro* '(lit.) has read a book'. The corresponding tree representation is as follows:

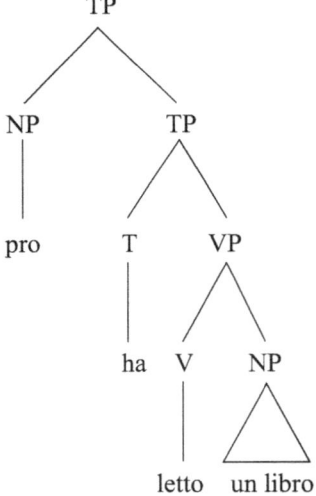

The reason for this choice is both theoretical and empirical. On the theoretical side, as I've noted, the need to keep sentence structure invariable is considered to be fundamental; the sentence is too important a linguistic structure to admit exceptions between languages (or within the same language). But this theoretical requirement would never have been accepted by the scientific community if empirical reasons hadn't been found that made it credible. Among these, two are worth noting.

The first involves the interpretation of pronouns—reflexive pronouns in particular. By adopting the null-subject hypothesis, it is in fact possible to show that linguistic phenomena associated with sentences that contain a pronounced pronoun—for example, *he*, *she*, and so on—are no different from those found in sentences with a null subject. For example, if a sentence contains a reflexive pronoun—which as we know needs an antecedent to be interpreted—as in *Maria sa che ammira se stesso* '(lit.) Mary knows that [he/it] admires himself/itself', the only way to make sense of it is to admit that the antecedent of *se stesso* 'himself/itself', which is to say the subject of *ammira* 'admires', is the equivalent of phonetically unexpressed *egli* 'it' or *lui* 'he'. Otherwise—that is, if the only available subject were *Maria*—the reflexive pronoun would only and *necessarily* be the feminine singular form *se stessa* 'herself' and the sentence *Maria sa che ammira se stesso* 'Mary knows that admires himself' would be just as ungrammatical as **Maria ammira se stesso* 'Mary admires himself'. Therefore, it's assumed that the position of the NP in the dependent clause is occupied by a singular masculine *pro*.

Besides this phenomenon involving the interpretation of pronouns, numerous other data support the null-subject hypothesis. Let's start from a general consideration: this single property of a given language—having or not having a null subject available in its lexicon—has cascading effects on that language's syntax; and, as it is immediately detectable, it gives children the immediate opportunity to acquire as a "result" many of the structural properties of the language they hear spoken (see Hyams 1986, Manzini and Wexler 1987, Wexler 1993, Guasti 2017, and the references cited therein). One of the properties that correlates with the ability to have a null subject is the ability to have the subject either to the left or to right side of the verb. But what properties does the subject

NP that follows the verb have in null-subject languages? For a verb like the one we're analyzing, *telefonare* 'to telephone', it's very important to note that when an NP follows a V as a subject, it doesn't behave like an NP that follows a V as an object. For example, we can't extract material from this NP; in this case, locality phenomena become an important guide for deciphering the structure, a genuine heuristic tool. To highlight this phenomenon, here I'll use the ability of Italian to extract part of an NP and replace it with the clitic (i.e., unstressed) pronoun *ne*. Let's take the two sentences *Hanno telefonato due amici di Giovanni* '(lit.) have telephoned two friends of John' and *Hanno incontrato due amici di Giovanni* '(lit.) have met two friends of John'. In the first case, *due amici di Giovanni* 'two friends of John' is the subject of the verb; in the second, it's the object. Extraction should behave differently because we expect that the two NPs occupy different positions in sentence structure. This is actually the case. When we extract *amici di Giovanni* 'friends of John' from the NPs of the two sentences and replace it with *ne* 'of-it/them', we get contrasting results: *Ne hanno incontrati due __*, '(lit.) of-them [they] have met two __', which is grammatical, and **Ne hanno telefonato due __* '(lit.) of-them [they] have telephoned two __', which is not. The fact that we can extract from the direct object isn't surprising, given the locality conditions on extraction, according to which we can extract from an NP only if it is adjacent to a V. But if we want to maintain the validity of these same locality conditions, we must also admit that the NP that follows *telefonano* '[they] telephone' isn't adjacent to V even if it's to the right of it. The only possibility is that this NP is found in a higher position, obviously still to the right of V. The minimum structure compatible with this hypothesis—and with the independent hypothesis that linguistic elements always and only combine in pairs—will be this (using as an example the sentence *Ha telefonato Giovanni* '(lit.) pro has telephoned John; John has telephoned'):

The Strange Case of Verbs without Subjects

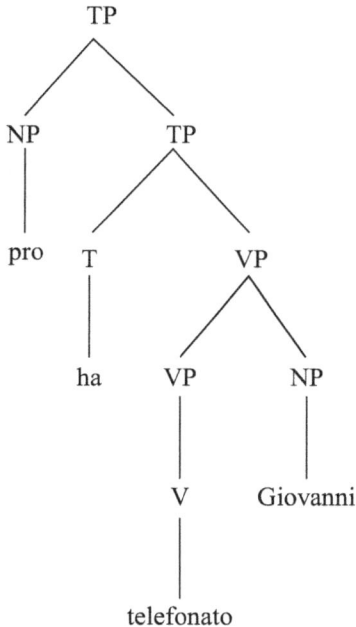

The subject *Giovanni* is connected with the verb but it's found, to use a physics metaphor, in a lower "orbit" compared to the subject's canonical position occupied here by *pro*; the NP *Giovanni* is technically the one defined as an "adjunct" of the VP, as the conventional double VP label indicates. In this case, the null pronoun *pro* partially shares the properties of reflexive pronouns, having as an obligatory antecedent the NP closest to it, *Giovanni*.

Similarly, when the subject of a sentence with a transitive verb, like *Ha letto un libro Giovanni* '(lit.) [pro] has read a book John', is located to the right of the verb, we still have a structure with the subject in the adjunct position. In other words, when it's in postverbal position, the subject in a postverbal position of an intransitive verb like *telefonare* 'to telephone' is in the same configuration as the subject of a transitive verb like *leggere* 'to read':

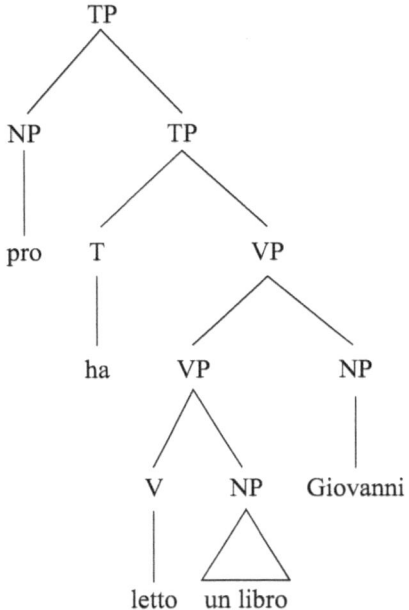

You may have already tried to construct other extractions from a subject that follows the verb. If you've tried with a transitive verb, like *leggere* 'to read' in the sentence *Hanno letto questo libro due amici di Giovanni* '(lit.) [they] have read this book two friends of John', you'll have noticed that the conclusion holds. In fact, it's not possible to say **Ne hanno letto questo libro due __* '(lit.) *of-them [they] have read this book two __', because the subject *due amici di Giovanni* 'two friends of John' isn't adjacent to the verb in either the hierarchical or the linear sense. But, if you tried with another intransitive verb, like *arrivare* 'to arrive', you'll have encountered a strange phenomenon, something totally unexpected, the kind of thing that's so simple it has always been ignored. Starting with the sentence *Sono arrivati due amici di Giovanni* '(lit.) [they] are arrived two friends of John; Two of

John's friends have arrived', with the subject to the right of the verb, you'll indeed get a completely grammatical sentence: *Ne sono arrivati due* __ '(lit.) of-them [they] are arrived two __; Two of them have arrived', where the extraction from the subject doesn't create any problems.

This phenomenon, observed systematically for the first time in the 1970s by David Perlmutter (1978), was implemented in the formal generative system and enriched by a great many new facts, some of which come from Italian dialects, in the influential work of Luigi Burzio (1986). This same phenomenon, and its implementation in the formal generative system, was reviewed in a radical way in the revolutionary theory of Ken Hale and Samuel Jay Keyser (2002). These observations have had enormous repercussions on syntactic theory. In fact, besides the canonical division into transitive and intransitive verbs—a division that dates back at least to the time of the Stoics—it immediately became clear that a new category was needed, the category called "unaccusative" constructions (and often, inappropriately, constructions with "unaccusative verbs"). If we adopt this category, in cases like *Sono arrivati due amici di Giovanni* '(lit.) [they] are arrived two friends of John', the expression *due amici di Giovanni* 'two friends of John' occupies the same position as the object of a verb—as in *Ho incontrato due amici di Giovanni* 'I have met two friends of John'—while not sharing all of the properties of a direct object. In fact, if on the one hand this expression is adjacent to V like a direct object, on the other it doesn't take what's called the "accusative case"—a particular ending that, in many languages, direct objects can take (which explains the label "unaccusative").[2] In many languages, such as Latin, German, and Ancient Greek, case is manifested morphologically on all nouns that make up the head of the noun phrase according to the role they play relative to the verb: in Italian, instead, case has been reduced to appearing only on pronouns, even if for the sake of simplicity one accepts that cases are obligatorily assigned to nouns in all languages. So, we say *Ho incontrato due amici di Giovanni* '(lit.) [I] have met two friends of John' and *Li ho incontrati* '(lit.) them [I] have met', with the pronoun *li* in the accusative case, but certainly not **Li sono arrivati* '(lit.) they [they] are arrived', starting from *Sono arrivati due amici di Giovanni* '(lit.) are arrived two friends of John'. We therefore assume that the postverbal NP in an unaccusative construction occupies the position of the direct object (i.e., that the NP is adjacent to V, because it's possible to extract material, as in *Ne sono arrivati due __* '(lit.) of-them are arrived two'), but it differs in that it can't be replaced by a pronoun in the accusative case. The structural formula assigned in Italian is [pro [T [V NP]]]; the corresponding tree representation for the example *È arrivato Giovanni* '(lit.) [he] is arrived John', is as follows:

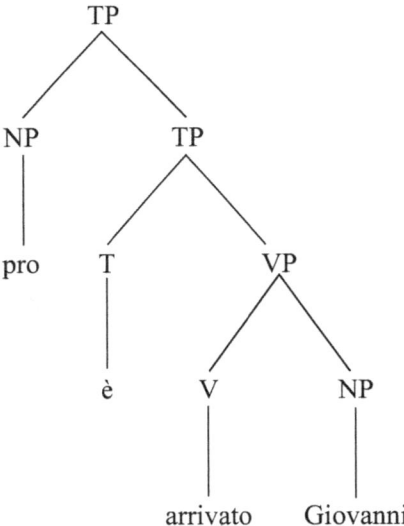

There are many other facts that justify this revolutionary tripartite division, and they may vary from language to language. Italian provides one in its use of different types of auxiliary verbs: *essere* 'to be' for unaccusatives and *avere* 'to have' for "pure" intransitives. Another is the possibility of using what are known as "absolute" phrases—that is, phrases independent from the rest of the sentence, as in *Arrivato Maria, siamo tutti partiti* 'Mary arrived, we all left' (but not **Telefonato Maria, siamo tutti partiti* 'Mary telephoned, we all left'). There are also Italian verbs that allow both auxiliaries, like *correre* 'to run' in *Sono corso allo stadio* '(lit.) [I] am run to-the stadium' and *Ho corso allo stadio* '(lit.) [I] have run at-the stadium'. In the first sentence, a person was outside the stadium and ran toward the stadium; in the second, the person was at the stadium and ran around inside the stadium. Also, in this case the extraction diagnostic using *ne* works: *Ne sono corsi allo stadio due __* '(lit.) of-them are run to the stadium two __' and **Ne hanno corso allo stadio due __* '(lit.) of-them have run at the stadium two __'. In other languages, such as English, that don't allow pronominal extraction, there are other syntactic phenomena that justify introducing a new class of constructions in addition to transitive and intransitive. For example, when we have an unaccusative construction with a verb that expresses a position in space (even metaphorically), the subject is allowed to occupy the direct object position, while a substitute element is inserted in subject position (technically called an "expletive," which we'll discuss in detail shortly): namely, *there*, as in *There arrived two friends of John* or *There exists an alternative theory*. Finally, there are some varieties of south-central Italian—explored for example in Chierchia 2004—in which verbs that in standard Italian are only unaccusative are also used transitively, resulting in a change of auxiliary (a phenomenon Chierchia calls "unstable valence"), as in *È sceso il gatto dal tetto* '(lit.) [it] is lowered the cat from-the roof' and *Ho sceso il gatto dal tetto* '(lit.) [I] have lowered the cat from-the roof': in the first case, *il gatto* 'the cat' is the subject, while in the second, it's the direct object and the sentence has a causative sense.[3]

Generally, I should add that many unaccusative verbs have a transitive variant; think of pairs of sentences like *È affondato un vascello* '(lit.) [it] is sunk a ship' and *Ha affondato un vascello* '(lit.) [it] has sunk a ship', where *un vascello* 'a ship' is the subject in one case and the object in the other.[4] Especially in the last two sentences, in line with what we've seen, movement is possible from the NP that follows the verb, as in *Ne è affondato uno __* '(lit.) of-them [it] is sunk one __' and *Ne ha affondato uno __* '(lit.) of-them [it] has sunk one __'; however, only in the transitive construction can an accusative pronoun substitute for the entire NP—as evidenced by the contrast between *L'ha affondato* 'It [it] has sunk' and **L'è affondato* 'It [it] is sunk'. Other interesting cases are provided by English, where a verb like *melt* can be used both transitively, as in *John melts the butter*, and unaccusatively—in which case, English not being a null-subject language, the NP moves to preverbal position: *The butter melts*.[5]

In conclusion, upon close examination unaccusative constructions make up a sui generis subclass within the class of "subjectless" verbs: they have a subject that shares many properties with the direct object, in particular the base position adjacent to the verb. We'll find out soon enough why sentences with the verb *to be* oblige us to substantially revise this theory. For now, let's keep in mind this reflection on the position of the subject, because in the discussion that follows we'll be dealing with a verb lacking a subject that shares many properties with the verb *to be*: the verb *to seem*. This verb is so close to the verb *to be* that often it's called the "quasi-copula." However, it also enjoys the defining property of verbs that give rise to unaccusative constructions, namely, that of not having a proper subject. So, as we'll see, the analysis of the quasi-copula will decisively influence that of sentences with the verb *to be*.

Let's start by comparing these two sentences: *He wants that John reach a goal* and *It seems that John reaches a goal*. In the first case, two individuals are involved: John and someone who wants John to reach a goal. In the second case, clearly not: it's not difficult to realize that *seems* is a verb without a subject. As a counterexample, just compare the sentences *They want that John reach a goal* and **They seem that John reaches a goal*; clearly, *to seem* can't have its own subject, at least not in the same sense in which *to want* can. However, if we expand our empirical range, we realize that there are two forms, somewhat similar to these, which seem at first glance more similar to each other than a careful examination shows: *John wants to reach a goal* and *John seems to reach a goal*. In this case, the sentences are the same with respect to the individuals involved. In both cases, in fact, there is only one individual: John. An adequate grammatical model must obviously take these insights into account. By definition, the speaker's competence must be reflected in the structural representations. How do we take into account these data involving the verb *to want* and the quasi-copula? To answer this question, we must further complicate the data and look at a special property of English. So far, we've considered the sentences *He wants that John reach a goal*, *It seems that John reaches a goal*, *John wants to reach a goal*, and *John seems to reach a goal*. However, English (unlike Italian, for example) also allows infinitives to have phonetically expressed subjects; so, in addition to the above sentences with the verb *want*, English has sentences like *John wants her to reach a goal*, which in Italian can only be created with a noninfinitive subordinate clause: *Giovanni vuole che lei ottenga un risultato* '(lit.) John wants that she reach a goal'. But the key thing is that, unlike in the case of *want*, the analogous sentence with the quasi-copula (the verb *to seem*) is utterly impossible in English as in Italian: **John seems her to reach a goal*. This rift between sentences with *want* and *seem* means that they cannot have the same structure.

One method of solving this hard-to-explain problem, now part of the standard model, is to admit this fundamental difference between the two verbs: actually, sentences with the verb *to want* always involve two subjects, of which the one that's dependent on the infinitive can be either a special, phonetically unrealized pronoun[6] or a phonetically realized subject in the accusative case; the dependent clauses with the verb *to seem* (or its Italian equivalent *sembrare*) don't have their own subject. The subject that appears in front of *to seem* in a sentence like *John seems to reach a goal* is nothing more than the subject of the dependent clause that moves into that position. Technically, this kind of movement is said to be an instance of subject "raising," where by "raising" linguists mean movement from subject position of the dependent clause to subject position of the main clause. We can see this more clearly by looking at the tree representation of the sentence in Italian where the verb *sembrare* 'to seem' appears with a compound tense, namely, *Giovanni è sembrato ottenere un risultato* '(lit.) John is seemed to-reach a goal; John has seemed to reach a goal'. In this tree, the dash represents the base position of the subject *Giovanni*, which has then raised into the main clause.

The Strange Case of Verbs without Subjects

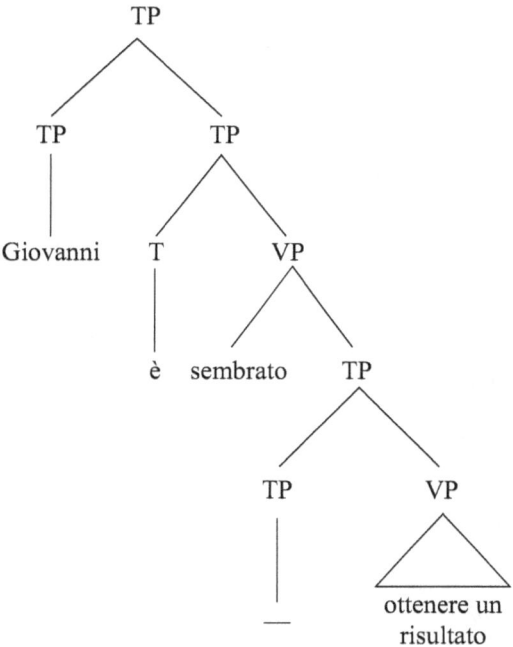

As an alternative to the raising strategy, of course there's the possibility that the subject doesn't move from the dependent clause. In this case, the verb of the dependent clause will be finite and a semantically null element will appear in the subject position: in English, this semantically null element is overtly realized by the pronoun *it*, as in *It seems that John reached a goal*. We'll certainly return to the issue of semantically null subjects, but this difference must be clear: raising will be central to the discussion of sentences with the verb *to be*.

In conclusion, the verb *sembrare* 'to seem' is a raising verb: it's a verb that doesn't have its own subject but lives—so to speak— parasitically on another sentence, taking that sentence's subject.

Looking at the situation from the point of view of the predicative bond, it follows then that the quasi-copula, like the copula, isn't the predicate: in Italian, when I say *Giovanni sembra un rivale* '(lit.) John seems a rival; John seems to be a rival', it's *un rivale* 'a rival' that acts as predicate to *Giovanni* 'John'. To corroborate the hypothesis that *un rivale* 'a rival' has a predicative role when it accompanies the verb *sembrare* 'to seem', we can resort to the interpretation of pronouns, taking into account what we've already observed about the verb *to be* in the "case of the two stars" in chapter 1: namely, that a pronoun contained in a predicate NP can't refer to the subject of the sentence of which it is the predicate. In fact, this is exactly the case here. The sentence *Giovanni sembra un suo rivale* '(lit.) John seems a his rival; John seems to be his rival' contrasts with *Giovanni odia un suo rivale* '(lit.) John hates a his rival; John hates his rival': in the first case, *suo* 'his' can't refer to *Giovanni* 'John' unless *sembra* 'seems' is interpreted as 'resembles' which is possible in Italian,[7] while in the second case, *suo* 'his' easily refers to *Giovanni* 'John'. This phenomenon can be explained only if *un suo rivale* '(lit.) a his rival; his rival' is the predicate of the sentence, which obviously excludes that the predicate could also be *sembra* 'seem'; the situation in the sentence with *odia* 'hates' is obviously different. Also, these two examples show that the sequence NP V NP conceals very different properties depending on the verb used. Now, let's move on to a case that will bring us directly to the solution.

3.2 *Is* and *There Is*

In this section, we'll be dealing with an especially thorny problem, already mentioned in the section of chapter 1 dedicated to Jespersen. Historically, the data we'll examine here have been the focus of linguistic debate from the outset. If we limit ourselves to the last two centuries, these data have served as a test bed for many fundamental reflections on the architecture of the language faculty in general, not only in Jespersen's work and in the nineteenth-century tradition but also in the entire tradition of generative grammar. For me, the subject is, if possible, even more delicate: I don't think the standard theory I will present is correct. I have made an effort in other instances (Moro 1988, 1997) to argue against this theory and to propose an alternative; I'll try to reproduce the reasons for my dissent again here. The curious thing is that part of the standard theory is still the basis of the alternative I've proposed. In any case, I'm compelled to cover this ground again. You—the reader—are of course free to stop here, though I hope that curiosity prevails and that you're open to listening to the alternative theory and, perhaps, to making it your own.

Let's start with a simple pair of sentences: *John saw that a man was in the garden* and *John saw a man in the garden.* The first is obviously a complex sentence; we'll turn our attention to the subordinate clause (*that a man was in the garden*). This clause is made up of a subject (*a man*) and a predicate (*in the garden*). It's hard not to see an analogy with the second sentence, which also has *a man* for its subject and *in the garden* for its predicate—and (it shouldn't surprise us at this point)—the predicate lacks a verb. Technically, the phrases that follow the verb *see* in the second sentence and form the predicative bond (*a man* and *in the garden*)— in turn realized as a phrase (*a man in the garden*)—are called "small clauses" (abbreviated SC). This term signifies that we're dealing with sentences, in that they contain a subject and a predicate, but incomplete sentences, in that the fundamental ingredient of time isn't indicated. In technical terms, a small clause like *a man in the garden* can simply be indicated as [NP PP], that is, a noun phrase followed by a prepositional phrase.

The next step comes from the analysis of a sentence like this one: *A man was seen ___ in the garden.* In this case, the subject of the verb *see* is raised from the small clause into the preverbal subject position; this is similar to what happens with the verb *seem* in sentences like the ones we looked at in the previous section (*John seems __ to reach a goal*). The fundamental point is that the relationship that associates *John has seen a man in the garden* and *A man was seen in the garden* has been considered on an analogical basis as the interpretive key to the following pair of sentences built around the verb *to be*: *There is a man in the garden* and *A man is __ in the garden*. The association between these two sentences would be (I say "would" because it's right here that my opinion diverges, but we'll return to this in the next section) that they're considered synonymous, the only difference being that, whereas raising takes place in the second case, in the first an element considered semantically null—namely, *there*—would be placed in the position of the subject. This element should indicate that the structure of the sentence in question adheres to the overall schema [NP [T VP]], with V having SC as its complement. To put it more explicitly, if we allow that *there* belongs to the category NP, with which it can commute, we'll have the raised variant [NP [T [V [__ PP]]] corresponding to *A man is in the garden* and then, with the insertion of the expletive element *there*, we'll have the variant [*there* [T [NP PP]]]] corresponding to *There is a man in the garden*. For the sake of clarity, I want to indicate the two structures with tree representations, with the T head (*was*) realized as an auxiliary to separate it from the V head (*been*). The first structure illustrates the raising of the small clause subject (*a man*) into subject position:

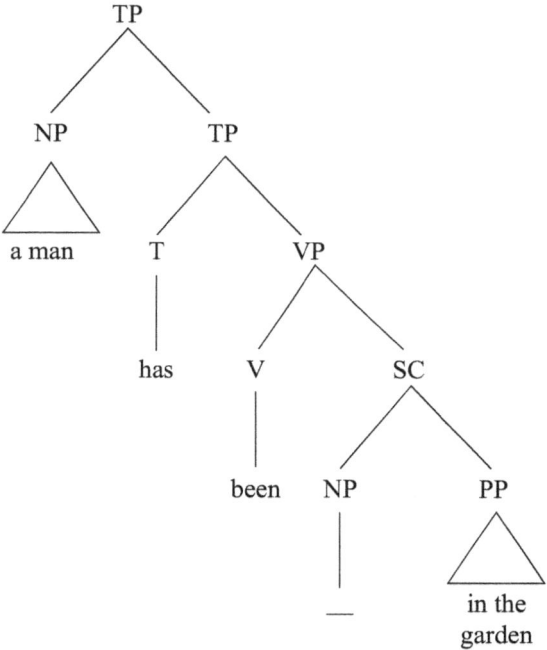

In the second structure, no raising takes place, but the expletive *there* is inserted in the subject position. Of course, this structure is generated from the same basic structure as the first one that contains the small clause:

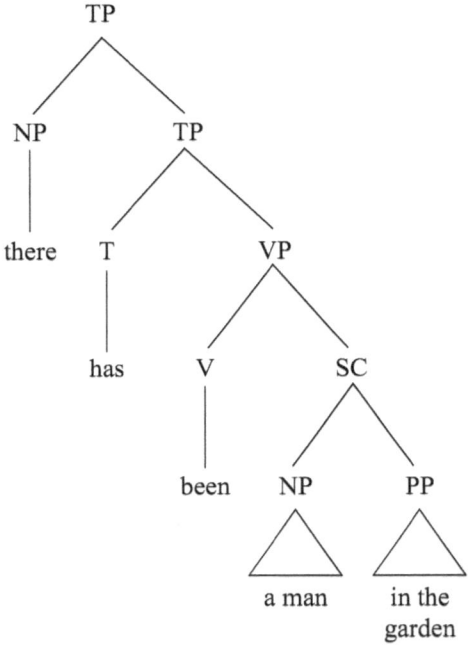

In linguistic tradition, especially in the twentieth century (as in Jespersen's work), elements like *there*, and its analogues in other languages such as Italian *ci*, have been labeled in various ways: "dummy subjects," "expletive subjects," "colorless subjects"—all terms that are meant to highlight that we're dealing not with "full-blown" subjects but with "placeholders" for elements with a purely structural, syntactic value, with no semantic impact. How scholars have dealt with these elements would itself be enough to build a history of linguistics around (again, see Graffi 2001 and the references cited therein). Within the generative grammar framework, it's worth remembering that the distribution of these elements was regarded as one of the substantive, empirical reasons for moving from *constructive* grammars toward *selective* grammars—that is, shifting from a vision of grammar in which sentences are built gradually, beginning with words, to one where, from among all possible combinations, the ungrammatical ones are filtered out, on the basis of general principles.[8] An explicit trace of this historic transition occurs in *Lectures on Government and Binding* (1981), where Chomsky proposes the principle "Insert *there* anywhere." The sentences where *there* can't appear are discarded on the basis of principles such as those governing the distribution of lexical categories or the assignment of thematic roles (see Hale and Keyser 2002). For example, the sentence **There read the book* is discarded because *there* can't receive the thematic role of agent of the action that is associated with *read*, unlike *Mary* in *Mary read the book*. However, the question was never completely resolved, and it has been, and still is, a source of debate. This is because even when the agent role is suppressed, as with verbs in the passive, *there* still can't appear (**There was read a book*), while the complement of the verb must obligatorily move to the subject position of the sentence, as in *A book was read*, except for a subclass of unaccusative verbs like *exist*, where *there* can appear in the place reserved for the subject (*There existed a book*). In Italian, a null-subject language, *pro* is usually possible as an expletive in the passive, but it remains to be explained why *ci* 'there' is impossible, as in **Ci fu letto un libro* 'There was read a book' (of course, excluding the interpretation where *ci* is the clitic version of the pronoun *noi* 'us' in the dative case, which by pure coincidence corresponds to the clitic version of *ci* used as a locative expletive).

At any rate, whatever the explanation is for the distribution of expletives like *ci* and *there* in subject position, it's clear that an explanation based on thematic role assignment isn't possible for the verb *to be*. In fact, the verb *to be* never assigns thematic roles; this is a prerogative of verbs that have predicative content, whereas the verb *to be* is only the manifestation of tense. In addition, even apart from the fact that the verb *to be* doesn't assign thematic roles, sentences with the verb *to be* accompanied by expletives are still perfectly acceptable, both in Italian (in a sentence like *C'è un fantasma*) and in English (in the corresponding sentence *There is a ghost*). Finally, we should take note of a very important fact that will be the focus of discussion in chapter 4: in Italian, which is a null-subject language, *pro* isn't always enough to make a sentence with the verb *to be* grammatical: the sentence **pro è Giovanni in giardino* '(lit.) pro is John in-the garden', in fact, is still ungrammatical without *ci* 'there'. The only possibility is to move *Giovanni* into subject position, as in *Giovanni è __ in giardino* 'John is __ in the garden'.[9]

Now it's time to summarize the discussion. The verb *to be*—as a verb without a subject—is considered an unaccusative verb (construction): with *to be*, it's possible either that the subject is an NP raised from a lower position, or that an expletive is inserted. We'll see that this way of analyzing structures with the verb *to be* not only is inappropriate from an empirical standpoint, but also requires sentence structure to be thoroughly reviewed from a theoretical perspective. It is, however, albeit with some simplification, the theory of sentences with *there is* or *there are* deemed valid until the mid-1980s and echoed by most contemporary works in syntax, including virtually all handbooks.

At this point, the door opens on two separate but almost inseparably related issues, both of them difficult and not yet fully resolved. On the one hand, the semantic questions: Is it really true that the two sentences *A man is in the garden* and *There is a man in the garden* are synonymous? Is it really true that the presence of *there* doesn't influence the interpretation of the elements associated with the verb *to be*? Why exactly does a locative adverb like *there*, and like *ci*, tend to appear in this position in various languages? Why are sentences with *there* called "existential"? On the other hand, the more typically syntactic questions: In Italian, a null-subject language, why should a subject expletive element, phonetically realized as *ci*, be present? What are the structural conditions that allow or force the appearance of *there* and *ci*? Do raising sentences and sentences with *there* and *ci* really have the same syntactic properties?

The semantic problems associated with sentences with *there*, and similar constructions in other languages, can easily be illustrated by concentrating on the name classically assigned to these types of sentences: "existential sentences." They're known by this name because we use them when we want to express the existence of something: *There are repulsive spiders*, *There are an infinity of prime numbers*, *There are stars*. It's clear, however, that this type of sentence with the verb *to be* isn't the only way to express existence: many languages, including English, have explicit, existential predicates, such as the verb *to exist*. That said, in linguistic tradition it's just sentences like those with the verb *to be*, which we're analyzing, that are defined as "existential sentences." What's special about existential sentences from a syntactic perspective? In my opinion, the linguist who came closest to a structural characterization of this class of statements was—not surprisingly—Jespersen, who we already encountered in chapter 1 regarding the study of sentences with the verb *to be*. After examining existential constructions in a broad sample of very different languages, Jespersen reached a generalization that we can now fully appreciate: "Whether or not a word like *there* is used to introduce [existential sentences], the verb precedes the subject, and the latter is hardly treated grammatically like a real subject" (Jespersen 1924, 155).

Without doubt, Jespersen fully captures the structural aspects that are specific to this construction. For him, it's not important whether a sentence includes a locative adverb like *there*. What's important is that the order of subject and verb be reversed when compared to the canonical order of the language in question, which is to say that, if normally the first precedes the second, in existential sentences the first should follow the second. It's enough to compare a significant sample of languages to realize that it's not necessary to have an expletive with locative content such as *there* or the verb *to be*. In Italian, for example, next to constructions with *ci* plus the verb *essere* 'to be' we also find constructions with *ci* plus the verb *avere* 'to have', as in *Non v'ha colta nazione a cui il nome di Francesco Petrarca non sia in pregio* '(lit.) not there has cultured nation in which the name of Francesco Petrarca not been in esteem; There has never been a cultured nation in which the name of Petrarch wasn't esteemed' (Ambrosoli 1831, 288). In German, existential constructions contain the verb *geben* 'to give' without a locative (*Es gibt viele Kartoffeln* '(lit.) it gives many potatoes; There are many potatoes'), comparable in some ways to the Italian *Si danno due casi* '(lit.) one gives two cases; Two cases are given'. Chinese speakers use an analogue of the verb *to have*, as in *You gui* '(lit.) you have ghosts; There are ghosts'. Besides the locative clitic *y* 'there', French has the verb *avoir* 'to have' accompanied by an expletive subject, *il*: *Il-y-a beaucoup de livres* '(lit.) it-there-has lots of books; There are many books'. Romanian has no phonetically realized expletive: for example, *Sunt probleme* '(lit.) are problems; There are problems'. Of course, it wouldn't make sense to maintain that it's only by chance that existential sentences in many languages use a locative-type predicate. We can interpret this fact calmly enough as if the predicate of existence was realized through a predicate of place—as if to say, "I'm in a place, therefore I exist." As we saw in the section of chapter 1 devoted to Aristotle, the verb *to exist* and the word *existence* contain a double locative reference, as their etymology indicates: next to the root *sist* (the causative form of *stare* 'to stay', as in Latin *sistere*), they have the preposition *ek* 'out of', indicating motion from a location, almost as if to say, "I come out." Syntactically, on the other hand, constructions with the Italian "verb" *esserci* 'to be there' give rise to the constellation of phenomena typical of unaccusative constructions: for example, they select the auxiliary *essere* (*Ci sono state molte feste in questo periodo* '(lit.) there are/have been many parties at this time'); they allow extraction of *ne* (*Ce ne sono state molte __ in questo periodo* '(lit.) there of-them are/have been many __ at this time'), while they don't allow the accusative pronoun to appear as subject (**Ce le sono state molte __ in questo periodo* '(lit.) there them are/have been many __ at this time'); and the past participle agrees with the subject in number and gender (*Ci sono stat-e molt-e fest-e* '(lit.) there are been-fem.pl. many-fem.pl. parties-fem.pl.; There have been many parties'). It's important to emphasize that, on the basis of these facts, in contemporary linguistic tradition it was decided to consider *to be* a verb that allows unaccusative constructions, because in the next section we'll see that this conclusion must be radically rethought, in a way that will even force us to rethink the notion of unaccusative.[10] Don't forget that in the analysis of existential sentences as sentences with an expletive subject, the predicate is considered to be the phrase that follows the subject: in the above example, the PP *in questo periodo* 'at this time'. Even this assumption, apparently taken as a given, must be rethought.

Starting from the analysis of the verb *to be* as a verb in unaccusative constructions, we'll find an explanation for the anomaly of copular phrases, before discovering in the end, among other things, that this hypothesis of the verb *to be* as an unaccusative verb doesn't hold up—indeed, that the very notion of the unaccusative needs to be revised. It shouldn't come as a surprise that if we start with a mistaken theory, we can use it to support a correct theory. In science, as in other areas, even misconceptions can be fertile seeds. Sometimes even a theory that was created to explain a specific phenomenon progressively evolves and is used to explain an entirely different phenomenon. This situation, mutatis mutandis, is reminiscent of what biologists call "exaptation" (on this topic, see

Gould 1991), where an organism's phenotypic trait evolves for a certain adaptive reason and then at some point the same trait acquires a new function and continues to evolve for different adaptive reasons. An interesting if controversial example (see Wesson 1991, especially the relevant passages therein) is the development of wings in certain insects: evolution led to a progressive increase in the size of the wings until it was possible to use them for locomotion, although if they were under a certain size they couldn't be used to fly. Of course, the fact that the wings grew in size, even though they didn't have the same function, can't be imputed to intelligent design or to any teleological purpose of nature. Evolution proceeds along random pathways and saves only what is not *exceptionally unfavorable* for the survival of an organism. Progressive growth would simply be due to selective pressure regarding a function different from that of locomotion: cooling the insect's body. Natural selection could obviously act on this function. The wings of these insects started out as fans and only later became blades to move them through the air. We can almost think that there exist phenomena of "scientific or cultural exaptation," whereby a theory that was developed for a certain reason is then recycled for other purposes. The theory of existential sentences could be a good example.

3.3 "Non-Euclidean" Grammars: Concerning the Rise and Fall of the Subject Postulate

We've finally arrived at the crux of this chapter and perhaps of the entire journey: the solution to the anomaly of copular sentences and the revision of sentence structure. To begin, we must rethink sentence structure in formal terms: [NP [T [VP]]]. We've noticed how this formula implements various notions of a clearly Aristotelian bent: first, that a sentence always needs a subject, a predicate, and tense; second, that this structure is asymmetric and in particular—among the various properties of this asymmetry—that it's only possible to extract material from the NP located adjacent to V; third, that the subject and predicate occupy fixed positions in the hierarchical structure, permitting a configurational definition of grammatical functions. Now let's briefly recall which elements make copular sentences unexpectedly anomalous. When we're faced with two copular sentences of the type *Una foto del muro fu la causa della rivolta* 'A picture of the wall was the cause of the riot' and *La causa della rivolta fu una foto del muro* 'The cause of the riot was a picture of the wall'—that is, NP V NP sentences that differ only in the order in which the same two NPs occur relative to the verb separating them—we observe phenomena that no other type of NP V NP sequence displays. In fact, when we try to extract a part of the NP that follows the verb using *ne* 'of-it', one sentence behaves exactly like a transitive sentence, while the other unexpectedly blocks the extraction process: for example, *Una foto del muro ne fu la causa* '(lit.) a picture of-the wall of-it was the cause' and **La causa della rivolta ne fu una foto* '(lit.) the cause of-the riot of-it was a picture'. This always happens with one of the two sentences of a pair in which it's possible to permute the two NPs that accompany the verb *to be*. Therefore, the explanation of this asymmetry can in no way be attributed in itself to a specific lexical property of the verb *to be* because, inexplicably, it deals with only *half* of these types of sentences.

At this point, we do know something more than when we first observed this anomaly: we know that the verb *to be* is analyzed as a raising verb, by virtue of its (presumed) unaccusative nature, shown by analysis of sentences with the expletive element *there* (*ci*). However, this advancement of the theory doesn't help us much. Even if we start from the assumption that the verb *to be* is an unaccusative verb that allows raising, we still don't see how this hypothesis can generate the two different behaviors that we observe: only one structure should be generated.

Before we proceed with the analysis, it's useful to simplify the structure in at least two ways, setting aside—so to speak—the elements that aren't immediately relevant. In particular, we can simplify the formula [NP [T [V NP]]] into [NP [T NP]], simply allowing that the verb *to be* is the direct expression of the head T, as we've already independently allowed for auxiliaries. Basically, this notation reproduces, in formal terms, Aristotle's insight that the verb *to be* is nothing more than the support for tense, where the morphology doesn't permit this to be expressed through the verb. A second simplification is instead due to the unaccusative nature of *to be*. The preverbal subject position is created empty, [__ [T [NP NP]]]; the subject is generated in a lower position, contained in the small clause, and is then raised into preverbal position, as in *A man was __ in the garden* (*There was a man in the garden*, derived by insertion of expletive *there*). This aspect of the hypothesis regarding the unaccusative nature of the verb *to be* will certainly be preserved. Even taking raising into consideration, the reasons for the anomaly of copular phrases still seem to persistently elude us: Why should the *same* structure give rise to such a conspicuous asymmetry? What's wrong with these formulas? Should we give up and think that *to be*, this verb alone of all the others, manifests properties that can't be derived from any structural principle? Or accept Russell's curse and think that there are two verbs *to be*? It's clear that if we were to admit this, it would be like giving up the idea that grammar is a "crystal" product of natural laws, accepting instead that it's just a chaotic accumulation of random exceptions: what could be the source of the regularities shown by copular sentences if not structure?

The turning point starts from a very general consideration regarding sentence structure, and we must trace it step by step. The structure [NP [T VP]] contains lots of information, as we've just seen: asymmetry under extraction, ability of the verb to engage in agreement processes, and so on—above all, the idea that the preverbal NP plays the role of subject and the VP plays that of predicate. All this information—of such different types—is in fact independent, in the sense that there's no necessary bond between these properties: none of them implies another. This is the moment to reflect on sentence structure. First, it's worth noting that this formula, [NP [T VP]], has been used in substantially the same way in all modern, formal treatises on syntax. From syntax textbooks (Haegeman 1991, Graffi 1994, Akmajian et al. 1995, De Mauro 2003, Carnie 2006, among others), to essays in linguistics applied to classical languages (De Mauro and Thornton 1985), to treatises on cybernetics and information theory (like the classic Hopcroft, Motwani, and Ullman 2006) or aphasia (Caplan 1992, Miceli 1996, Basso and Cubelli 1999, Denes 2009, to name just a few)—as far as I know, virtually all authors of all schools treat sentence structure in this same way, apart from formalism, which of course can differ significantly. The salient property in this case is that which relates the grammatical functions (subject and predicate) with structural positions in the tree representation: in summary, the sentence is always at least an NP and a VP, where NP is rigidly assigned the role of subject and VP that of predicate.

When a coherent system consists of multiple properties irreducible to each other, it's typical of scientific practice to try and verify whether the system remains coherent even when one of the properties is suspended. A paradigmatic case is that of so-called "non-Euclidean" geometries. Classical geometry—or "Euclidean" geometry as we know it from textbooks and elementary introductions—is the result of a canonization that dates back to the Alexandrian period. The adjective refers to Euclid, who lived during the reign of Ptolemy I in the fourth century BC and who wrote a treatise on mathematics in thirteen books known as *The Elements*. The success of this book is incalculable; it is perhaps second only to the Bible for the number of its editions, one of the most influential texts of all time. Even today, all schoolchildren learn the rudiments of geometry from this colossal systematization.[11] In it, the whole structure of geometry is derived from five postulates put forth in a constructive form and in such an elegant way that they haven't needed retouching. For example, the fifth postulate states, "If a line segment intersects two straight lines forming two interior angles on the same side that sum to less than two right angles, then the two lines, if extended indefinitely, meet on that side on which the angles sum to less than two right angles." The history of the attempt to derive this postulate from the other four is fascinating (see, for example, the compelling account in Asimov 1972) and constitutes in itself the subject of a treatise (for philosophical implications, see Casati and Varzi 1994). However, the reason I mention this axiom is linked to the failure of such attempts, a failure that led two nineteenth-century mathematicians, the Hungarian János Bolyai and the Russian Nikolai Ivanovich Lobachevsky, to verify whether the system of geometry remained coherent even without the fifth postulate, founding non-Euclidean geometry in the process.

Keeping this methodology in mind, we can now return to sentence structure and the properties used to describe it. If these properties don't necessarily imply each other, an interesting test is to see whether the system remains coherent even if we deny the validity of any one of them. This was the theoretical starting point for the solution to the anomaly of copular sentences originally proposed in Moro 1988. The property we can try "suspending" is the one according to which the grammatical function of the subject is invariably identified with the highest NP in the hierarchical structure captured by the tree representation.

As we've seen, this property has been viewed as inextricably integrated into the formal system that represents sentence structure, as evidenced by the critical consideration quoted earlier from

Lepschy 2000. Interestingly, although originally this property was stated as a postulate, there was someone who actually attempted to derive it on a formal basis, as a theorem. Following a proposal by Susan Rothstein (1983), Chomsky (1986b) "derived" the obligatory nature of the subject's position on a logical basis, in partial contradiction to the insight according to which the structure of natural languages doesn't follow the structure of formal systems. In this work, Chomsky advanced the idea that the subject of a sentence is comparable to that of an "argument of a function" in mathematics. According to this view of things, the syntactic structure of the sentence is nothing other than the linguistic manifestation of the Fregean-type notion of a logical-mathematical function. In fact, Chomsky explicitly used the phrase "saturation (in ... the Fregean sense)" (Chomsky 1986b, 116) for the position of the phrasal subject, where "saturation" means assigning a value to a given function's variable. In other words, the role of a (preverbal) subject NP would be similar to that of the variable x in a function of the form $f(x)$—where the function would be linguistically expressed by the verbal predicate VP. This "linguistic function" would have a position that must be filled—or saturated—exactly as, generally, the argument of a function should receive a value that is a member of the domain in which the function is defined. Therefore, according to this perspective, *Jane eats* has a structure similar to 17^{22}. In the first case, the predicate expressed with the word *eats*—sometimes referred to as *eat(x)*—is defined relative to a certain set of individuals and applies to the individual named *Jane*, resulting in *eat(Jane)*. In the second case, however, the predicate $f(x) = x^{22}$, defined, for example, relative to the set of whole numbers, applies to the number 17, resulting in 17^{22}. The result of 17^{22} is a number; the "result" of *eat(Jane)* is the truth value "true" or "false," depending on whether Jane eats or not.[12]

That's the point. In fact, if the syntax of a language contained only verbal predicates, it's difficult to see why we should depart from this postulate of sentence structure: leaving aside the problems that still arise when the subject is an expletive, why would we ever abandon the idea that the highest NP in sentence structure is a subject, or, in logical terms, the individual or group of individuals to which the function expressed by the verbal predicate is applied? However, the reasonableness of this postulate fails as soon as, alongside sentences constructed with verbal predicates, we take into account those built with nominal predicates, and in particular NP-type predicates. If in fact we eliminate the postulate according to which only subjects may appear in preverbal position, and we leave as the only remnant of this postulate the requirement that there must be an NP in the preverbal position, we immediately give nominal predicates the ability to appear in this position, since they are, of course, NPs in every respect. So, once again the verb *to be* creates a crisis in sentence structure, to the point of undermining the central postulate. What effects does the elimination of this postulate have on grammar? In what follows, I'll try to briefly illustrate the benefits of what we might call a "non-Euclidean" grammar in resolving the anomaly of copular sentences and more generally contributing to a better understanding of how sentences work.

Our first and most immediate result is that, from the base structure that's valid for sentences with the verb *to be* ([__ [T [NP NP]]]), we can derive *not one but two* structures: one where the subject is raised, which I'll call "canonical copular sentences" because they represent the well-established option, and one where the predicate is raised instead, which for obvious reasons I'll call "inverse copular sentences" and which represent the innovation of this unified theory. We'll see tree representations of these two structures shortly. First, let's look at the representation of the basic structure of the copular sentence with *a picture of the wall* as subject and *the cause of the riot* as predicate. Before the syntactic movement, we have this structure:

The Strange Case of Verbs without Subjects

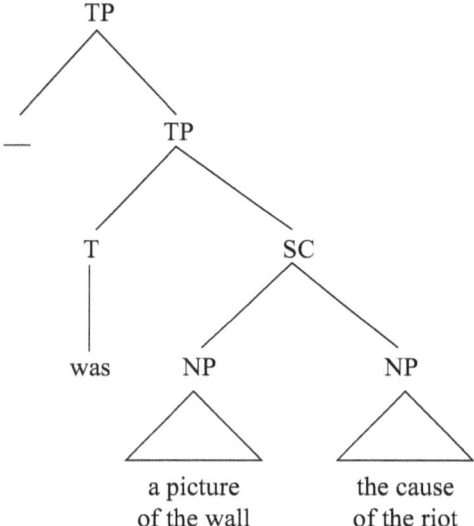

In chapter 4, I'll discuss the reasons why the NP must move. For now, simply note that declarative sentences such as *Is a picture of the wall the cause of the riot*,[13] *Is a man in the garden*, and *Is Helen an algebra student* aren't grammatical, while *A picture of the wall is the cause of the riot*, *A man is in the garden*, and *Helen is an algebra student* are. In formal terms, after the NP moves to preverbal position, we'll have two structures. Starting from the above tree structure, first of all we have [NP [T [__ NP]]] for the canonical copular sentence, or, in tree representation:

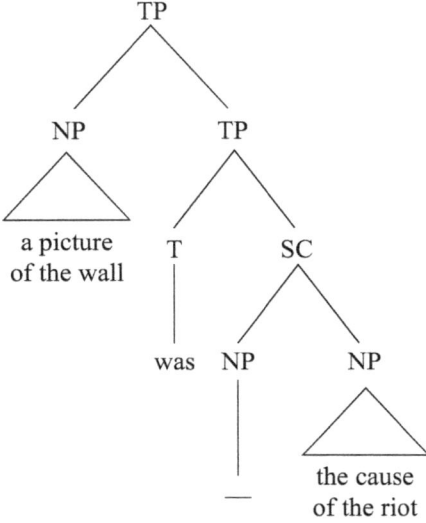

In addition to this structure—and this is the crucial point—since we've eliminated the subject postulate, we'll also have a second, new structure, one that's in a sense symmetric with respect to the first, at least where the lower portion is concerned. In fact, the canonical structure is no longer the only one that can be generated. In the model without the subject postulate, we can *also* generate the structure [NP [T [NP __]]], where the other NP (the nominal predicate *the cause of the riot*) is raised, while the subject (the NP *a picture of the wall*) remains in the lowest position, contained in the small clause, and (in linear order) appears postverbally:

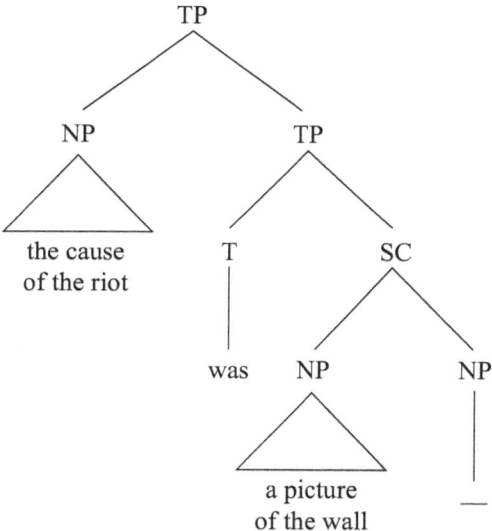

With this, we dismantle the standard hypothesis of formal linguistics according to which division into chunks of the form NP VP constitutes the division between subject and predicate: in the case of inverse copular sentences, in the sequence NP VP the predicate is the NP and the subject is the NP contained within the VP. This is the innovation.

3.4 The Unified Theory of Copular Sentences

What benefits does this new analysis without the subject postulate offer? Even at first glance, this dual derivation gives us hope in the effort to decipher the anomaly of copular sentences; the NP V NP sequence of the two copular sentences presents itself in two asymmetric variants, after movement of the NP. Meanwhile, we immediately note that these two structures have a significant effect on the Russellian quarrel. In fact, this double structure somehow does justice to Russell's concern, even while dismantling the essence:

there aren't two verbs *to be*; the verb *to be* is always the same, even if the NP that follows the verb *to be* can be referential (i.e., need not necessarily be predicative) on condition that a predicative NP has been raised into the position traditionally reserved for subjects. The innovation with respect to the important descriptive results obtained in previous studies (especially, as noted earlier, Ruwet 1975, Higgins 1979, Longobardi 1985) is that we now have a unified theory, a theory that, starting from the same basic structure, is able to trace the anomalies to the interaction of the same principles normally adopted in syntax. In particular, as Longobardi (1985) proposed despite not reaching a unified theory, the verb *to be* is always accompanied by two NPs with different grammatical functions (one playing the role of subject, the other the role of predicate). To sum up, the unified theory of copular sentences suggested here does nothing other than combine this hypothesis with the analysis of the verb *to be* as an unaccusative raising construction and transformationally binds the two final structures into to a single "starting" structure; this is made possible by abandoning the axiom of subject position in sentence structure.

At this point, we need to verify concretely whether this expectation is confirmed—that is, whether this asymmetry is sufficient to derive the anomaly on the basis of independent principles. Let's focus first on the phenomenon of extraction. To review the facts: in the canonical sentence, we can extract material from the NP that follows V (as, for example, in the case of the Italian clitic pronoun *ne* 'of-it': *Una foto del muro ne fu la causa* '(lit.) a picture of-the wall of-it was the cause'); in the inverse version, we cannot (**La causa della rivolta ne fu una foto* '(lit.) the cause of-the riot of-it was a picture'). The locality conditions on extraction from an NP predict that extraction is only possible if the NP is adjacent to V—that is, in formal terms only if the structural formula [V NP] obtains. As additional proof, consider the following fact. Starting from a sentence such as *Mangio un piatto di spaghetti* '[I] eat a plate of spaghetti', we can say *Ne mangio un piatto __* '(lit.) of-it I eat a plate __'; while, starting from a sentence such as *Metto il formaggio su un piatto di spaghetti* '[I] put the cheese on a plate of spaghetti', we can't say **Ne metto il formaggio su un piatto __* '(lit.) of-it [I] put the cheese on a plate __'. Therefore, the first result we can bank on, if we adopt the two asymmetric formulas for copular sentences, is that extraction from an NP that follows the verb *to be* is impossible when this NP is the subject, because this NP is not adjacent to V: in this case, V, the verb *to be*, is adjacent to the small clause, not to the NP. Ignoring irrelevant details, we have the structure fragment ... V [NP ..., where V and NP clearly aren't adjacent; adjacency would be represented as ... [V NP] ..., and this isn't the structure we have. This immediately explains the data without having to resort to an ad hoc hypothesis, even though we must come back to this point to refine the theory.

But a new question arises at once: why can we extract from the NP that follows V in a canonical copular sentence, since it isn't adjacent to a V either? The reason in this case is always traceable without additional assumptions to the locality conditions that come into play here. As we've already noted, to explain the extractability of the VP it's been assumed that such conditions simply don't apply to predicates; they only apply to the arguments of predicates. Now, since the NP that follows the verb *to be* in a canonical copular sentence is a predicate, we can simply say that extraction of material from the NP that follows the verb *to be* in canonical copular sentences isn't blocked by the locality condition, exactly as it isn't blocked in the case of a VP: they're both predicates.[14]

Summarizing, we've finally understood that the NP V NP sequence, when V is the verb *to be*, can't be ascribed to a single structure. Unlike what happens with other verbs, in this case the sequence contains too little information: in fact, we must always verify whether we're dealing with a canonical ([NP [T [__ NP]]]) or an inverse ([NP [T [NP __]]]) copular sentence. Of course, that's not always possible or easy. In the case of the two NPs in the above examples (*a picture of the wall* and *the cause of the riot*), the asymmetry is clear: *cause* is predicated of *picture* and not the other way around, in the sense that a picture can have the property of causing something, but a cause can't have the property of photographing. There are of course cases that aren't so clear-cut, where it's not possible to recognize an asymmetry of this type. Jespersen's two examples *Miss Castlewood was the prettiest girl at the ball* and *The prettiest girl at the ball was Miss Castlewood* are indistinguishable. In this case, we simply agree with Jespersen that "we cannot decide which is the subject and which is the predicate" (Jespersen 1924, 136), or we try to help ourselves out with the use of pronouns, as in the case of the two stars. On the other hand, there exist very interesting phenomena where this asymmetry helps us understand the syntactic relationships between elements. In this case, Italian syntax is extremely useful. Let's see why.

In English, as we've seen, in an NP V NP sequence the verb agrees with the NP to the left (for example, *Cain kills Abel* and *Cain kills Abel and Pinocchio*, contrary to **Cain kill Abel and Pinocchio*). In Italian, this NP can be dislocated to the right, as an adjunct (for example, *Uccide Abele e Pinocchio Caino* '(lit.) [he] kills Abel and Pinocchio Cain'). The verb *to be* constitutes, even with respect to this easily recognizable property, a unique and important exception. If we pluralize *a picture of the wall* and we say *two pictures of the wall*, we'll have *Two pictures of the wall were the cause of the riot* but also **The cause of the riot were two pictures of the wall*! We can see with the naked eye that, in the case of inverse copular sentences, the NP V NP sequence is completely anomalous: the verb agrees with the NP to the right. For Italian, it's enough to allow that the verb always agrees with the subject NP, even, without exception, when the latter is located to the right of V.[15] And note that here we're not dealing with a subject adjoined to the right, as in our Italian example *pro uccide Abele e Pinocchio*

Caino '(lit.) [he] kills Abel and Pinocchio Cain': the equivalent case naturally also exists in copular sentences, but the order is different from NP V NP, as in *pro furono la causa della rivolta queste foto del muro* '(lit.) pro were the cause of-the riot these pictures of-the wall'.

Another particularly interesting case consists of sentences like *What fascinates me is a prime number* (technically called "pseudocleft" sentences to distinguish them from plain cleft sentences like *It is Abel and Cain who Pinocchio kills*). How can we distinguish between subject and predicate in this pseudocleft sentence, which displays no differences in number? Must we also give up in this case, as in the case of Jespersen's examples? Is being a prime number the property that I'm predicating of that which fascinates me, or vice versa? In this case, independently of any semantic considerations, comparing this sentence with two others removes all doubt. To start, it's easy to show that *what fascinates me* is the subject. It's enough to take the sentence *What fascinates me is strange*, where the presence of an AP (*strange*) is compatible only with the idea that *what fascinates me* is a subject. To resolve the dilemma and decide whether, in the original example, the verb *to be* is followed by a nonpredicative NP, it's sufficient to pluralize *a prime number* and verify what happens to the verb agreement. The resulting sentence is *What fascinates me are prime numbers*. In this case, agreement with the NP on the right reveals the inverse copular structure of the pseudocleft sentence: here *what fascinates me* is without doubt a predicate, since the verb *to be* shows agreement to the right.[16]

An important theoretical consequence is provided by the verb *to be* when *pro* is used. Recall that *pro* is traditionally called a "null subject (pronoun)." This terminology has held since it was proposed, and there was no reason why it should be changed. But when predicative NPs and inverse copular sentences enter the picture, obviously, things do change. The possibility of having a sentence like *pro sono io* 'pro am I' next to *pro è me* 'pro is me' illustrates the situation well. In the second case, the first person verb is accompanied by a nonnominative, first person pronoun (*me*). This pronoun can't function as a subject (think for example of *Me arrivo '*Me arrive'); so, we're dealing with a canonical copular sentence and *pro* plays the role of subject. But in the case of *pro sono io* 'pro am I', the rightward agreement unequivocally indicates that this is an inverse copular sentence—that is, that the appropriate structural formula is [*pro sono* [*io* __]] '[pro am [I __]]', or that the tree structure is as follows:[17]

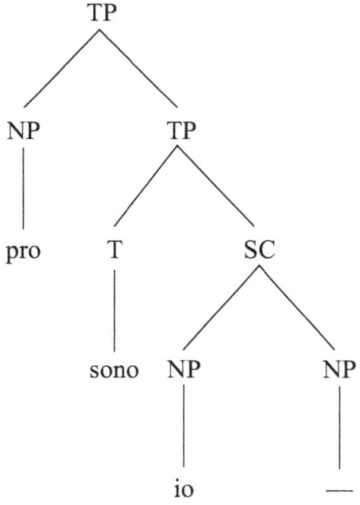

If this weren't so, we could change *pro* to third person and say *pro è io '*pro* is I', certainly an ungrammatical sentence in Italian (cf. the canonical version *pro è me* 'pro is me').

This simple bit of data then has very important repercussions from a theoretical point of view: it implies that the element *pro* can't be called "null subject," as it can also play the role of null predicate. This shouldn't be surprising; the opposite would be worrisome, since *pro* is an NP and it's not possible to say whether an NP plays the role of subject or predicate until it's used in a sentence. It would be absurd to ask whether the phrase *the cause of the riot* is a subject or a predicate until it's inserted into a structure. It's a predicate in *A picture of the wall is the cause of the riot*, but it's a subject in *The cause of the riot is surprising*. Furthermore, as Abelard noted, it's precisely because of this ability that the verb *to be* necessarily enters into syllogisms. Once more, the verb *to be* enables us to refine our understanding of syntactic facts, allowing us to normalize the function of *pro*: this element can no longer be considered a "null subject"; rather, it's simply a null pronoun, able to play both the role of subject and that of predicate. Note that in Italian the sentence *pro sono io* isn't simply the symmetric variant of another sentence with its subject to the right (technically called an "inverse subject construction"—like the pair *Io telefono* 'I phone' and *Telefono io* '(lit.) phone I'—in that the sentence **Io sono* 'I am' is incomplete (or elliptical, as Abelard maintained). In fact, the element *pro* can't appear except in a preverbal position; this is certainly connected with the fact that the inflection helps identify the features of gender and number of the subject but not of the object, even though this condition isn't universal, as in Chinese, which has *pro* but lacks inflected verbs, to say nothing of languages where the verb agrees with the object. In languages that lack *pro*, such as French, there are alternative strategies in the case of inverse copular sentences. If we take a sentence like *Mme Bovary c'est moi* 'Mme Bovary is I', we can clearly see that the propredicative element is phonetically expressed with the element *c'* (contracted form of the demonstrative pronoun *ce*), *moi* 'I' being the subject of the sentence. This propredicative element is mandatory in French only in inverse copular sentences, as this pair of sentences shows: *Cette jeune femme (c')est ma passion* '(lit.) this young woman this is my passion; This young woman is my passion' and *Ma passion *(c')est cette jeune femme* '(lit.' my passion this is this young woman'. The fact that the asterisk appears outside the parentheses, signaling the ungrammatical nature of the phrase should *c(e)* be omitted, indicates that only the second sentence shows this asymmetry.

The unified theory of copular sentences brings yet another interesting property to light. Generally, with a verb other than the verb *to be* the interrogative pronoun *who* is only compatible with the third person: for example, one cannot say **Who I telephone?* With the verb *to be*, this restriction falls by the wayside and a sentence like *Who are they?* is completely grammatical. Why? It's because we're dealing with a canonical copular sentence that has *pro* as its subject: the element *who* doesn't play the role of subject here; rather, it plays that of an *interrogative predicate*. This conclusion is particularly interesting because it shows that the role of predicate isn't reserved for lexically full elements, that is, open class words— be they subjects or objects—but may very well be available to operators, at least interrogative ones. It's also interesting to note that the sentence *Chi sono?* '(lit.) who am' is nothing more than the interrogative version of the sentence *pro lo sono* 'pro [so] am', where the predicate is created using a clitic pronoun *lo* 'so'. Both sentences contrast with *Sono io* '(lit.) am I; It's me', which, even intuitively, differs from them in interpretation, since, unlike them, it's an inverse copular sentence.

Finally, the unified theory of copular sentences allows us to resolve many seemingly mysterious issues in many languages, and more generally to understand why the verb *to be* isn't necessarily present even in languages that have it. Let's start with a fact of English syntax that at first seems inexplicable. We'll consider the sentences *I believe a picture of the wall the cause of the riot* and *I believe a picture of the wall to be the cause of the riot*. Both are acceptable; the verb *to be* is completely optional. Reversing the order of the two postverbal NPs leads to an unexpected contrast: **I believe the cause of the riot a picture of the wall* is ungrammatical; *I believe the cause of the riot to be a picture of the wall* is grammatical. In this case, the verb *to be* is mandatory. Adopting the unified theory of copular sentences provides a natural and immediate explanation for this phenomenon. The basic order (*a picture of the wall the cause of the riot*) is possible both in the presence and in the absence of the verb *to be*. However, when the predicate crosses over the subject, it needs to have an available position where it can "land"; this is provided by the verb *to be*, which comes with an available specifier position. That's why, unlike in the pair with canonical order, in this pair the verb *to be* is mandatory. This phenomenon isn't so obvious in Italian for reasons that are not yet well understood and that seem to be linked to the possibility of having subject inversion even in small clauses: for example, in Italian one can say *Maria vide cantare Giovanni* 'Mary saw singing John' and *Maria vide Giovanni cantare* 'Mary saw John singing', while in English only the second construction is grammatical. At any rate, it's difficult to imagine how to explain the English data if we don't adopt the proposed flexible structure for the architecture of the sentence.

The hypothesis that the verb *to be* only performs the role of providing a landing site for movement of the predicate implies that this role must necessarily be played by a verb. This expectation is confirmed in Hebrew, a Semitic language. Edit Doron (1986), developing an idea in Berman and Grosu 1976, as noted in Shlonsky 2000, captures a similar contrast. In Hebrew, the verb *to be* doesn't exist: its function is realized by a pronoun that isn't always required. For example, in the sentence *Dani (hu) xaveri hatov* '(lit.) Dani him friend the-good; Dani is my best friend' the pronoun is optional. However, in the inverse copular version *Xaveri hatov *(hu) Dani* '(lit.) friend the-good he Dani; My best friend is Dani' the pronoun becomes obligatory, exactly—mutatis mutandis—as with the verb *to be* in the infinitival English examples. Doron proposes analyzing the pronoun as a functional head, that is, as an element without lexical value; this analysis can easily be imported into the unified theory, and it explains the facts in a natural way. When the predicate crosses over the subject, it requires a landing site: this is why the pronoun is obligatory in inverse copular constructions of the Hebrew type. Asya Pereltsvaig (2007) reaches similar conclusions from detailed analysis of Russian data (which I won't illustrate here for reasons of space). Even Russian—so interesting because the copula isn't expressed in the present indicative tense—in fact shows that the unified theory of copular sentences explains many seemingly atypical data.

Interestingly, the unified theory of copular sentences has also had nontrivial effects in areas other than sentence structure. For example, Richard Kayne (1994) uses the analysis of inverse copular sentences to propose that even NPs display cases of internal predicate raising. The prototypical cases are expressions like *that idiot of (an) Andrea* where a predicative bond is evident between *that idiot* and *Andrea*, as in *Andrea is that idiot*. The presence of a preposition, in this case, certainly isn't necessary to determine possession (in the correct reading); it only serves to allow the predicate *that idiot* to raise and cross over *Andrea*. In other words, the preposition only serves to supply a landing place for *that idiot*, analogous to the function performed by the pronoun in Hebrew inverse sentences. In the context of NPs, the following cases are interesting. If I say *Francesca has chosen books of these types*, of course I know the direct object of *choose* is *books* and *these types* modifies *books*, just as a predicate modifies a subject in a sentence like *The books were of these types*. If I say *Francesca has chosen these types of books*, even though the order is different and *these types* can be the complement of *choose* (for example, in *Francesca has chosen these types, not those*), the global intuition is that *books* continues to be the direct object of *choose* and the subject of *of these types*. A natural way to understand this intuition is to say that both *books of these types* and *these types of books* are generated from the same structure: the difference is that in one case *books* raises and lands in the specifier position made available by the preposition *of*, while in the other case *these types* raises. The analogy with canonical and inverse copular sentences is immediately obvious.

Let's summarize the facts we've analyzed so far. The anomaly of copular sentences was resolved by eliminating a postulate of sentence theory—namely, that the NP preceding the verb is always and only the subject of the sentence—leaving as remnant the requirement that this position be occupied by an NP. This hypothesis, which normally has no effect when it comes to verbal predicates, raises the possibility that the NP preceding the verb *to be* is a predicate while what follows is the subject, giving rise to inverse copular structures. Therefore, the sequence NP V NP can't be associated with a single tree structure. More information is needed; that is, we must always check whether what is raised to the preverbal position is a subject (canonical copular sentences) or a predicate (inverse copular sentences). On the basis of independently required locality principles, the anomalous facts then follow naturally and oblige us to redefine some syntactic notions—among them the hypothesis that *pro* plays the role of null subject, since in fact this element can play the role of null predicate. The unified theory of copular sentences also seems to adapt to other languages and other structures, suggesting that raising the nominal predicate is much more common in the syntax of natural languages than was first imagined.

3.5 *There Is*, or "And Yet It Moves"

We're not finished yet: we need to deal with another not-so-small matter. The "verb" *to be* preceded by *there* as in *there is* or *there are* returns to spoil the fun. It's curious, but this single syllable—*there* (and its Italian equivalent *ci*)—plays a crucial role throughout the construction of the unified theory, not least because no previous works have attempted to account for the anomaly of copular sentences in conjunction with the properties of existential ones—at least it wasn't attempted with respect to many of the locality phenomena that we'll examine in this section.

Let's start with a theory-internal question; later, the argument will touch on matters independent of the theoretical framework. The theory-internal question refers to a locality phenomenon. As we've seen, one of the main reasons for analyzing sentences with the verb *to be* as unaccusative constructions with raising was the similarity between sentences like *There are many solutions in this book* and *Many solutions are __ in this book*. Along with the subject-raising strategy, the current theory—but also independent traditions, such as Jespersen's—allows insertion of an expletive subject, which in Italian is *ci* 'there'. This in itself may not be a problem. The problem arises from the fact that starting with a sentence like *Ci sono molte soluzioni in questo libro* 'There are many solutions in this book' and extracting from the NP following the verb, we can get a sentence like *Ce ne sono molte __ in questo libro* '(lit.) there of-them are many __ in this book'. How is it possible to extract from the subject, *molte soluzioni* 'many solutions', which hasn't been moved? This contrasts completely with what we saw before: from *La causa della rivolta fu una foto del muro* 'The cause of the riot was a picture of the wall', we certainly couldn't derive **La causa della rivolta ne fu una foto* '(lit.) the cause of-the riot of-it was a picture __'. The subject NP from which we've extracted in *Ce ne sono molte __ in questo libro* is in exactly the same structural position—that is, inside the small clause. Must we stop and record an exception? Of course, this would greatly weaken the proposed theory; like theories in other scientific disciplines, linguistic theories always aim to minimize the number of exceptions. Therefore, we must radically rethink the role of elements like *there* and *ci*. To do this, we'll start with data—often overlooked or completely ignored[18]—not immediately compatible with the hypothesis of raising the subject as an alternative to inserting the expletive. On the whole, regardless of this, there's still the lingering suspicion that this theory is wrong simply because in a null-subject language such as Italian, it shouldn't be necessary to have a phonetically expressed subject expletive such as *ci*. In fact, by definition *pro* should be enough—but this simply isn't true, as shown by the ungrammaticality of **È un uomo in giardino* '(lit.) is a man in [the] garden' compared with the grammaticality of *C'è un uomo in giardino* '(lit.) there's a man in [the] garden'.

In any case, there are many independent facts that make this theory dubious, regardless of the question of locality. Let's review a few of them. First, the element *there* can only be inserted if the predicate of the small clause is a PP or an AP, that is, only in a sentence like *There are many solutions in this book* or *There are many difficult solutions*. If the predicate is another NP, as in **There are many solutions a hoax*, the sentence is ungrammatical. The analogous sentence with subject raising is entirely acceptable, however: *Many solutions are __ a hoax*. How can a subject—moreover, a subject without semantic value like *there*—select the lexical category of its predicate? The second problem rears its head in the sentence *There are infinite numbers*. It's a grammatical sentence, but, if we're serious about the theory of the expletive, it's a sentence lacking a predicate, which should be a PP or an AP; in fact, if we build the analogous structure with raising, we get **Infinite numbers are*, certainly not a grammatical sentence. A third difficulty comes from languages that allow infinitival constructions with overt subjects. As noted earlier, unlike Italian, English allows sentences like *I consider many solutions to be a hoax* and *I consider many solutions a hoax*. With *there*, the English equivalent of *ci*, it's possible to construct infinitival sentences: *I consider there to be many solutions*, but not **I consider there many solutions*. Even in this case the theory of *there* as subject expletive doesn't provide immediately interpretable data and, what's worse, it doesn't even allow us to see a natural way to correct the theory, if we don't change the underlying assumptions.

These problems concerning structures with *there* (and *ci*) have very different theoretical statuses, although very clear ones: on the one hand, these sentences run counter to the proposed solution because of the impossibility of extracting material from the subject NP of inverse copular sentences; on the other, independent of the unified theory of copular sentences, we have data that don't add up, like those regarding the possible types of predicate. The situation can be resolved, however, if we allow that the preverbal NP position doesn't necessarily have to be occupied by a subject, that is, if we adopt the hypothesis that a preverbal NP can be a predicate. Starting from this, I propose that we completely reverse the traditional analysis of existential sentences and say that elements like *there* and *ci* aren't *subject expletives* but *predicate expletives*—or, in technical terms, that existential sentences are a special type of inverse copular sentence. So, a sentence like *There was a picture of the wall in the garden* won't have the traditional structure corresponding to the following tree:

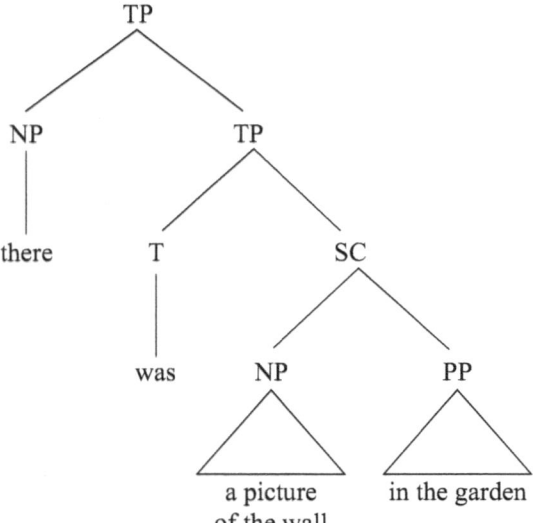

The Strange Case of Verbs without Subjects

Instead, it will be as follows, where the predicate—realized by the pronominal element *there*—is generated in the small clause and then raised to preverbal NP position, while the subject, generated in the small clause, remains there and thus appears in postverbal position (shortly we'll see the new structural role of the PP *in the garden*):

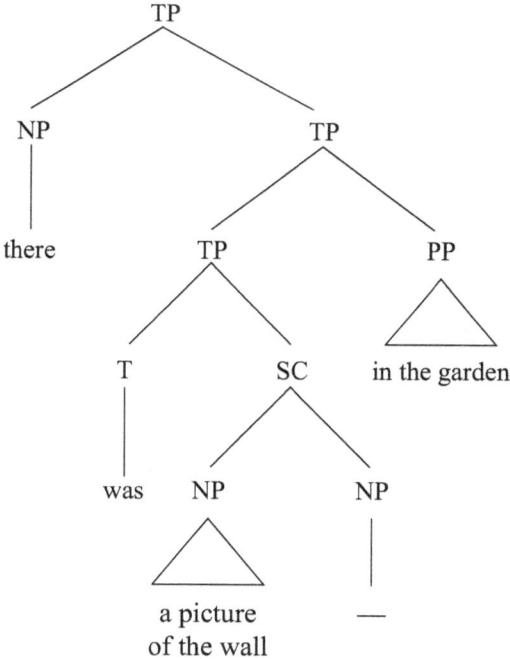

The abandonment of the subject postulate, motivated by the anomaly of copular sentences of the NP V NP type, therefore has disruptive effects on the delicate structure of existential sentences: not only does the predicate appear in preverbal position, but the element that follows the subject—the PP *in the garden*, in these examples—is, so to speak, downgraded to an adjunct role and no longer plays that of predicate. We'll see proof of this in just a moment. Above all, we'll see how this new perspective, diametrically opposed to the traditional one, can solve the above-mentioned problems, starting with the last one. Meanwhile, let's note a first, immediate success: that in a null-subject language, the fact that the preverbal NP must be phonetically expressed is no longer a paradox. In Italian, for example, the preverbal element *ci* 'there' isn't the subject expletive; rather, it's the predicate expletive, or better yet it's a pronominal element with a predicative function. So, it has nothing to do with the null-subject property. It's like the clitic object of obligatorily transitive verbs: starting with the verb *gradire* 'to appreciate', for example, which can't be used in an absolute way (that is without a direct object), I can only say *Maria li ha graditi* '(lit.) Mary them has appreciated; Mary has appreciated them', not **Maria ha graditi* 'Mary has appreciated'. It's no surprise that the clitic is obligatory and, above all, there's no need to have recourse to a parameter.

The fact that English *there* can't appear in an infinitival sentence without the verb *to be* can then be traced immediately to the fact that if the predicate is to be raised, there must be a position where it can land—no additional hypotheses are needed. This isn't an ad hoc hypothesis: we already know that this is the way things stand because of contrasts like that between *I consider a picture of the wall (to be) the cause of the riot* and *I consider the cause of the riot *(to be) a picture of the wall*. Existential sentences are inverse copular sentences, so *there* must have a place to move to if it is to appear in preverbal position, and this place is made available by the verb *to be* in its infinitive form.

The unified theory of copular sentences also allows us to immediately explain the contrast between two sentences like **Infinite numbers are* and *There are infinite numbers*. In the first sentence, the absence of a phrase accompanying the subject is due to the omission of the predicate: if I say *Infinite numbers are in the hands* *of the spies*, the sentence is acceptable. By contrast, the second sentence (*There are infinite numbers*) is always acceptable, whether *in the hands of the spies* accompanies the subject or not. According to Edwin Williams (1984) and James Higginbotham (1987), this fact would constitute a strong proof that *there* really is a subject in its own right. In their analyses, the NP following the verb *to be* in a sentence like *There is a chef* would play the same role as the NP following the verb *to be* in a sentence like *John is a chef*. Apart from the difficulty of accounting for this choice in semantic terms—in fact, it's not clear how one could interpret the expletive in a referential way—a number of syntactic barriers would still make this hypothesis totally unviable. One is the fact that in Italian, and in Romance languages in general, a postverbal predicative NP in a copular sentence can be expressed with an uninflected clitic pronoun. For example, in Italian the sentence *Giovanni è un cuoco* 'John is a chef' can easily be associated with *Giovanni lo è* '(lit.) John it is; John is so'; if, however, we start with *C'è un cuoco* 'There is a chef', the version with an uninflected clitic pronoun is utterly ungrammatical, *Ce lo è '(lit.) there it is'. The possibility that sentences with *esserci* 'there is, there are' can be canonical copular sentences is doubtless to be discarded, at least on an empirical basis.

But if the lexical material following the NP in an existential sentence isn't a predicate, what *is* its grammatical function? As the structural representation indicates, the only remaining possibility is that this element constitutes what's technically called a "secondary predicate." To understand what we're dealing with, consider the sentence *Mary calls the president as a physicist*. This sentence contains two predicates: the main one conveyed by the verb (Mary calls) and a secondary one, linked by the predicative marker *as* (Mary is a physicist). If *as* were absent, the sentence would be ungrammatical under the relevant interpretation: **Mary calls the president a physicist*. In the same way, one can say *There are* *many solutions as alternatives*, where the secondary predication (*alternatives*) is expressed by the element *as*. Note, however, that if the secondary predicate were expressed not by an NP but by a PP or an AP, there would be no need for an intermediary: *Mary calls the president from this station*, *Mary calls the president proud of the results*. This asymmetry explains the facts about existential sentences without additional assumptions, as long as we adopt the proposed hypothesis regarding inverse copular sentences: the phrase that follows the subject in an existential sentence isn't the primary predicate; rather, it's the secondary one, sometimes called an "adjunct." It can be omitted and, if it's not a PP or an AP, it must be accompanied by a predicative marker like *as*.

There is also indirect evidence that the phrase following the NP of an existential sentence is an adjunct. It's well known that extracting material from adjuncts yields ungrammaticality. Take for example two unrelated sentences like these: *They say that John left without meeting the followers of Jeshua* and *They say that John liked meeting the followers of Jeshua*. In the first case, the sequence *meeting the followers of Jeshua* is clearly an adjunct; indeed, I can omit the entire sequence and simply say *John left*. On the contrary, in the second case this phrase isn't an adjunct, but a complement: if I omit it, I have the ungrammatical sentence *John liked. If I try to extract material from the NP in this sequence, I will obtain two different results: an ungrammatical sentence in the case of the adjunct (**Of whom do they say that John left without meeting the followers __?*) and a grammatical one in the case of the complement (*Of whom do they say that John liked meeting the followers __?*). Now, if we adopt the hypothesis that existential sentences are inverse copular sentences and that the phrase (PP or AP) that follows the subject is an adjunct, then, consistent with the overall architecture of grammar, we expect that extraction from that phrase will yield a worse outcome than in the case of raising. This prediction is correct. **Of whom do they say* *that there are many people indebted to John followers __?* is certainly worse than *Of whom do they say that many people indebted to John are followers __?* Once again, the alternative hypothesis, based on the unified theory of copular sentences and ultimately on abandoning the postulate that the preverbal NP is the subject of the sentence, gives a positive empirical result, without additional hypotheses.

There's still an important factor to explain: if existential sentences are inverse copular ones, why is it possible to extract material from the subject NP, while in other existential sentences this isn't possible? Clearly, the importance of explaining this fact doesn't just lie in an attempt to explain the facts about existential sentences on the basis of independent principles: failure to do so would actually undermine the unified theory, because the reason why extraction from the subject NP is impeded in the case of non-existential sentences would no longer be clear. To understand this, we must reflect on the conditions governing extraction from NPs. On the basis of considerable empirical data, we've seen that the ability to extract from an NP depends on two syntactic conditions: either the NP is a predicate (equal to a VP) or the NP is adjacent to a V. In the case of inverse copular sentences, Italian speakers immediately know that one can't say **La causa della rivolta ne fu una foto* __ '(lit.) the cause of-the riot of-it was a picture __'. What changes if the predicate is *there*—in other words, if one says instead *Ce ne fu una foto* __ '(lit.) there of-it was a picture __'? The crucial thing is to understand what generally makes the relationship between V and an NP complement special, or at least why this relationship allows extraction from the NP, unlike the relationship between NP and other syntactic elements. There are two concomitant facts. The first is the proximity of V to the NP: for extraction to be possible, V can't be too "far" from the NP. For example, starting with *Maria conosce un bellissimo porto della Corsica* 'Mary knows a beautiful port of Corsica', I can say *Maria ne conosce un bellissimo porto __* '(lit.) Mary of-it knows a beautiful port __'; but starting with *Maria conosce una spiaggia vicino a un bellissimo porto della Corsica* 'Mary knows a beach near to a beautiful port of Corsica', I can't say **Maria ne conosce una spiaggia vicino a un bellissimo porto __* '(lit.) Mary of-it knows a beach near to a beautiful port __'. The second fact is that the verb selects the complement. Consider these two sentences, for example (which take advantage of the ambiguity of *volte*: 'vaults' and 'times'): *Michelangelo dipinse due volte nella cappella Sistina* 'Michelangelo painted two vaults in the Sistine Chapel' and *Michelangelo dipinse due volte lo stesso affresco* '(lit.) Michelangelo painted two times the same fresco; Michelangelo painted the same fresco two times'. Only in the first case does the verb select the following noun phrase (that is, *dipinse* 'painted' selects the direct object *due volte* 'two vaults'); in the second case, *due volte* 'two times' is an adverbial and, if anything, is selected by the semantic properties of the event expressed by the verb. In fact, we can say *Michelangelo ne dipinse due__ nella cappella Sistina* '(lit.) Michelangelo of-them painted two __ in-the Sistine Chapel; Michelangelo painted two of them in the Sistine Chapel' but not **Michelangelo ne dipinse due __ lo stesso affresco* '(lit.) Michelangelo of-them painted two __ the same fresco'. So extractability from a subject NP (or more generally from an NP that is the argument of a predicate) rests on a combination of two factors: the presence of a V in a local configuration, and a relationship of selection between V and the NP. It's important to add at this point that a verb selects not only for its complement, but also for its subject—for example, with respect to its thematic role, that is, the way the subject is involved in an event. We know this because we can say, for example, *John breaks his arm* and *John breaks the piggy bank*: here, the thematic role of the subject *John* differs depending on whether the predicate is *breaks his arm* or *breaks the piggy bank*. The intentionality of the gesture is implied only in the second case; in the first, on an unmarked reading, the break is something that happens to John, not something that John makes happen voluntarily.[19]

Keeping all of this in mind, let's return to our two crucial cases. Obviously, it can't be the second factor—proximity to a verb—that accounts for the difference between inverse copular and existential sentences. In both cases, the verb *essere* 'to be' is exactly the same "distance" from the NP: **La causa della rivolta ne è una foto__* '(lit.) the cause of-the riot of-it is a picture __', *Ce n'è una foto__* '(lit.) there of-it is a picture __'. So, we can narrow the field and ask ourselves whether there's a good reason why *ci* 'there' is different from an NP like *la causa della rivolta* 'the cause of the riot'. Given these premises, it's not unreasonable to think that the hypotheses that existential sentences are inverse copular ones, and that *there* and *ci* are predicates and not subjects, can help in understanding the difference. If *there* were an expletive subject, we wouldn't have much to say: the subject certainly has no selective capacity over itself (or nevertheless over the subject NP associated with it insofar as it's an expletive). However, if *there* is a predicate, then— as we've seen—it selects the thematic role of the subject. Thus, *there* qualifies a priori as an element capable of making the NP barrier permeable. Just as a verb generally makes the barrier of the direct object NP that follows it permeable because, as a predicate, it selects that NP (and because it's close to it), so does *there* in its role as a predicate. In other words, it's as if *there is* were the verb that selects the subject NP of an existential sentence: the subject being sufficiently close in hierarchical terms, the extraction becomes possible. Once again, it's worth pointing out that the alternative theory whereby *there* is a subject expletive wouldn't help solve this problematic contrast. That a full NP like *the cause of the riot* isn't able to transform the verb *to be* in the same way, on the other hand, is reasonably attributable to the fact that the head of the predicate *cause of the riot* is too deeply embedded in the NP to be able to interact directly with the verb *to be* and thus result in a new verb, the verb *there is* (*esserci*); *the cause of the riot* is a predicate, but its head isn't close enough to the subject contained in the small clause to have an effect on it.[20]

Among other things, this analysis has an important theoretical repercussion: the verb *to be* doesn't *necessarily* produce an unaccusative construction; it does so only in the presence of *there*. This contrasts with the way *there* was generally treated in the early works on this important issue, starting at least with the research of David Perlmutter (1978) and Luigi Burzio (1986). In fact, without *there*, not all diagnostic traits for the unaccusative are satisfied, in particular that of extractability from a postverbal NP in inverse copular sentences. In contrast, with the Italian verb *esserci* 'there is, there are', we have a construction that fulfills the diagnostic criteria for unaccusatives: in other words, it must be concluded that it's the verb *esserci* that is unaccusative, not the verb *essere* 'to be'. On the theoretical level, this consequence must also have repercussions regarding the general nature of the unaccusative. Because I'm only dealing with the verb *to be* here, I won't start down this new road; I simply note that the defining properties of unaccusative constructions are dissociated, which obliges us to conclude that they can't be derived from a single factor.[21]

Also on the interpretive side, the theory of existential sentences as inverse copular ones seems to have attractive (though less stable) advantages. To see these advantages, we'll start with a simple example. Let's take the sentences *There are many prime numbers* and *Prime numbers are many*, which are synonymous in a certain intuitive sense. In fact, we understand that the "real predicate" of the sentence *There are many prime numbers* is *many* and the "real subject" is *prime numbers*, just like in the sentence *Prime numbers are many*. The element *there* doesn't seem to contribute to the sentence's meaning in any crucial way, so much so that we can ignore it in the paraphrase; this is why we've defined it as a "predicate expletive." On the other hand, we know that *many prime numbers* is an NP and that the verb *to be* isn't a predicate. We must fit the pieces of this puzzle together: subjects that don't behave like subjects, predicates that seem to spring from NPs, a verb that's not a predicate, and a predicative element that's not interpreted. The last fact isn't too surprising. It's similar to what we find in the sentence *Le farfalle lo sono* '(lit.) the butterflies so are; The butterflies are like that': the pronoun *lo* is interpreted as a predicate, but only structurally, as is the case with gendered pronouns, except that *lo* doesn't even display agreement in gender and number.

Let's take seriously the intuition that the predicate of an existential sentence determines the subject NP. To a first approximation, we may thus define an existential sentence as a minimal syntactic construct where a prenominal element (for example, *many* in *There are many prime numbers*) becomes the predicate of the noun to which it refers. So, an existential sentence should be seen as a syntactic mechanism that takes an NP of the type [Det N] and returns a proposition that has Det as predicate and N as subject: an existential sentence is, so to speak, a mechanism that "splits" the NP to build a predicative structure. If the NP is followed by a PP or an AP, it will be interpreted as a secondary predicate, like the AP *drunk* in the sentence *A man telephoned drunk*. Pursuing this line of reasoning, we run into an unexpected fact noticed by many linguists: in many languages, such as English, an existential sentence can't have a subject introduced, for example, by a definite article; one can't say **There is the dog in the garden*, because the prenominal element *the* preceding *dog* can't act as a predicate.[22] This is called the "definiteness effect." And note that this effect doesn't depend only on the presence of a prenominal element that can function as a predicate: if, for example, rather than saying *many dogs*, I say *many of the dogs*, the sentence is unacceptable, even though *many* is present (**There are many of the dogs*), since *many* can't function as a predicate (we need only note **Dogs are many of*).

Evidently the definiteness effect doesn't hold in Italian, because one can say *Ci sono i cani in giardino* '(lit.) there are the dogs in [the] garden'. Although a detailed explanation would take us far afield, I'll outline the argument briefly. A sentence like *C'è Giovanni* 'There is John' certainly can't be interpreted as an existential sentence. In other words, the element *ci* is interpreted as the only predicate, there being no element within the subject NP able to perform that function; therefore, the only possible reading is the locative one. We can think that, because Italian (unlike English) permits the subject to be dislocated to the right (as in *Telefona Giovanni* '(lit.) calls John'), the sentence *C'è Giovanni* 'There is John' is entirely analogous to *Giovanni c'è* '(lit.) John there is', with the subject shifted to the right. The presence of an additional expression, like *in biblioteca* 'in [the] library' in *Giovanni c'è in biblioteca* '(lit.) John there is in [the] library', would make this sentence substantially similar, mutatis mutandis, to a sentence of the type *Giovanni lo legge, un libro* '(lit.) John it reads, a book', that is, to a "clitic left-dislocation" structure in which a phrase like *un libro* 'a book' is duplicated by the clitic pronoun *lo* 'it'—a much-noted structure in formal linguistics, studied in detail beginning with the pioneering works of Guglielmo Cinque (1990).[23] The possibility of having the subject to the right plus a clitic left-dislocation structure would generate the sentence *C'è Giovanni in biblioteca* '(lit.) there is John in [the] library'. This solution would allow us to discard Chomsky's (1977b, 52) hypothesis that the definiteness effect is a semantic restriction, and thus to postulate the existence of a semantic parameter for this crosslinguistic difference, certainly a very delicate operation (see Moro 1997).

To sum up, the assumption that an existential sentence is nothing more than a minimal construct with which a language produces a proposition from an NP seems to hold up well. As a rebuttal, we need only negate the existential sentence *Ci sono molti numeri primi in questo codice segreto* 'There are many prime numbers in this secret code' and interpret the result: *Non ci sono molti numeri primi in questo codice segreto* 'There aren't many prime numbers in this secret code'. It's clear that the unmarked interpretation is that the prime numbers in the secret code are few, not that many prime numbers are excluded from the secret code.[24] This fact is easily interpreted only if we start with the hypothesis that existential sentences are a mechanism for producing a predication from an NP. Another interesting case—which replicates the case of the earlier example of the definiteness effect in English, *many of the dogs*—is the contrast between *There aren't many unicorns* and **There aren't many of the unicorns*. If the first expression can be paraphrased in a natural way by saying that the unicorns aren't plentiful, the second can only mean that many of the unicorns aren't present at any given place; it can't mean that there aren't many of them in existence. Of course, the scenario is a bit simplified: for example, I haven't explained why one can say *There is a problem*, when we know that the indefinite article can't act as predicate (**Problem is a*), but these issues would lead us too far afield. It's enough for us to know that the indefinite article can also function as an "existential quantifier," as in the expression *I have met a butcher*, which can be paraphrased by saying that a butcher exists such that I have met him, highlighting in this way the existential operator function of the indefinite article.

Finally, it's worth noting that, in Italian, sentences with *ci* and the verb *essere* can be followed by an entire sentence, as in *C'è che mi sono innamorato di te* '(lit.) there is that I am enamored of you; It's that I'm in love with you'. What structure do we attribute to this sentence? Under the unified theory, we have only two options: either it's a canonical copular sentence, in which case we'd be forced to admit that the sentence *che mi sono innamorato di te* 'that I am in love with you' is a predicate and *ci* 'there' a subject; or the sentence *che mi sono innamorato di te* 'that I am in love with you' is a subject, *ci* 'there' is a propredicate, and the sentence *C'è che mi sono innamorato di te* 'It's that I'm in love with you' is an inverse copular sentence. Even on an intuitive level, the hypothesis that the sentence *che mi sono innamorato di te* 'that I am in love with you' is a subject clearly seems more plausible. In general, sentences can't function as predicates, unless they contain a "gap," which is to say that not all arguments compatible with the predicate are present in the sentence. This is nothing more than a rather unintuitive definition of a relative clause. If we look at English, it's easy to see the logic behind this definition. Let's take the sentence *John loves these books*. This sentence can never play the role of predicate, but if we take away the direct object of the predicate *loves these books* (that is, if we take away *John loves __*), this incomplete sentence can act as a predicate in a sentence like *These books John loves __ are fascinating*. The sentence stripped of an argument functions as a predicate, which must be saturated by an argument in a different position. None of this applies to *C'è che mi sono innamorato di te* 'It's that I'm in love with you'. In fact, the sentence *che mi sono innamorato di te* is complete; it has no gap that can make it play the role of predicate. Therefore, discarding all other possibilities, the least plausible must be true and the tree structure of this sentence is as follows, where the sentence—which for simplicity I continue to represent as TP[25]—is the subject of the small clause and *ci* is the propredicate raised to the canonical subject position:

The Strange Case of Verbs without Subjects

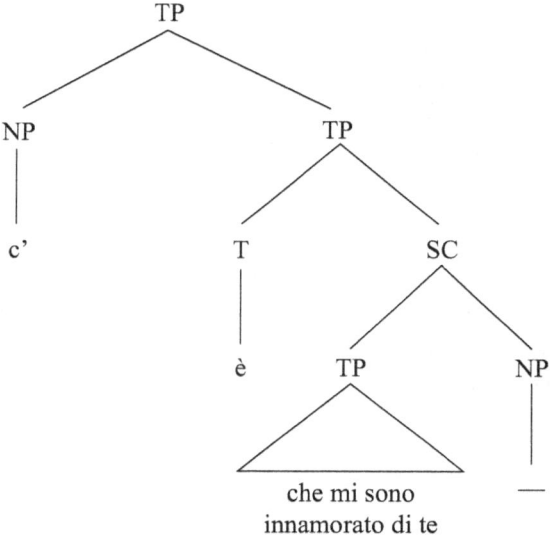

The preceding discussion also offers some very interesting possibilities for reexamining constructions with the verb *to seem* followed by a sentence in finite form. In this case, English provides examples where the structure is, so to speak, transparent. Let's first imagine this short dialogue:

"What is it that bothers you?"

"It's that I don't want to leave."

What's the difference between *I don't want to leave* and *It's that I don't want to leave*? The difference is that *it* stands for *what bothers me*; in other words, *it* is a pronominal-type predicative element that allows the speaker not to repeat the entire predicate as in *What bothers me is that I don't want to leave*.

Starting from this analysis of the element *it* as a predicate pronoun with the verb *to seem*, it becomes possible to radically rethink constructions involving the quasi-copula. In a sentence like

It seems that John left or its Italian equivalent *Sembra che Giovanni partì*,[26] the elements *it* and *pro* preceding the quasi-copula are no longer subject expletives but predicate expletives, and the finite sentence that follows the quasi-copula is no longer the complement of the quasi-copula but the subject of a small clause complement of the quasi-copula, as in the case of *C'è che mi sono innamorato di te* 'It's that I'm in love with you'. In other words, we could say that the sentence *It seems that John left* has the same structure as an inverse copular sentence. The English example would thus have the following tree representation, where the pronominal element *it* is raised and generated as a propredicate in the small clause and then raised (T is omitted from the tree):

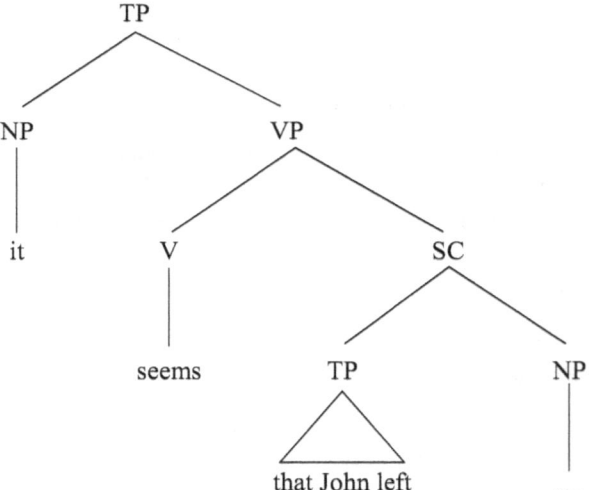

This structure is very similar to the one with the verb *to be*, underlining once more the common nature of copula and quasi-copula. The traditional representation is as follows, where the clause *that John left* is represented as a complement to *seem*, as with any transitive verb (for example, *say* in *Mary said that John left*):

The Strange Case of Verbs without Subjects

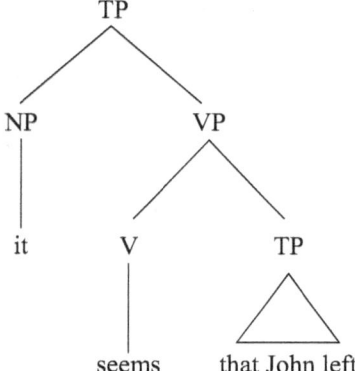

If this analysis proves correct, the class of inverse sentences should include other sentences in addition to copular ones.[27]

Before concluding our journey, we still need a clarification regarding the verb *to be*. A naive question—which, as often happens with naive questions, doesn't lend itself to a naive or easy answer—is this: are the two copular sentences generated with the verb *to be* really synonymous? It's not easy to realize this immediately, but in fact the two sentences convey completely different information. Let's take two simple sentences built from our usual examples. First, *A picture of the wall is not the cause of the riot but the cause of the restoration* is entirely grammatical; the adversative conjunction *but* is negating the predicate nominal. Second, in the inverse sentence *The cause of the riot is not a picture of the wall but a picture of the tower*, it's the subject that's being negated. Now, it's easy to verify that adding the adversative conjunction is always allowed, but the NP that's being negated isn't uniformly the subject or the predicate in both sentences. To check this, consider the contrast between these sentences: **A picture of the wall is not the cause of the riot but a picture of the tower* and **The cause of the riot is not a picture of the wall but the cause of the restoration*. The contrasts considered here are based on the process of focalization. This phenomenon has been studied a good deal with respect to subject inversion in Italian. For example, the pair of sentences *Giovanni canta* 'John sings' and *Canta Giovanni* 'sings John' differ precisely because of the focalization of the subject. In the second case, in fact, I can say *Non canta Giovanni ma Pietro* '(lit.) doesn't sing John but Peter'; in the first case, however, I can't say **Giovanni non canta ma Pietro* '(lit.) John doesn't sing but Peter'. Similarly, I can say *Giovanni non canta ma declama* 'John doesn't sing but recites', but not **Non canta Giovanni ma declama* '(lit.) doesn't sing John but recites'. So the two copular sentences—the canonical and the inverse—don't constitute a case of redundancy in natural language; rather, the movement produces different interpretive effects, allowing us to better understand the mechanisms that lead to a selection between two alternative movements.[28]

Let's summarize the path of this last leg of our journey—rough, intricate, full of bumps, perhaps tortuous, but (I hope) coherent. We saw that the verb *to be* had been analyzed as a verb without a subject, an unaccusative construction that involves movement of a subject NP into a lower, preverbal position. Alongside the canonical version, where the NP that moves is always and only the subject, we examined an alternative proposal, the inverse variant, in which the predicative NP moves. This alternative was made possible by eliminating the postulate requiring the highest NP in a sentence's structure to be the subject, in favor of a more flexible structure that simply requires the presence of an NP in that position. The unified theory of copular sentences that emerged from this framework allowed us to think about existential sentences in a new way, viewing them as inverse copular sentences, and to reconsider the nature of *to be* as an unaccusative verb. The repercussions of this theory are both empirical (deriving the anomaly of copular sentences on the basis of independent principles and interpretation, and discovering new phenomena on a comparative basis) and theoretical (revising the theory of sentence structure and the notion of the unaccusative). In particular, contrary to the standard model adopted both in linguistics and in related fields, it's no longer true that the sequence typically associated with sentence structure, NP VP, is identified with the grammatical functions of subject and predicate. With the verb *to be*, the NP in the sequence NP VP can be a predicate, and the subject can be contained in the VP, in postverbal position.

At this point, we can finally tackle the problem raised by Russell and see it in a new light. Although we must reject the hypothesis that the verb *to be* is a predicate of identity (and existence), it remains true that the NP that follows the verb *to be* doesn't necessarily play the role of predicate: on the basis of considerable data, some originally collected by Giuseppe Longobardi (1985), we see that the verb *to be* can actually be followed by a referential NP with the role of subject, but that in this case the preceding NP is a predicate, not another referential NP. The unified theory of copular sentences proposed here should be seen as a transformative solution that connects all of the data together; that is, starting from a single basic structure, it allows all the properties of sentences with the verb *to be* to be derived naturally, on the basis of universal and independent syntactic principles (including sentences with expletives, which weren't included in previous models). All of this was possible only on the condition of completely reviewing sentence structure and abandoning the axiom according to which the NP that precedes the VP in a sentence is always the subject.

Our journey to the center of the sentence ends here. The verb *to be* has guided us through the time and space of linguistics. We began with Aristotle; we heard the words of Abelard; we passed through the Port-Royal school in order to arrive in the twentieth century and grasp the fundamentals of the biggest revolution in the history of linguistics, which combines the essence of structuralism with a mathematical and biological vision of language. We focused on a particular type of sentence with the verb *to be*, showing that the explanation of certain anomalous data undermined the central dogma of sentence structure: namely, that the sequence NP VP is invariably identified with the functions of subject and predicate. This theory doesn't justify Russell's invective; rather, it shows that the verb *to be* can be followed by an NP that isn't a predicate, as long as the NP preceding it is. Obviously this isn't the final stage. Quite the opposite: the journey can continue through the work and intelligence of those who find these ideas fascinating. In parting, I'd like to touch on a number of crucial points that, for me at least, could form the basis of future studies on and around the verb *to be*. So what follows won't be a single epilogue but several epilogues, pointing out the kinds of questions that come to mind.

I don't know if I was able to convince you that the verb *to be* isn't "a disgrace to the human race"; I hope it's at least clear that if we must concern ourselves with disgraces, it would be best to turn our attention elsewhere.

4 Epilogues between Language and Necessity

Mad is he that is so bold he casts his mind beyond our compass.
—Masuccio Salernitano, *Il Novellino*

In our journey to the center of the sentence, guided by the verb *to be*, we've realized the complexity of the hidden web of threads that binds the words of natural languages together. It's the sense of wonder that strikes us when we look at a tapestry: from the front, the figures seem to be made up of adjacent points of color, but when we turn the tapestry over, we see that these points are really small sections of a continuous thread, which appears and disappears in an unexpected and seemingly chaotic flow, linking apparently unconnected parts of the image we see on the finished surface. To find an answer to the anomaly of the verb *to be*, we've also had to bring the hidden web of threads supporting the structure to the surface. Moving beyond the deceptive nature of linear sequence, we've treated words as atoms and sentences as molecules, trying to decipher their regularity, the primitive elements that make them up, their geometry, and the invariable laws that form the basis of all natural languages. At the end of the journey, we turn and look back at what we've gathered; however, it's impossible not to realize that the number of new questions is also greater than the number of answers. We mustn't let ourselves be discouraged by this. Only presumption leads to thinking of research as a closed loop; a theory that generates questions is always preferable to one that doesn't. If anything, we must take care to select from among all the questions those that, in principle, allow for an experimental response.

Starting from this perspective, we can group the questions raised by this brief history of the verb *to be* into at least three distinct research areas: questions about the formal mechanisms that interact in structuring sentences; questions about how these mechanisms are implemented physically in the brain; questions about what these sentences tell us in general about natural language as a biologically determined phenomenon and ultimately about the position of humankind itself in nature.[1] So we'll move forward, groping through a narrow, uncertain passageway—but we already know what the walls of this passageway are made of: on the one hand, the necessity imposed on the forms of language (i.e., the reasons—be they physical or biological—that determine its structure); on the other, all of the linguistic regularities we don't (yet) know how to explain but that are nonetheless true, even if they could simply be traced back to accidental, historical reasons. Language can't be anything but the equilibrium point between these two conditions: in this sense, linguistics once again becomes a much more general model. Rather than just a simple investigation of the structure of a communication code, it becomes an opportunity to explore the specific nature of humankind.

It won't be possible to tackle these issues in a comprehensive way—and not just for lack of space (all too often, lack of space has become an alibi for not clearly stating the ultimate consequences of one's own analysis), but mostly because we still know too little about the nature and the architecture of human language and, perhaps, we may never know everything about it. That's why I've titled this chapter *epilogues* and not *an epilogue*: because we don't exactly know what the next move will be, the next decisive result that will lead to a significant advance in our knowledge. But the curiosity that our wonder in the face of reality naturally evokes inspires us to try to identify possible questions for each of the above-mentioned lines of research, taking into account what we've seen in our journey through the history of the verb *to be*.[2]

4.1 The Form of Grammar: Between Linearity and Hierarchy

Let's start from the formal properties of grammars, those regularities that we express in syntactic formalism and that we can't justify on the basis of any independent reason. On the path toward constructing a formal theory of sentences with the verb *to be*, and generally throughout the presentation of syntactic structures, we've consistently held two hypotheses, more or less explicitly. The first: that words are combined in pairs, resulting in asymmetric and recursive structures (phrases). The second: that some portions of the structure are copied into higher positions and only the copy in the highest position is pronounced (syntactic movement). The first extraordinary fact is that these two properties of the human communication code—phrases and movement—are not to be found, either alone or in combination, in the communication code of any other living species (in this regard, see among others Anderson 2008, the references cited therein, and Corballis 2007). We don't know the reason for this species-specificity. Certainly it isn't only the evolutionary pressure of the environment or skills such as motor coordination—as suggested for example by Corballis (2003)—otherwise, these same structural properties would also have to be found in the communication codes of other species that share the physical and biological conditions of our world as well as our motor skills. As we'll see in a moment, we must be highly cautious in hypothesizing an equivalent of our code in other species. However, the question remains: why are these two structural properties, phrases and movement, present in the code of *our* species?

A brief aside before diving into the formal issues: whatever the answer to this question is, the structure of language makes human beings a special case in the natural world, with incalculable consequences. Although this is intuitively obvious, nevertheless it's not easy to identify which phenomena can be unambiguously linked to the presence of human language. Of course, if we exclude the presence of written material, on what basis could one ever affirm that a certain group of individuals possess a language with properties comparable to that of our own? I'm not sure there's a clearcut answer: certainly it's not merely the ability to communicate (in fact, all animals communicate, even among different species), nor is it social structure (ants and wolves, for example, are well organized socially), nor even the elaborate building of architectural structures (spiderwebs and beehives are objects whose construction doubtless requires very complex "calculations"). In my opinion, a reasonable hypothesis can be found in the human ability to pass on the experience of preceding generations to succeeding ones, that is, in the ability of a species to make progress in the absence of changes in the biological structure of the organisms belonging to it—in short, the ability to have a "history." In this sense, the difference between humans and all other species is enormous. When a spider hatches, it doesn't build on the webs of the spiders that came before it and make a better one; it's condemned to start from scratch, driven only by instinctual and perceptual mechanisms encoded in its genome. On the contrary, a child doesn't have to start from scratch—let's say by discovering fire at two, inventing the wheel at three, writing at five, and penicillin at six. Simply, with a degree of variability that certainly depends on the ambient society and individual capabilities, children extend the path of those who preceded them. Whatever the causes and consequences that make humans human, these can't reasonably be dissociated from the structure of the communication code and, in particular, from the ability to produce potentially infinite structures to use as a basis for communication. Of course, there could be different ways to implement this linguistic ability that don't generate recursive structures like the ones found in phrases and syntactic movement, but these are the facts. So, having cleared the field of peripheral issues, one question still stands out: why is it that these *two* properties are present in our species' communication code? A theory could consider these two facts (phrases and syntactic movement) as independent and simply not bother to look for an answer. There have been phases of research in which linguists have attempted to describe and explain each of the two phenomena separately, both theoretically and empirically: of course, these preliminary phases were very important, but what I would like to illustrate here is the possibility that these two facts both derive from a *single* source. Naturally, the verb *to be* is at the heart of this proposal.

To illustrate this unified theory, we can start with a simple question: why, in a structure of the type [__ T [NP NP]], must one of the NPs move into the preverbal position to create [NP T [__ NP]] or [NP T [NP __]]? That is, why can't both stay in the positions where they were generated?[3] We certainly can't hypothesize that this is due to the absence of *pro* in a language's lexicon.[4] If this apparently simple and immediate explanation were true, raising in structures of this type would be obligatory in languages that do *not* include *pro* in their lexicon, such as English, but not obligatory in languages where *pro* is available, such as Italian. This difference between languages isn't found in the data: even in Italian, in fact, one can't say **Sono molte foto del muro la causa della rivolta* '[pro] are many pictures of-the wall the cause of-the riot', except perhaps in marginal contexts and with a particular intonation.[5] It's clear, then, that one of the two NPs must move into the preverbal position whether or not a language's lexicon includes *pro*. Why? We can attempt to explain this fact by applying a weak version of the antisymmetry theory originally formulated by Richard Kayne in the mid-1990s (Kayne 1994; see also Cinque 1996). Let's see how.

First, let's look at the canonical version of antisymmetry theory. According to this theory, the hierarchical order of phrases is unambiguously mapped into the linear order of words and vice versa (the Linear Correspondence Axiom or LCA). Simplifying: If a phrase X is hierarchically "prominent" over another phrase Y in a tree structure, the words contained in X precede those contained in Y in the sentence's linear sequence;[6] conversely, if a word w linearly precedes a word w' in a sentence, it means that there exist a phrase X containing w and a phrase Y containing w' such that X is prominent over Y. An important theorem follows from the LCA: namely, two (or more) phrases can't be positioned symmetrically; if they are, the words they contain can't be organized in a linear sequence. In its original version, antisymmetry theory was valid for any syntactic structure in any language: from the moment the first words are combined to the moment the structure is being interpreted by the semantic and phonological components, the asymmetry between phrases (and parts of phrases) must always be preserved. This theory—although not free from problems that don't appear completely resolved—has substantial theoretical and empirical advantages.[7]

On the empirical side, there are many comparative-type confirmations of this theory that account for, among other things, the absence of symmetric transformations relative to linear order, both in different languages and in the same language (for a detailed review, in addition to Kayne 1994 and Cinque 1996, see the updated summary in Kayne 2010). Antisymmetry theory explains, for example, why there are no languages where interrogative movement takes place to the right, contrary to the Italian example. Since movement always lifts a phrase (or part of a phrase) from a lower position to a prominent position, the elements in this phrase always precede those of the phrases contained in the lower position.[8]

On the theoretical side, antisymmetry theory derives all of the properties of phrase structure from a single axiom, the LCA. For example, it explains why a phrase can't have two adjacent heads: the two heads would be in a symmetric hierarchical configuration—neither would be prominent relative to the other—and as a result, it wouldn't be possible to arrange the elements contained in the phrases into a sequence. Also on the basis of the LCA, antisymmetry theory explains why a phrase can't have two complements, XP and YP: the two phrases would also be in a symmetric configuration (in this case, one would be prominent over the phrases contained in the other); therefore, XP would precede YP and vice versa, which of course is impossible. The theory has notable advantages in terms of the simplicity of the overall system; in addition, the reduction of phrase structure to a single axiom has important consequences for the study of spontaneous language learning in children. We no longer need to think—at least with regard to phrase structure—that the guide preceding experience contains a heterogeneous list of properties that would specify, for example, that each phrase must have just one head and just one complement; it's enough that it contains the LCA. The absence of LCA-violating errors during the spontaneous language-learning phase also supports, albeit indirectly, the plausibility of the LCA derived from comparative syntax studies (on this topic, see Guasti 2017).

A weak version of antisymmetry theory plays the central role in the proposed unified theory of syntactic movement and phrase structure.[9] Unlike the original version proposed by Kayne, this weak version admits that the grammar of human language imposes structural restrictions on syntactic configurations in a more parsimonious way. The central idea is that syntactic configurations should satisfy the LCA *only* at the point when a sentence must actually be pronounced, that is, only when the words must necessarily be arranged in a linear sequence:[10] before this happens, syntactic configurations are free to form symmetric structures. How is it possible that the weak version is acceptable if the configurations must be compatible with the LCA, albeit only when the sentence is pronounced? The proposal is to assume that syntactic movement is nothing more than the "rescue mechanism" that syntax uses to return structures to an asymmetric configuration compatible with placement in a linear sequence. One of the two elements constituting the symmetric configuration that violates the LCA is moved; that is, a copy of it is created higher up in a prominent, and therefore asymmetric, position. The lower copy isn't pronounced, thus allowing the words contained in these constituents to be arranged in linear order. Only by adopting the weak version of antisymmetry can we also explain, without resorting to additional or extragrammatical hypotheses, why syntactic movement (usually) involves deletion of the lower copy's phonological content: this happens because the lower copy can't be put in linear order in the position it occupies, on pain of violating the LCA.

Often, in theories that don't adopt the weak version of antisymmetry, it is said that only one copy is pronounced in order to reduce articulatory effort. In that regard, Chomsky in particular invokes an extragrammatical principle of economy (minimal computation) that's not well defined:

The Delete operation presumably—at least, arguably—is coming from the outside. If you want to minimize computation, if you want to spell things out as little as possible, you will spell out only one of the two identical elements, either the new one introduced by the operation (the "higher one" in the configuration) or the one in the "base" position of initial Merge (the "lower one" in the configuration). The higher one cannot be deleted, or there will be no distinction between overt and covert Move. So therefore the lower one must be deleted. These considerations should derive from outside the language faculty, from general principles of minimal computation. (Chomsky 2004, 153)

This is a "solution" that doesn't seem well founded from any perspective—quite the opposite. Meanwhile, as of yet we don't have a model that explains the exact "energy costs" of pronouncing a word, in a neurophysiological sense: for example, the opposite hypothesis could be valid and there could be an energy cost in *inhibiting* the pronunciation of a phrase. Regardless of any speculation of this kind, though, language certainly contains many redundancies that are exactly the opposite of the hypothetical explanation based on economy criteria. If just one copy of syntactic movement were pronounced for reasons of economy, we would still need to explain a fact from Italian that we examined in discussing the redundancy principle: namely, *quella strana nuova bellissima ragazza bionda simpatica* 'that strange, new, beautiful, nice, blonde girl', where the morpheme that expresses the singular feminine in Italian, -*a*, is pronounced no fewer than seven times.[11]

Finally, let's return to the verb *to be* and the requisite raising of the NP in structures of the type [__ T [NP NP]]. It's precisely this empirical case that provides the fundamental fact underpinning weak antisymmetry theory, and it's also the first to have been discussed. Because this theory would explain the movement in this structure, we need to find independent empirical reasons that lead to admitting that the two NPs appearing with the verb *to be* are directly linked to the basic structure, without the intervention of a head that makes them asymmetric. In formal terms, this means finding empirical reasons to admit that the two NPs of a sentence with the verb *to be* combine immediately as [NP NP], and not as [NP [H NP]] (where H stands for any head). In a tree representation, the bond between the two NPs—subject and predicate within a small clause before raising—will be as follows:[12]

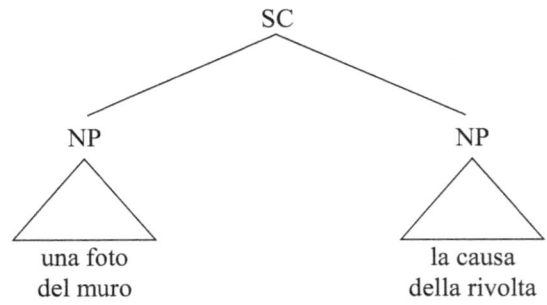

'a pictureof-the wall'   'the cause of-the riot'

One justification for the symmetry hypothesis is based on the possibility of cliticizing the predicative NP in Italian. Let's look at these two sentences: *Giovanni considera queste foto del muro la causa della rivolta* 'John considers these pictures of the wall the cause of the riot' and *Queste foto del muro sono la causa della rivolta* 'These pictures of the wall are the cause of the riot'. If we try to cliticize the predicative NP in the two sentences, we get **Giovanni lo considera queste foto* '(lit.) John it considers these pictures' and *Queste foto lo sono* '(lit.) these pictures it are; These photos are so'. The contrast is stark. To explain it, one can make use of what's known as the *Head Movement Constraint* or HMC, originally proposed by Lisa deMena Travis (1984), according to which a head can't move up to another head by skipping over an intermediate one.[13] English auxiliary movement offers a typical example. Questions containing an auxiliary are formed by moving the auxiliary to the front of the sequence. For example, from the sentence *You have read the book* we get *Have you __ read the book?*, and from the sentence *You would read the book* we get *Would you __ read the book?* Therefore, both *would* and *have* can move. However, if both auxiliaries appear in the same sentence, only the first can be moved: from the sentence *You would have read this book* we can get the question *Would you __ have read this* *book?*, but not **Have you would __ read this book?* The ungrammaticality of the last sentence is attributed to the fact that *have* jumps over the head position occupied by *would*, thus violating the HMC. In parallel, the ungrammaticality of **Giovanni lo considera queste foto* '(lit.) John it considers these pictures' can be viewed as a violation of the HMC: the bond between *queste foto* 'these pictures' and *la causa della rivolta* 'the cause of the riot' when they are preceded by the verb *considerare* 'to consider' is therefore mediated by a head without phonological content.[14] The grammaticality of *Queste foto lo sono* '(lit.) these pictures it are; These photos are so' shows that this sentence involves no HMC violation and therefore there aren't any heads between *queste foto* 'these pictures' and *la causa della rivolta* 'the cause of the riot' in the small clause. Raising is thus required to neutralize the breach of the LCA due to this symmetric configuration.

In conclusion, having seen the essential role played by sentences with the verb *to be* in the formulation of weak antisymmetry theory, we can get back to the question that launched this long discussion, a question regarding the formal properties of grammars: why is it that two properties as different as phrase structure and syntactic movement are present together in the structure of human language? The advantages of adopting the weak version of antisymmetry are certainly already evident. This theory, which derives movement from conditions imposed by the LCA on linearization (and that's why it's called "*dynamic* antisymmetry"), connects movement phenomena with the theory of phrase structure, or rather with the geometry they must respect in order to produce temporal sequences of words. The coexistence of these two structural characteristics no longer needs to be explained, because they are in fact the result of a single requirement—that of linearization imposed by the LCA, active only when necessary.

Of course, in order to accept dynamic antisymmetry (and more generally, in order to accept antisymmetry theory), we need to resolve all the theoretical and empirical problems that come along with it, and show its advantages. This complex assessment can only happen after the scientific community scrutinizes and examines much more data than is currently available (see, for example, Moro 2004, Barrie 2006). It's enough to point out once more that sentences with the verb *to be* become the driving force of research, as has often happened in the long tradition of linguistic thought. One may wonder why these sentences continue to pose new challenges and provide the impulse for new theories. The inability to trace the raising of NPs back to the presence of *pro* is just one of many recalcitrant phenomena exhibited by the verb *to be* relative to canonical models. Certainly, it can't be considered chance: as we've seen, the verb *to be* is the only verb, or at least the prototypical verb, whose predicate and subject can belong to the same morphological category, a category usually reserved for subjects and complements of V and of P—the NP. So, sentences with the verb *to be* are the only ones where the predicative link can't rely on categorial or morphological asymmetry: the *glue* between subject and predicate must therefore be structural and syntactic, not morphological or categorial. That sentences with the verb *to be* pose questions regarding symmetry in natural languages is therefore independent of one's choice of theoretical framework: symmetry resides in the facts—or better, in the fact that the subject and predicate are both NPs. Sentences with the verb *to be* are therefore the ideal laboratory for understanding how the predicative bond is implemented in grammar, once irrelevant empirical residues are eliminated.

We began this chapter by talking about two antithetical forces that shape the structure of language: the needs (1) of extralinguistic conditions and (2) of the form of language itself, unrelated to any immediate physical or biological reason. These two forces are quite evident when it comes to understanding the nature of syntactic movement: on the one hand, there's the need to build linear sequences of words in time; on the other, there's the need to encode syntactic elements in recursive binary combinations. Syntactic movement, one of the characteristic aspects of the human communication code, thus arises as a point of equilibrium between these two forces. Finally, notice that the link between the need for linearization and the recursive and hierarchical structure of syntax is less intuitive than one would think with respect to language acquisition: in syntax, the rules only see hierarchical structures; to the child, what is immediately available as sensory data is only the linear structures. If language were designed to facilitate communication, and therefore learning, this paradox would be very difficult to justify—too difficult, in fact. Again, it's the brain that needs to combine the pieces of these independent worlds: the ear hears words, the brain sentences.

4.2 Language in the Brain

All of this naturally leads us to set aside the problems of theoretical linguistics and to turn to the second question posed earlier, regarding the neuropsychological mechanisms underlying the formal principles of grammars. This section is a necessary excursus: asking ourselves whether the verb *to be* is represented somehow in the brain first requires us to more broadly understand what aspects of language structure we relate to what we know about the brain's architecture and functioning. It's an embarrassing question. It's embarrassing because although we know full well that the human ability to communicate on the basis of a grammar is somehow represented in the brain, even today the order of complexity and knowledge of the two domains seems almost incommensurate despite enormous research efforts. To tell the truth, even the point of departure—quite obvious to us now—hasn't been easy to grasp over the long course of history; in the absence of technology and in-depth studies, understanding that language is processed in the brain isn't as intuitive as it might seem. Certainly, no one has assumed that this ability is related to the gallbladder—but in the past, understanding that language isn't an "expression" of the heart, for example, was neither as simple nor as obvious as it seems to us today. Basically, when we hear or say things that move us emotionally, we first feel that sensation in our hearts, and what's more, it's when our heart stops beating that we stop being able to speak. None other than the great Aristotle fell for this physiological illusion and considered the brain neither more nor less than the body's radiator; instead it was the heart, according to him, that was the seat of cognitive abilities. It's because of this illusion that many languages still have what one might call "cardiocentric" lexical fossils—as in English where, certainly not for romantic reasons, when we memorize something we're said *to know it by heart*. Even today, when it seems we know a lot more about the brain—to return to the issue of the incommensurability of the two empirical domains—things aren't much better. Indeed, perhaps the advancement of knowledge in neuropsychology accentuates the contrast even further: just consider the complexity of the human brain in microscopic and quantitative terms. The data in our possession appear to surpass anything we can imagine and provoke an epistemological vertigo worthy of certain Borges-esque images, as in the following case. Gerald Edelman, winner of the 1972 Nobel Prize in Physiology or Medicine, has calculated that the number of circuits that can form in a human brain is 10 followed by at least a million zeros, while the number of particles in the universe—that is, of all the components of all of the atoms of which all the galaxies in the known universe are made—is 10 followed by *only* seventy-two zeros (Edelman and Tononi 2000; see also Boncinelli 1999 and Martino 2009 for an assessment of the complexity of the brain and the nervous system in general). It's not only that the proportions between the physical mechanisms and descriptions of grammar are so unequal; the issue is that, independent of the problem of how to reconstruct the networks underlying the complex syntactic system, we don't even have the vaguest idea of how to map the minimum elements of language—phonemes, morphemes, words, phrases—into the functional and anatomical topography of the brain.

However daunting this state of affairs, it means neither that linguistics is a dead letter nor that it's a temporary taxonomic activity, only useful in eventually reducing the discipline to neuropsychology. In the same way that Newton didn't hold back in presenting his theory of gravity, even though this phenomenon didn't fit into the Cartesian mechanism, contemporary linguists never stop seeking out the fundamental principles underpinning the complexity of linguistic phenomena even if these principles aren't readily traceable to known neuropsychological processes. The legitimacy of theoretical concepts such as "phrase" or the LCA is based on the fact that they allow known phenomena to be explained and new phenomena to be predicted: they exist insofar as they play a role in explanation. Asking anything more would be asking linguistics to provide a metaphysics, or an ontology, things that aren't required of any other empirical science.[15]

Recently, however, neuroimaging techniques have given unexpected glimpses at possible pathways, although in this area of research they are to be traversed with caution. Regarding syntax, at least two steps have been taken. On the one hand, there's the discovery of a selective neural network for syntax involving what's known as "Broca's area" (a portion of the cerebral cortex in the left inferior frontal gyrus) and a deep part of the brain (left caudate nucleus), constituting an integrated system. On the other hand, there's the discovery that when learning a language that *doesn't* respect the common principles of natural languages—in particular, an artificial language that doesn't adopt the recursive system that generates phrases in a hierarchical fashion—the brain unconsciously uses networks other than the ones dedicated to syntax, and activity in Broca's area significantly decreases (for a presentation of these experiments see Moro 2006b, 2016 and the references cited therein).[16] The fundamental problem with regard to research in this area is both technical and methodological. Neuroimaging techniques provide a measure of the brain's hemodynamic activity—in a broad sense—which is then related to the metabolic activity of neurons. Excepting pathologies, all parts of the brain are always active—albeit exhibiting different metabolic activities and modulated by environmental conditions—so, in order to acquire selective data on a specific cognitive task, data that are free from any basal brain activity and from any interference, it's always necessary to make a comparison between two different tasks (subtractive method) or between different stages of the same task (parametric analysis; see Perani and Cappa 1996, Friston 1997). So, isolating the hemodynamic—hence metabolic—activity related to just one aspect of a cognitive task is highly challenging, sometimes even simply from a theoretical perspective (just think of how hard it is to properly define the different types of what's commonly called "memory"). From an empirical standpoint, given the complexity of neural networks, it's well understood that hoping to have even an approximate knowledge of the networks underpinning linguistic tasks (but also others), when the only available data is hemodynamic activity in the brain, is like imagining that we could map the world's cities by observing airport passenger flow rates from outer space. The task is practically impossible, even if we can find some bits of information: we can confirm, for example, that there's no big airport and therefore no big city in the heart of the Sahara; or that, on the contrary, there must be large urban centers on North America's East Coast, given the presence of large airports. But this isn't always true: there are airports located next to insignificant towns just because these towns are located at the crossroads of well-frequented routes or because they're easily accessible from congested cities. As far as we know, our brain's neural networks could be like train stations that seem disproportionately large compared to the cities where they're located because that's where the tracks connecting major cities converge. Broca's area could eventually turn out to be *just* a congested crossroads. Perhaps nothing "happens" in that area; perhaps its centrality is only the effect of the involvement of other paths that converge in that location for neurophysiological or neuroanatomical reasons that escape us. Bearing this caveat in mind, it's still possible to make nontrivial deductions about the relationship between the brain and language. As mentioned, we can exclude the idea that not all conceivable grammars are realized in the world's languages because of a mere historical accident or the result of an arbitrary convention, given that the selective network for natural language syntax is deactivated when an individual learns an "impossible" language, that is, a language that doesn't implement the recursive system typical of all natural languages.

So, the "boundaries of Babel" exist and they are traced in our flesh, in the neurophysiological and neuroanatomical structures of our brains. The dominant thesis in the first half of the last century— so well summed up by the words of the famous American linguist Martin Joos (1957), "Languages differ from one another unpredictably and without limit," words written, ironically enough, in the same year in which Chomsky's *Syntactic Structures* was published— was therefore completely and definitively overturned. This was made possible by the combination of experimental results, especially those based on neuroimaging data, and results from theoretical and comparative linguistics. By now the convergence is clear and complete: natural languages are biologically determined and invariable structures, excepting accidental modifications, and obviously excluding the association between signifier and signified that remains largely arbitrary in the sense and to the extent defined by Saussure. Seven centuries have passed since the *doctor mirabilis*, Roger Bacon, said "Grammatica una et eadem est secundum substantiam in omnibus linguis, licet accidentaliter varietur"—that is, "Grammar is, in its essence, one and the same in all languages, even though it differs in superficial features" (Jakobson 1963, 209)—and his insight, albeit transformed into neurobiological terms and no longer expressed in theological ones, takes on a new life in modern thought.

Let's continue with our overview. A second recent field of research, still in the area of studies on the relationship between language and the brain, is related to reports that the neural networks involved in language interact in the brain with other specialized networks. Following the line of research begun by the group led by Giacomo Rizzolatti on what are called "mirror neurons," and related research,[17] it was noted that when the brain interprets action sentences, the same motor circuits that activate when physically performing the same action are simultaneously activated (Tettamanti et al. 2005). This correspondence (technically described as "somatotopic") is striking: sentences involving the hand (like *I grab the knife*) activate the areas of the cortex that control the hand, while sentences involving the leg (like *I kick the ball*) activate areas that control the leg, and sentences involving the mouth (like *I bite into the apple*) activate areas that control the mouth. This process clearly shows a connection between different modules of the brain: those organizing linguistic expression and those overseeing motor control, with significant involvement of Broca's area. Some researchers even consider this connection the phylogenetic basis of our species' language capabilities: the role of organized movement—and in particular the use of the hands—seems important enough that it might even be possible to trace the birth of human language back to it (see, for example, Corballis 2003, 2010).

Personally, I don't think there are sufficient empirical or theoretical grounds for this conclusion. Regarding syntax in particular, on the contrary it seems reasonable to assume that any explanation that aspires to trace the emergence of the structure of this special and unique component of human language to elements related to motor control is *inherently* inadequate. In my opinion, there are at least two types of reasons for this. First, the type of recursion observed in syntax—a nontrivial recursion,[18] that is to say, one characterized by weak self-similarity properties, as we saw in previous chapters—can't reasonably be seen as isomorphic to any motor activity; even if we imagine that an action such as walking is recursive, in the sense that it can be described as the iteration of a potentially infinite movement, it doesn't appear that any movement can be nested in a structure (or procedure) of the same type, as is the case with the production of phrases in every human language. In addition, with regard to language learning, the acquisition of syntactic structures seems to be much less subject to an explanation linked to motor control, even if combined with the hypothesis of mirror neurons. All that syntax outputs in the motor domain, and that speakers can therefore perceive, is a linear sequence of words, and we've seen that this feature is exactly the one that *none* of the rules of syntax explains: syntax is based only on hierarchical relationships and these, by definition, are invisible in physical linguistic data—compressed or, so to speak, "flattened" in the linear sequence. But independent of these considerations, a more radical objection to the hypothesis that the origins of language structures are to be found in motor control remains: had language emerged from our motor control ability, obviously in a nontrivial sense, the mere fact that primates or animals with sophisticated motor control don't speak using a recursive syntactic system would be very difficult to explain, or at least it would be necessary to resort to additional crucial assumptions. And the problem would just be shifted.

Aside from these reflections, there are also empirical data showing that language structures can't in any way be *completely* traced to a sophisticated emancipation from motor control structures, while also admitting that the latter might have a recursive structure. A recent study (Tettamanti et al. 2008a) showed that when participants were interpreting action sentences expressed both in the positive and in the negative (so, alongside sentences like *I kick the ball, I grab the knife, I bite into the apple* were their negative counterparts *I don't kick the ball, I don't grab the knife, I don't bite into the apple*), the motor circuits associated with the interpretation of action sentences were partially inhibited in negative sentences. This result has disruptive consequences; one concludes that in fact it's negation that modulates a part of the motor control system and not the other way around. To grasp this conclusion, we need to see one point clearly: the negation pertains only to the level of pure linguistic representation *of* the world; it is not *in* the world. Which is to say that negative facts don't exist; rather, all that exists are (all of the) other facts that aren't those negated by our imagination or, if we want to keep the conversation on a neuropsychological level, there are no negative facts that can constitute sensory stimuli—only positive facts can do so.

So, the data on the effects of negation in the brain reasonably lead us to conclude that grammar nevertheless has primacy over representations or, if we want to be more conservative, to conclude that there is at least one central aspect of language, syntax, that may not be entirely attributable to the representation of the world, be it sensory-motor or not. Taking a closer look, we find that we're fundamentally dealing with a neuropsychological interpretation of the most radical of the dichotomies that have always characterized the debate over the nature of language, in both the ontogenetic and, more recently, the phylogenetic sense: the dichotomy between those who consider language to be derived from the structure of the world (like the Modistae in the Middle Ages) and those who consider language to be a phenomenon that develops in a (partially) autonomous way from the structure of the world (like the Cartesian linguists in the seventeenth century).[19] Tettamanti et al.'s (2008a) experiment with negation can therefore be counted as a point in favor of those who believe that the structure of language can't derive entirely from the structure of the world. Negation isn't the "shadow" cast on the brain by any physical event; if anything, it's the brain that casts shadows on the world. There's much to discuss about this issue, far more than I can do here, but it isn't inappropriate to highlight that these data regarding a single linguistic fact seem to have significant general implications regarding the interaction between the mind and the brain.

Finally, it's interesting to note that negation isn't part of any other animals' communication codes. Of course, an animal can refuse to do something, and in this sense construct a form of negation, or it can recognize that a given event doesn't occur and act accordingly, but it's the *formal* aspect of denial that's missing; in particular, there's no interaction between negation and recursion. However hard we try to imagine an equivalent to negation in animal communication, I'm not aware of any research demonstrating the possibility of recursive interpretation of multiple negatives in the same utterance, something that's immediately available in human languages. To take a simple example, a human has no difficulty in understanding *I don't think I can't do it* as meaning 'I think I can do it', where the two negatives neutralize each other. Imagining that an animal can do this is definitely possible: thinking that it's plausible is decidedly less so.

A third type of research on the physical implementation of the grammatical system consists of studies on genetics and language. Ignoring the current of research that simply shows how the distribution of language families and of genes can be superimposed (on this topic, see the pioneering works of Luigi Luca Cavalli-Sforza; among others, Cavalli-Sforza 1996), there are interesting studies carried out around the so-called "language gene", or FOXP2 (for the link between genetics and linguistics, see Benítez Burraco 2009). It's difficult to imagine a more unhappy term for this gene: it was quickly realized that the gene in question was involved in language (and many other systems, as are all so-called "master genes") but that, at most, it is a gene able to control only peripheral aspects of linguistic expression, such as those that calibrate the delicate mechanism controlling oral-facial coordination for the pronunciation of sounds. However, beyond this first false alarm there are still a number of preliminary issues that need to be addressed before a research program into the genetic basis of language can even be undertaken. Among these are at least two central issues, of different orders of complexity.

The first is easily resolved, and it's very clear to geneticists: one must avoid confusion between "genetically determined" and "universal." In this regard, the enlightening words of Peter Medawar, Nobel Laureate in Physiology or Medicine in 1960, come to mind:

One of the gravest and most widespread aberrations of geneticism is embodied in the belief that if any characteristic is enjoyed by all individuals of the community, it must be genetically underwritten. Thus, if it should turn out that a certain basic linguistic form such as the Aristotelian subject/predicate form is an element of all the languages of the world, then its usage must be genetically programmed. (Some of Noam Chomsky's writings are not guiltless of this assumption, which is also a disfigurement of sociobiology as it steers its precarious course between the twin perils of geneticism and historicism.) It may be well to repeat in this context the reason why this supreme canon of geneticism is not satisfactory: if any trait is to be judged "inborn" or genetically programmed, then there must be some people who *lack* it. The ability to taste phenylthiocarbamide, for instance, is known to be genetically programmed because there are those who *lack* it. (Medawar and Medawar 1983, 109; emphasis mine)

So, when it's said that modern linguistics studies the universal aspects of natural language grammars and identifies its invariant principles, it shouldn't be implied that these principles are the result of the identification of specific genes, unless the term "gene" is devoid of its true empirical value: "genetic" in this case means simply "biological." Even before we can raise the molecular biology issue, today we're still miles away from a "Mendelian linguistics"—a linguistics that has identified (statistical) genetic regularities expressible, for example, in the formal terms of modern syntactic theory—precisely because we haven't yet identified the significant traits with respect to grammar (and to syntax in particular) that are *not* possessed by some human being. It's important to note, however, that the absence of a Mendelian linguistics may not be simply a matter of lacking technique and luck and that therefore it's not enough just to wait until the time is ripe. There could be other issues that must be subjected to the critical scrutiny of science.

The second issue is much more delicate and logically presupposes the validity of what has been said with regard to the first. The fact that not all features are genetically determined can correspond to (at least) two distinct situations. Let's proceed step by step. When I observe a feature of a living being, if this feature isn't genetically determined, one possibility is that it is, so to speak, the effect of the interaction of other features that *are* genetically determined. Take, for example, an easily recognizable feature of the human body: the armpit. We know quite well that there are no armpit genes; if anything, there are genes that govern the construction of the body and the arms. So, the armpit exists, it's perceptible and nameable, but it's not the result of direct genetic expression: it's the result of independent genetic interactions that follow specific instructions for building the torso and the arms. This position was taken by Stephen Jay Gould and Richard Lewontin in a famous essay inspired by the spandrels of Saint Mark's Basilica in Venice (Gould and Lewontin 1979), those ornately decorated wall segments formed at the juncture of two arches that share a column. Gould and Lewontin observed that the spandrels had never been *designed* by an architect; they were simply what happened at the juncture between two arches, which on the contrary were themselves the result of a purposeful and precise plan. Therefore, it isn't enough to recognize a feature and give it a name in order to assume that it's the direct execution of a genetically determined design: this feature could in fact be the result of an interaction between two independent designs. If we keep this way of viewing things in mind, we can allow that language is like an "armpit of the brain": like armpit genes, language genes don't exist, and the absence of a Mendelian linguistics (at least for the time being) could be a consequence of this complex state. It could be that genes whose synergy results in language also express other constituent traits (pleiotropia), such as vital organs or vital aspects of metabolism; should even one such gene fail to be expressed, it could result in the inability to complete the formation of the fetus or could even prevent embryogenesis, and therefore language would be so deeply rooted in the genetic structure of human beings that it might be impossible to trace the molecular basis that controls its expression. Certainly, this state of affairs, if true, has substantially contributed to protecting the human species: in fact, it would be like saying that humans couldn't be born with mutations that made them identical to normal humans in every way except for the ability to use language. Obviously, I'm not referring to capacities peripheral to language (such as the use of vocal cords or gestures), but to the ability to combine a finite number of signs in an infinite way according to the rules that are typical of human grammars, in particular recursive syntactic ones. An individual of our species is only born if he or she is also equipped with the language faculty.

However, upon reflection, the issue at hand could hide a state of affairs that's even more complex and, in some ways, disconcerting. Let's begin once more with a visual example, similar in part, but not completely, to that of the spandrels of St. Mark's given by Gould and Lewontin; this example will help us to better understand the bond between an organism's features and their genetic basis:

Epilogues between Language and Necessity

The figure reproduced here is called the "Kanizsa triangle" after the Italian psychologist Gaetano Kanizsa, who invented and studied it in the 1950s (Kanizsa 1955). Surprisingly, when viewing the figure with our human eyes, we can't avoid seeing an equilateral triangle with one point upward. However, the triangle isn't there. It's illusory; it's constructed *in* our brains and *by* our brains "completing" those physical traits that are available and perceived by our eyes according to our brains' own laws, inaccessible to our conscious minds. Taken individually, the pieces of the figure that together make us perceive the triangle don't cause us to perceive "parts" of the triangle, as the following figure shows:

What if human language is more similar to the Kanizsa triangle than to a spandrel? Could it be that it's a type of "cognitive mirage" like the Kanizsa triangle? Obviously, I'm not simply saying that language isn't a monolithic block but rather the result of the interaction of independent modules, such as phonology, morphology, syntax, and semantics; this is a given in modern linguistics. Nor am I saying that the effects of language are illusory; linguistic communication exists, of course. Nor am I reframing Gould and Lewontin's analogy in order to say that language has no dedicated genes but results from the interaction of independent genes. I'm suggesting, instead, that we can't rule out the possibility that the regularities that we perceive in natural languages—at any level of abstraction—are actually produced by our cognitive system on the basis of stimuli that do *not* contain the regularities that we seem to perceive. Under this view, sensory data would be unavoidably and unconsciously completed by the brain, just as we can't avoid seeing the Kanizsa triangle even though not even one complete side of the triangle exists. Finding the genes responsible for this mirage—be it a dedicated or a derived genetic design—would coincide with finding the genes that express our cognitive system in its entirety, a task that is most likely far beyond the reach of human intelligence. To use the simplest case involving visual perception, it's almost as if, in order to understand the structure of a triangle, it were necessary to discover the genetic basis underlying the neurophysiological mechanisms that cause us to inevitably "see" it even when it's not there.

Finally, there is another interesting difference between the two models. In the case of the spandrels, even if there's no dedicated design on the basis of which they were built, all we need to know is the design of the arches to infer the spandrels. The spandrels are real objects; their form—albeit with some variation—must be one that allows for the connection between the two arches. It's like saying that, given a universe, I can define a set that belongs to this universe both directly (for example, by listing the elements that belong to it) and indirectly, by defining the complementary set (by listing all of the elements that *don't* belong to it). But in the case of the Kanizsa triangle, the situation is very different: given that the triangle exists only in our minds, even if I were to have the designs of the elements that allow the image's components to be perceived, the image itself wouldn't emerge as a necessary complement. The triangle isn't a "solution" external to our minds, like the spandrels of Saint Mark's. Perhaps language isn't even the only solution to a series of stimuli. At least to me this seems neither clearly evident nor a given: for example, we can easily imagine a language with no recursive rules, only rules based on linear order. In other words, what would remain of the triangle if the same image were seen with the eyes of, say, a fly? And what remains of language if the individual listening is of a different species?

So we're a long way from the technological and, retrospectively, simplistic vision that equates the brain with a computer's hardware and cognitive abilities with software. If in fact we really wanted to maintain the technological metaphor, we would at least have to admit that our cognitive software isn't set up to run on the hardware that is our brain: instead, it's the characteristic expression of it— indeed, the only possible expression, almost as if flesh itself were *lógos*. One wonders whether it wouldn't be appropriate to postulate, at least temporarily, a different level of representation of cognitive facts, a level that, independently of how we describe the brain in neurobiological terms and of the formal regularities that describe individual cognitive systems, is arranged according to its own laws: a *mindware*, so to speak, a reality with laws not reducible either to what we know of neurophysiology and neuroanatomy or to what we know of complex systems, in the formal sense.

Considering everything we've noted so far in this delicate but necessary preliminary reflection on the possibility of a neurolinguistic study of the verb *to be*, we understand very well that the ability to detect the neural network that houses the verb *to be* through experiments qualifies as a dream that can't be dignified with the word hope. We know of course that the verb *to be* must be in the brain, but we have no idea where it is, or whether we'll ever be able to know where it is; moreover, we don't know where any other single word is either. Meanwhile, it's only reasonable to admit that words aren't trivially implemented in isolation but are found within structures, this time not only as Saussure intended the term.[20] However, we don't have to completely give up.

4.3 Losing and Acquiring the Copula

An unexpected hope for being able to link the verb *to be*, precisely the verb *to be*, with physical—which is to say neuropsychological—aspects of linguistic codification comes from the clinical study of brain pathologies, both degenerative ones and those due to "focal" lesions (i.e., lesions that occur following an injury, an infection, a tumor, or a vascular incident such as a stroke or heart attack, which damages a limited part of the brain tissue). There's a linguistic pathology belonging to the aphasic category, which consists in the omission of what are called "functional" words or, as they would have been defined by an ancient grammarian, "syncategorematic" ones—that is, words without an autonomous content, fixed in number, that serve as logical connectors (like articles, prepositions, auxiliaries, and conjunctions) or inflected morphemes (like those that in many languages indicate the gender and number of a noun or inflection in a verb). The patient speaks using so-called telegraphic speech—sometimes referred to as "titlese" (the language of headlines, shortened for reasons of space)—producing utterances like *Yesterday student buy book* rather than *The students bought the books*. This condition, known as "agrammatism," provides the missing link, allowing us to at least acknowledge that somehow the verb *to be* is visible as a distinct entity in the brain, distinct from other verbs and likened to functional words, including auxiliaries: there are patients who omit the copula but not other verbs and say *Mary physicist* and not *Mary is a physicist* (on the topic of agrammatism, see among others Caplan 1992, Miceli 1996, Basso and Cubelli 1999, Denes 2009). Whatever its cause, agrammatism shows that the verb *to be* isn't a verb like the others, which is to say it's not a predicate, corroborating in a surprising way the hypothesis Aristotle began to formulate twenty-four hundred years ago.

And that's not all: the verb *to be* behaves in a special way during spontaneous language acquisition in children. A notable illustration comes from the research project on language learning and aphasia coordinated by Kenneth Wexler at MIT, where participants studied English-speaking children's acquisition of canonical and inverse copular sentences. They found that not only is the copula learned differently from other verbs, but the two types of sentences are associated with different acquisition rates (Hirsch and Wexler 2007, 2008; for an overview of data on the acquisition of the copula, see also Becker 2000, Franchi 2006, and the references cited therein).

In turn, the study of children's spontaneous language acquisition inevitably leads to questions of an evolutionary nature, the last of the three topics in this collection of epilogues. Once we accept, as Noam Chomsky has often emphasized, that "the acquisition of language is something that happens to you; it's not something that you do" (Chomsky 1988, 174), it's impossible not to wonder why this thing—the spontaneous acquisition of a language with syntax comparable to our own—doesn't happen to individuals of any other species (see Corballis 2007, Anderson 2008, and the fundamental study on chimpanzees reported in Terrace et al. 1979).[21] It's useless to deny that to date we're unable to provide a "linguistic paleontology": as we've seen, if we exclude writing—which takes us back around six thousand years at most, too short a time to hypothesize significant genetic changes—we have no sure traces that can lead us to hypothesize what groups of hominids or primates were equipped with the human capabilities that we call "language." The whole question of whether animals can speak is in some ways reminiscent of another, namely, whether computers can think—and both questions appear meaningless. In this regard, the great British mathematician Alan Turing expressed a definitive opinion:

I propose to consider the question, "Can machines think?" This should begin with definitions of the meaning of the terms *machine* and *think*. The definitions might be framed so as to reflect so far as possible the normal use of the words, but this attitude is dangerous. If the meaning of the words *machine* and *think* are to be found by examining how they are commonly used it is difficult to escape the conclusion that the meaning and the answer to the question, "Can machines think?" is to be sought in a statistical survey such as a Gallup poll. But this is absurd.... The original question, "Can machines think?" I believe to be too meaningless to deserve discussion. Nevertheless I believe that at the end of the century the use of words and general educated opinion will have altered so much that one will be able to speak of machines thinking without expecting to be contradicted. (Turing 1950, 433)

So far, Turing's prophecy hasn't come to pass, but his words are still reasonably current, maybe not so much in likening machines to humans, but vice versa in the more-or-less explicit attempts of biological reductionism that seek to make humans, indeed every person, coincide with the complete profile of their genetic heritage. Having said that, while taking this important caveat into account, there are some considerations that I can sketch out, with the aim of preparing the ground for a time—if it comes—when it will be possible to date the emergence of language. I don't think it would make much sense to add "the emergence of language in the human species," given that language is a defining capacity of our species.[22]

First of all, given that the primary characteristic of human language is the ability to manipulate a finite number of signs in a potentially infinite way (recursive and hierarchically organized), this ability can't be *partially* present: infinity is there or it isn't; there can't be just a piece of it. Note that from the ontogenetic perspective, it doesn't even make sense to think of a phase in an individual's linguistic development where recursion isn't present. In the first place, there are good reasons to believe that even in the babbling phase, babies "play" with a recursive production of signs (sounds and gestures, as shown in Petitto et al. 2001). The same argument is valid regarding the question of precursors in other species: if the distinctive feature of language is the infinity generated by recursive procedures, this infinity can't exist in embryonic form. Once again: it's there or it isn't. In short, to put it in terms that biologists prefer: we're not even in a position to assume that, with regard to language, ontogeny recapitulates phylogeny, which is to say that the development of language acquisition in a child mimics the historical stages of language development in our species. This simply means that it makes no sense to look for language precursors—sometimes called "protolanguages"—either in our species, or in others, unless we twist the meaning of the term "language," thus confronting the same danger that Turing warned us about regarding the term "thought."

To sum up, human language, understood as the structure of the communication code, is a phenomenon unique to humans: there is no other living being capable of syntax, as we understand it to exist in human language; and, in the case of the human species, it does not make sense a priori to talk either about protolanguages or about protosyntaxes, if we assume that the central feature of syntax is recursion. In this sense, syntax turns out to be a genuine leap that happens in nature, to reverse the Linnaean adage (on this topic, see Berwick 1997). But it's not a leap that could possibly be bridged by an unexpected discovery, just as infinity can't be achieved simply by discovering a very large number and adding it to another. Whether all this places language outside the theory of natural selection—that is, makes it more akin to physical systems than to biological ones, as Chomsky (2004) seems to suggest—I can't say for sure, although certainly we're dealing with a biological system sui generis (as we saw in reflecting on the question of the genetic basis of language). At any rate, it would be impossible for Darwin's words not to come to mind: "If it could be demonstrated that any complex organ existed, which could not possibly have been formed by numerous, successive, slight modifications, my theory would absolutely break down" (Darwin 1859, 189; see the illuminating comment in Gould 2002, 150–51). Perhaps this conclusion doesn't apply to language or, better yet, perhaps the appearance of syntax in human languages was *prepared* by numerous, successive, small mutations, gradual and silent. However, and this is the most important thing, there is no doubt that, precisely because of its defining characteristic—the ability to produce infinite structures—it must have appeared in a complete form: the infinite can only emerge in its entirety, not arrive a piece at a time.

Another decisive point concerning evolutionary issues lies in the fact that syntactic structures are totally unjustified: there's not a single aspect of grammar that can be called *functional* to communication. Obviously, this doesn't mean to say that language isn't useful and, if you will, *suitable* for communication; what it means is that syntactic structures aren't "designed to communicate well." They simply represent an acceptable equilibrium point, just like any other biologically determined trait. Our spinal column isn't *well designed*—indeed, in some ways, it's very fragile—but for the organism in which it has developed, it's evidently a favorable compromise, providing clear advantages: for example, it leaves our hands free while we're walking. One might indeed ask why grammars contain (so many) formal restrictions, as we've seen in the case of locality. To take a concrete example, why is it that, starting from an affirmative sentence like *John wants to consult an exorcist before meeting the wizard*, I can make an interrogative like *Which exorcist does John want to consult __ before meeting the wizard?* but not **Which wizard does John want to consult an exorcist before meeting __?* And note that nothing prevents me from moving the same NP after *meeting* when it's in a different syntactic structure: *Which wizard do you consider meeting __?* In fact, it's not hard to imagine what that second, ungrammatical sentence might mean—yet it's completely unacceptable. Honestly, it's not hard to imagine a possible world where the second interrogative sentence was grammatically correct rather than the first, or one in which both were correct. This locality restriction is purely a structural fact, not a semantic one; it depends on the fact that it's not possible to move a constituent that qualifies as an adjunct. The phrase *before meeting the wizard* isn't a verb complement but a circumstantial expression. The same thing happens with other types of adjuncts, such as what are called "locative expressions." For example, consider these two sentences: *Francesca has photographed a neighborhood of Barcelona* and *Francesca has taken some pictures in a neighborhood of Barcelona*. Movement is possible in the first case, giving *Of which city has Francesca photographed a neighborhood __?*, but it isn't in the second case: **Of which city has Francesca taken some pictures in a neighborhood?* (obviously, *of which city* can be referring to *pictures*, but if we insert a complement to *pictures*, we can see how truly ungrammatical the correct interpretation of the sentence is: *Of which city has Francesca taken some pictures of a beautiful girl in a neighborhood __?*). This also occurs because the phrase *a neighborhood of Barcelona* is a complement of the verb in the first sentence but an adjunct in the second (and, perhaps, a complement of the preposition *of*). Moreover, the same locality principle is at work in sentences constructed with words without a lexical root, like **Which grok does the gulc prib the pitang to gangle the brals before eganning __?* Clearly we don't have any reason connected to meaning or to communication that motivates us to select one of the two structures as acceptable. Potentially, they could both be acceptable or the acceptability could be reversed. As we've already noted, a "perfect" language—or at least richer one, in purely combinatorial terms—would be one where *all* word combinations were interpretable; certainly the amount of information conveyable by linguistic expressions would be greater than in a language that selects only some of the possible combinations as interpretable. Also in this case we can better grasp this conclusion by way of the simplified model outlined in chapter 2, where it was proposed that one could at least imagine one "monstrous" language in which all word combinations were associated with different interpretations. But, as we've already observed, there's no need to jump to the conclusion that restrictions are always and entirely useless, if not harmful.

In fact, it's reasonable to assume that the presence of (universal) restrictions contributes significantly to making it possible for children to learn languages spontaneously and in a reasonable amount of time (although biologically limited to the first years of life), as evidenced by, among other things, the absence in infant language of mistakes that violate these restrictions. Imagine if the retina of a human eye perceived the entire range of electromagnetic waves: at birth children would find themselves immersed in a chaotic fog, and this kind of stimulus would lose all meaning, resulting in the inability to orient oneself in space unless by using other senses. If there were no restrictions on grammars, the same thing would happen in the process of language acquisition: deciphering a system where every combination is interpretable would be just too complex. It's much easier to have a filter that discards some forms. First, the child tunes in to human voices and distinguishes them from other sounds—for example, not interpreting the pattering of rain on windowpanes as part of the communication code—then gathering linguistic regularities according to patterns that are independent of experience (see, among others, Nespor, Gervain, and Mehler 2005). In this sense, locality becomes, together with recursion, the basic nucleus of human language syntax: the latter ensures the potentially unlimited development of structures (hierarchical, which is to say phrases); the former selects, from among the immense number of structures that can be generated, only those consistent with the experience-independent principles that make them learnable. How recursion and locality are implemented—in formal, descriptive, and neuropsychological terms alike—remains, however, entirely unexplained.[23]

Certainly, one could argue that once humans become adults—which is to say capable of highly complex abstractions—these restrictions become unjustified, and one could easily learn and therefore disseminate any kind of language. I'm not sure there's a persuasive answer to that argument at present, but a comparison might be helpful. If future archaeologists were to find only modern computer keyboards, they would be faced with a very difficult puzzle: why are the letters arranged the way most of us are currently familiar with? For example, why aren't they arranged alphabetically? Wouldn't that make it easier to learn to use a keyboard? In fact, this objection isn't entirely unreasonable, as anyone who has sat down to type for the first time knows, but there *is* a reason; it's just that to understand it we have to know how the first typewriters were built. The earliest models, which date back to the second half of the nineteenth century, ran into a mechanical problem. The letters were printed on the paper by a series of metal bars arranged in a semicircle, operated by pressing keys on a keyboard; these bars moved forward one by one to strike an ink-impregnated ribbon, leaving an imprint of the letter on the paper. The bars all hit at the same spot; a carriage mechanism and a cylindrical roller moved the paper back and forth, up and down, as the typist typed. A typical and frequent drawback was that, when someone was typing quickly, the bars that were close to one another stuck together and jammed the machine. There were only two alternatives: either type very slowly and decrease the benefits of mechanical writing, or arrange the letters so that the most frequent combinations weren't adjacent on the keyboard and therefore the bars weren't adjacent. This is the reason for the seemingly abstruse arrangement of letters on current keyboards, often identified as "qwerty" keyboards because of the first six letters on the top left.

Once mechanical typewriters were replaced by electronic ones, the motive for choosing *one* of the possible combinations convenient for the mechanics of the time was no longer operative, but the system was already widespread and habit made the reintroduction of an easier layout impracticable (see Liebowitz and Margolis 1990). Maybe neuropsychologists and contemporary linguists are in the same situation as our future archaeologists: the reason why certain conceivable grammars aren't present in languages can't be explained if we're not able to figure out the reason behind the ones we have.

If this reason is ease of learning or, more directly, a reason connected to the development of neuroanatomical architecture, we don't know that now but, as noted earlier, we can at least rule out the purely conventional reason. Moreover, it could be that the reason forcing a certain type of grammar is related not to a phylogenetic fact but to an ontogenetic one; this would complicate the situation even more because ontogenetic reasons aren't easily accessible to evolutionary investigation. In fact, even disregarding the neuropsychological issues, we know that spontaneous language learning happens only once, and only during a limited phase of our lives: in this sense, learning a language resembles a phenomenon we all know and that's so familiar it doesn't surprise us anymore. Over a lifetime, all of our body's tissues are renewed at the atomic level by introducing new atoms into the body, essentially through food and breathing. Although opinions differ on this, it seems that total tissue renewal takes place over a period of about a decade. At the level of our organs, however, there are no wholesale changes: only our "baby teeth" start falling out when we're about six or seven and are replaced with a new and more numerous set of teeth. Clearly, it's not simply about wear; it would be very handy to have new teeth every time the old ones became worn down or fell out. (This happens in other species, like sharks.) So why don't we have "baby eyes"? To put it simply, we're programmed to get new teeth but not new eyes once in a lifetime and during a specified period, and this must have been established as a good thing in the course of evolution, because of the anatomical advantage it offers compared with the growth of the jaw, for example. Anyone observing human growth might wonder why we don't get a new language the way we get new teeth, or acquire a more powerful one while maybe keeping the same vocabulary. There's no answer to this question, but there's also no answer to the question about the renewal of other organs. We just have to be content to think that the random mutations that led to this state of affairs constitute a *not unfavorable* change for individuals of our species. We can't say more precisely than that.

In such a complex scenario, the questions seem to become infinite and impossible. Faced with the fact that all languages share the same syntactic principles, for example, we have to wonder why there are different languages, or why we don't understand all of them. And again: how does a language change? These questions certainly aren't new, but perhaps we can approach them in a new way if we start from the point of view that the human language system is anchored to its neurobiological structure and that this structure is unique among living species. Of course, we wonder why there are different languages, since it doesn't make much sense from a biological point of view; or, at least, one might as well wonder why there are different species. Meanwhile, as molecular genetics has taught us, living species appear to be qualitatively different, as we perceive them, but if we analyze the difference between an elephant and a butterfly at a molecular level, it's only in the order and amount of four different nitrogenous bases, the nucleotides of DNA. In addition, it's one thing to ask why there are different languages, and another to wonder how this state of affairs has helped to create equilibrium for individuals of our species on earth. If we pursue this second perspective, then it's plausible to think that having languages that aren't mutually comprehensible has helped to avoid overly large clusters of human population: in the early stages of our species' development, it was one thing to manage a village; it would have been quite another to manage a megalopolis. Without language barriers, the tendency of humans to congregate in the same place would have been devastating for our survival. But this conjecture, which reframes the catastrophe of Babel as a precious gift to humanity, only tells us that the system was sufficiently elastic to permit the emergence of grammars that are apparently totally different although substantially identical in structure; what it doesn't tell us is *why* these grammars exhibit degrees of variation, albeit minimal. On the other hand, no biologist asks *why* there are different species, or why there are exactly *these* species; biologists only ask *how* these species can be traced to a common pattern and what natural laws or random occurrences have operated to give them the form they have.

Also, the fact that languages change (subtly) over time becomes a new problem if we accept the biological perspective on language. However, we must resist the temptation to think about the changes in a "Darwinian" way, at least with the meaning, often caricatured, that this term appears to have in contemporary language. In fact, languages may (perhaps) mutate randomly, but language mutation differs substantially from biological mutation because, in the latter, mutant traits are inherited by the descendants of the mutant while, in the former, there's no guarantee of transmission. On the other hand, if linguistic mutation is by definition triggered by single individuals and must be transmitted through channels other than those of biological parentage, one might ask, Why are languages so stable, since each individual can produce mutations in isolation? What preserves the unity of a grammatical system? It's clear that the questions are becoming too unwieldy; we need to avoid the snowball effect. In science, as in all efforts to attain truth, it's necessary to proceed without being overwhelmed.

This long digression on the relationship between language and the brain therefore ends here, and we can get back to the central theme of our journey.

In all this, what role does the verb *to be* play? I certainly can't respond to such big questions about the source and nature of language and its relation to the brain. However, if we adopt the unified theory of sentences with the verb *to be*—which actually formally implements Aristotle's intuition that we're talking about the support for grammatical tense in a sentence—at least two general points become clear. First of all, the verb *to be* shows not only that references to our way of seeing the world (time) have become part of the human language, but also that such references are harnessed in the architecture of grammar in a systematic way that follows the natural "grain" of our neurobiological structure. In fact, grammatical tense isn't a simple linguistic reflection of physical time. Rather, it constitutes an interpretive structure specific to this "phenomenon": present, past, future, aorist (or indefinite tense), and verbal aspect aren't notions that we use to *measure* the reality of our world; rather, they're notions that we use to *project onto* the reality of our world through grammar. Furthermore, the fact that it's grammatical tense, not the verb *to be*, that's universal, leads us to conclude that the verb *to be* doesn't have a specific importance but is only, so to speak, an opportunity—albeit an extremely valuable one—that we've been given to understand the nature and the structure of language; in fact, any other element could function to express time. The central insight of Ferdinand de Saussure's linguistic thought—namely, that an element is visible in a grammatical system to the extent that it differs from the others—finds its extreme expression in this phenomenon. Thus, the verb *to be* is empty, like all the elements that make up a grammar are empty. It only has a role because it stands out from other elements, and any other element could play the same role, if it differentiated itself in the same way within its native grammatical system. So it can no longer come as a surprise that "the verb *to be*" may not have a corresponding word in a given language, as in the case of the present tense in Russian: even an empty space in a grid may in fact have significance if it contrasts with everything else, like an empty chair at a table full of friends. So, I end this book as I began it, hoping that this time the same words will have taken on a new meaning, or at least a clearer one.

We don't see the light. We only see the effects that it has on objects. We know of its existence only because it's reflected by what it encounters in its path, thus making objects visible that we wouldn't otherwise see. So a nothing, illuminated by another nothing, becomes something. Words work the same way: they don't have content in and of themselves, but if they encounter someone who listens to them, they become something. Analyzing language is like analyzing light. We find ourselves in the same situation: we learn to know that what's scrolling under our eyes right now has a meaning only because our brains are built to comprehend these sentences as instructions to produce meaning, not because meaning resides in the sentences.

Afterword

The devil doesn't stink like shit,
he makes you doubt the rose's sweetness.
—Anonymous

So, we've come to the end of our journey through time and through the geography of the verb *to be*. Perhaps nothing about the journey is noteworthy except for enjoying the company we've kept and the information we've shared, me talking, you listening. But all of this will have been useless if it hasn't left you with the curiosity to take other journeys, at the end of which I'll do the listening and you'll do the talking. No one should let themselves be intimidated by the knowledge of others, be it scientific knowledge or knowledge of any other kind. The great scholar Abelard—who, as we've seen, was so interested in the verb *to be*—wrote about language research: "In fact, the perfection of ancient authors is not such that the doctrine would not also need our studies; nor can science grow to such a degree amongst us mortals that it cannot continue to increase" (Abelard, *Dial.*, 535). So, there's room for anyone who wants to take part—and naturally, room for mistakes as well. In science as elsewhere, nihilism is the worst choice a person can make, and often nihilism is nourished by doubt, grows with doubt, manifests itself through doubt: not methodological doubt, but the kind of doubt that paralyzes you, makes you think you're destined to fail, and convinces you to never take a risk. This obviously doesn't imply either that we'll be able to decipher all the mechanisms that underlie human languages (in both the formal and the neurobiological sense) or that we'll ever understand why language has arisen only in our species. The way I see it, and for what it's worth, there's more science in recognizing the mystery than in maintaining that it's possible to explain everything, because science should not become the opium of the people.

Notes

Chapter 1

1. From the etymological point of view, the Italian word *essere* 'to be' derives from the Indo-European root **es-*, which in Italian is part of the paradigm of the verb *essere* in forms such as *sono* 'I am', *essente* 'existent', *sarà* 'be', and is found as well in the German infinitive *sein* 'to be' or in the ancient Greek *estín* 'is'. The conjugation of *to be* in Indo-European was, however, made up entirely of different roots (a phenomenon technically called "suppletion"). So, it was not a regular verb like the Italian *amare* 'to love', whose conjugations all have the same root *am* (*amo* 'I love', *amavo* 'I loved', *amerai* 'you will love', etc.), and in fact it is not regular in English or Italian: *sono*, *ero*, *fui* 'am, was, was'. Among the roots used in the conjugation of the verb *to be* in the various Indo-European languages are **sta–*, which we find, for example, in Italian *stato* 'been' and in French *été* 'been'; **was–*, which we find in German *war–* 'was' and English *was*; not to mention **bheu–/*bhu–*, located in practically all branches of the Indo-European family, from Italian *fui* 'was' to English *be*. Finally, it's interesting to note that the infinitive of the Italian verb *essere* may be inflected as a noun (*l'essere* 'the being' and *gli esseri* 'the beings'), where the plural is understood to mean "esseri vivente" or *living beings*.

2. The tradition of philosophical studies on "being" is extensive: in the Italian arena alone, one might mention, among others, the volume in honor of Emanuele Severino *Le parole dell'Essere* (Petterlini, Brianese, and Goggi 2005) or refer directly to the ideas expressed in Severino's essay (1992).

3. Regarding the concept of time in physics and perception of time, see the essay by Enrico Bellone (Bellone 1994) and the references cited therein.

4. It should be added that the properties that render an event fully completed or not are not only related to the grammatical system; they can also depend on the semantic nature of the lexical root. To a first approximation, we can distinguish at least two categories: for example, the verb *to sneeze* refers to an event that has an inherent end (i.e., is punctual, or *telic*, to put it in technical terms), whereas the verb *to read* doesn't, because reading has no intrinsic end (it's *atelic*). This second way of understanding aspect as a lexical and not a grammatical phenomenon is defined by a German term, *Aktionsart* (the 'way in which the action takes place'). Of course, it's interesting to note that the verb *to be* is neither telic nor atelic: since it is not itself a predicate, its properties, as we'll see in detail, depend entirely on the predicate with which it's combined, such as *reader* in *Paula is a big reader*, or on the type of "quantification," such as *the* as opposed to *a* in the sentences *Paula is a winner* (atelic, meaning 'Paula is the kind of person who wins') and *Paula is the winner* (telic, in that 'Paula has won a competition'). (For a critical examination of the notion of aspect and related themes, see Comrie 1976, Bertinetto 1986, Dahl 1994, and the references cited therein.)

5. The use of an asterisk to indicate an ungrammatical phrase, and also to denote reconstructed forms, is common in contemporary linguistics. In general, this diacritical mark has been used extensively in linguistics, even before this stage (for a history of the asterisk in linguistics, see Graffi 2002).

6. Perhaps it's worth remembering that the notions of "signifier" and signified, which Ferdinand de Saussure established in the modern era, were already implicit mutatis mutandis in the system of the Stoics, as evidenced in the terms *semaínon* and *semainómenon*, respectively (regarding this proposition see, among others, Robins 1967, Lesky 1996, and the references cited therein), as well as one that is difficult to interpret, *lektón* (roughly defined as 'what is said when you use an appropriate expression', to a first approximation, as a deverbal adjective from *légein* 'to say', 'to speak'; regarding this point, see Frede 1994).

7. Often it's stressed that instead of "learning" it would be more appropriate to talk about language "acquisition"; personally, I don't find this shift in terminology particularly enlightening. I'll use both terms depending on

how useful they are in a specific locution: for example, I certainly wouldn't say "learn knowledge of English," but rather "acquire." It remains understood that, whichever verb is used, what leads to mastery of one's native language is not entirely a process of importing external structure; instead, it is in large measure dependent on a biologically determined plan—a subject I will address several times.

8. For the translation of Aristotle I've primarily used Ackrill's (1963) classic English-language version—still a benchmark even today (see, for example, Goldin 1998)—because it is the one most naturally adaptable to linguistic terminology. Some choices from the prestigious Italian Colli edition—such as the translation of *hypokeímenon* (for example, in *De int.*, 3, 16b, 7) as *sostrato* rather than the more traditional *soggetto* (Lat. *subjectum*; Eng. *subject*)—would have risked introducing suggestions and concerns not immediately relevant to the exclusively linguistic nature of the discussion about the verb *to be* developed in this book, and would have ultimately made the understanding of crucial points less clear. I refer to the Colli edition here only in regard to a controversial point, where, moreover, Colli doesn't differ substantially from Ackrill.

9. Aristotle was aware that even this definition, as restrictive as it is, isn't immune to problems: given a declarative sentence in the future tense, for example, like *Tomorrow there will be a naval battle*, it's not possible to say whether it is true or false. We can limit the damage by admitting that a moment does exist—tomorrow—in which it will be possible to verify whether the battle really takes place and thereby distinguish this sentence from an interrogative one like *What time is it?*, where it never makes sense to ask whether it's true or false.

10. It's difficult to overstate the importance of Boethius in the philosophy and history of Western thought. Of his extensive and important works—which, in addition to the *Consolatio philosophiae*, one of the most widely read texts in all of Christendom, perhaps equaled only by St. Augustine's *Confessions* (see Chadwick 1981), include writings on mathematics and music—here we're interested in noting his translation of Aristotle's *Organon*.

11. If we wanted, here we could open up a boundless philological, philosophical, and theological question, which it would be impossible to deal with in depth. For example, this might lead us to assert that the famous passage from the Gospel of John (1:14) *kaí ho lógos sàrks egéneto* would be properly translated as 'and the word became flesh' and not (as it is in

Italian) 'and the verb [*verbo*] became flesh'. The Italian version is based on Jerome's Vulgate, which is a translation from the original Greek into Latin (*et verbum caro factum est*). In Italian, *verbo* doesn't mean 'parola/ word' unless taken as a Latinism. Indeed, I would hazard that one could even consider translating the passage from John as 'and reason was made flesh', given that in Greek *lógos* also means 'reason' in the sense of connected, constructed thought (from the root *leg-/log-*).

A well-attested alternative is to translate *lógos* with *sermo*, meaning 'discourse', 'language', or 'sentence', as noted by Vecchio (1994), cited in Arduini 2004 (see also the references cited therein). More generally, however, the reason for the antonomastic choice of *verbum* in Latin for 'word'—rather than, for example, *nomen* in a hypothetical and strident *nomen caro factum est*—remains to be understood.

12. It's true, however, that the lexicon of many languages, like the Indo-European ones, contains a verbal predicate that expresses existence—precisely, *to exist*: this complicates things a bit. If it's true that existence cannot be a predicate, the only consistent hypothesis is that such verbs actually mean 'to be present', but this solution has the feeling of a last-minute bailout: we should therefore keep the issue of the verb *to be* separate from that of a different verbal predicate.

13. Regarding this as well as a great deal of other information on the history of linguistic thought, I am indebted to Giorgio Graffi.

14. On the very delicate issue of the relationship between linguistic and logical form in Russell, see Di Francesco 1990 and the references cited therein; on the different meanings of the term "logical form" in analytic philosophy and in the cognitive sciences, see also Graffi 2001. Certainly the fact that only one label has been used to identify two such different ideas as the disambiguation of languages by the analytical philosophers and the semantic investigation of natural languages did not and does not aid in the debate (one might say that it is a disgrace).

15. Russell's knowledge of philosophical tradition was unquestionably vast; one need only refer to his *History of Western Philosophy* (Russell 1945). Decisive in its effect on his thinking, in addition to his contact with Frege, was his contact with the philosophy of Leibniz, with whom he shared a passion for "perfect" (artificial) languages, as evidenced by the language project *characteristica universalis*. In the essay that he dedicated to Leibniz (Russell 1900), he came to the conclusion that for Leibniz every

proposition is ultimately reducible to a subject-predicate relationship. Curiously, Ishiguro (1990) notes that for Leibniz even a proposition like *Cicero is Tullius* is considered to express a predicative relationship, making the issue of Russell's consistency even more delicate.

16. Technically, according to traditional grammars, when referring to *her* we are talking about a "possessive adjective," but modern formal grammar would predominantly say "pronoun" *tout court*. This difference in terminology is immaterial to the argument that we are going to verify.

17. Someone might suggest that in this case the verb *to be* is "implied"; however, that person would have to construct a theory of implied verbs that is not just a descriptive reformulation of the available data. I'm not aware of anyone who has fruitfully pursued this avenue (in this regard, see also Graffi 2001).

18. On the whole, generative linguistics is still in good shape, or perhaps the best possible shape among linguistic schools of thought, but I can't fail to note that, compared with the first 30 years after the publication of Chomsky 1957, the picture it presents is sometimes less clear, as if the generativist *koiné* were fragmented (which isn't necessarily a bad thing). I don't know if we're witnessing the natural epilogue of a paradigm or only the merging of this paradigm with new streams of empirical data coming from the neurosciences. It brings to mind the words of Anna Morpurgo Davies regarding the end of the so-called "Neogrammarian" model that enjoyed a strong influence in the second half of the nineteenth century: "The success of the Neogrammarians depends in part on the fact that they could easily instruct their students on how to apply the model. … The aversion toward them, however, was due in part to the fact that a good number of their followers applied the model mechanically, without making much effort to call the foundations into question" (Morpurgo Davies 1996, 346). If this is happening in formal linguistics, it certainly isn't due to the work of Chomsky, which, as evidenced by the development of research in generative grammar, was the first to challenge the theoretical model.

19. In generative grammar, it's customary to refer to terms like "agent" (but also "patient," "beneficiary," and "experiencer") as "thematic roles" or "theta roles," and the theory that deals with them as "theta theory." Theta theory addresses at least two important and closely related questions. First, why are there so few thematic roles in the world's languages? Second, is it possible that these roles are derivable from the syntactic structures where

they occur? A unified response to these questions was provided by Ken Hale, an American linguist and polyglot active at MIT over the last three decades of the previous century, who made fundamental contributions to the development of generative grammar (Hale and Keyser 2002). The number of thematic roles is limited and universal because it derives from the configurations in which noun phrases can be found; from this perspective, therefore, the geometry of syntax is the basis for this surprising and interesting phenomenon.

20. Truthfully, not even a sentence like *Peter believed him to have killed him* is well suited to the theory whereby the subject is recognized on the basis of agreement, because in this case the predicate is a verb in the infinitive, which doesn't agree. We can ignore this last difficulty, noting inter alia that in languages where the infinitive is inflected in number or kind—such as the future infinitive in Latin—Jespersen's diagnostic criterion is once again acceptable.

21. We'll see that in reality things are, if that's possible, even more complicated: for example, in Italian one says *I ragazzi sono la causa* 'The boys are the cause', but *I ragazzi sono i colpevoli* 'The boys are the culprits', showing that it's not always necessary to have agreement between the two noun phrases accompanying the verb *to be*, since *i ragazzi* is masculine plural and *la causa* singular feminine. (For a detailed discussion of these topics, see Moro 1997.)

22. From now on, I'll almost always use the term "copula" in its adjective form (as in *copular sentence*), to keep the discussion clear in case we should need to distinguish between various types of verbs.

23. It's worth noting that the strategy of applying the theory of pronominal coreference that was proposed in the previous section doesn't suffer the same blow; an indirect way to recognize the subject may therefore be based on this phenomenon. (For more on this, see Moro 1997.)

Chapter 2

1. In this form, the quote is taken from an unpublished lecture: the same content, expressed in a less synthetic way, can be found for example in Chomsky 2004, 155.

2. Sometimes, as Jaegwon Kim says, "[A]s systems acquire increasingly higher degrees of organizational complexity they begin to exhibit novel

properties that in some sense transcend the properties of their constituent parts, and behave in ways that cannot be predicted on the basis of the laws governing simpler systems" (Kim 1999, 3). This can happen in any structure or system, including the system of numbers—where, for instance, it could be argued that the real-number system has different properties than the "bricks" of which it is, in a sense, composed, the natural numbers; for example, it's dense and continuous. Similarly, a grammar has different properties than a lexicon, while "emerging" from it, in a certain sense. For a critical discussion of emergentism, see Di Francesco 2007.

3. To be precise, each property must divide the whole into two exact halves, combining the partitions (understood as the properties, and therefore their division) in an adequate way, unless of course the properties are not already so overabundant as to satisfy the taxonomic need to distinguish all of the individuals among them. I'm grateful to Umberto Manfredini for bringing this critical point to my attention.

4. For example, in standard Italian—where the number of vowels is relatively limited—we have the following matrix (taken from Nespor 1993, 61) valid for seven vowel sounds: i, u, e (for closed e), o (for closed o), ε (for open e), $\mathopen{}\mathclose\bgroup\originalleft.\aftergroup\egroup\right.$ɔ$ (for open o), a:

Vowels	i	u	e	o	ɛ	ɔ	a
Rounded	−	+	−	+	−	+	−
High	+	+	−	−	−	−	−
Low	−	−	−	−	+	+	+
Retracted	−	+	−	+	−	+	+

It's interesting to note that in addition, although this is not an immediate consequence of the structuralist approach, even though the vowels are actualized on the basis of a continuous space—in fact, it's possible to pass from one vowel to another without a disconnect, for example when pronouncing i, e, a, o, u—they are discrete elements when they become linguistic entities. If we look at the words *pit*, *pet*, *pat*, *pot*, and *put*, for example, there isn't an infinite number of other words corresponding to the positions intermediate between the vowels in each pair of words.

5. The difference between signified and signifier is one of the concepts central to Saussure's thought. As we've already had occasion to note, it was in some ways anticipated by the Stoic grammarians: the signifier is the base material that makes up a sign, and to this a meaning is arbitrarily

associated. This link is arbitrary (except in onomatopoeia), not only because the same meanings can correspond to different signifiers in various languages, but also because in a single language a fragment of the signifier can be combined and recomposed with other elements so that it expresses a different meaning. So, the signifier *pound* presents a complex situation: it's associated with the meaning 'a unit of weight and mass' in *a pound of oranges*, but also with 'hit' in *I pound the nail into the wall*. Moreover, neither of these two meanings is present in *compound* 'composed of two or more parts', as in *the chemical compound*. Arbitrariness is therefore at the core of a fundamental property of the human communication code, the so-called "double articulation" (see Hockett 1960).

6. The definition of "phoneme" is delicate and complex and cannot be given on a physical basis, but should be understood only in relation to the linguistic notion of "sign" (see, for example, Kenstowicz 1993, Nespor 1993, De Dominicis 2003, Albano Leoni 2006). When two sounds occur in the same position in two words that are otherwise identical, and the meaning of the two words differs, we say that the sounds realize two different phonemes—for example, the first sounds of the words *part* and *dart*, written in linguistic notation as /p/ and /d/. In some cases, a phoneme can contain sounds arising from different articulations, the choice of which is entirely determined by the context; in these cases, it is said that the phoneme is chosen from a set of allophones. An example is the nasal phoneme /n/ in Italian, which incorporates at least three different allophones, depending on the context, as in *anche* 'also', *anta* 'door', and *anfora* 'amphora', which contain respectively the allophones [ŋ], [n], and [ɱ]. Therefore, although in many cases a phoneme is realized by a single phone, the phoneme shouldn't be viewed as a physical entity (acoustic or articulatory): the phoneme represents a class of sounds and is essentially a psychological phenomenon.

Moreover, not all languages have the same phonemes or the same number of phonemes—a fact that can only be understood if we admit that the distinctive nature of a sound is psychological rather than physical. In English, for example, the nasal allophones found in Italian *anta* ([n]) and *anche* ([ŋ]) constitute two different phonemes: in fact, there are pairs of words that change meaning with only the commutation of these sounds, like *sing*, which is pronounced [siŋ], and *sin*, which is pronounced [sin]. In the case of Chinese, however, the pair of Italian phonemes [r] and [l] never constitute a phonemic opposition. It's interesting to note that sensitivity to phonemes is lost after a period of spontaneous acquisition ending roughly at puberty; later, it's very difficult and certainly not natural to perceive phonemic differences.

7. The calculation that gives us this number is simple: to find out how many combinations of n phonemes there are, even with repetitions and in any order, given a number k of phonemes, we raise k to the nth power (k^n). In the case of standard Italian, we have 30 phonemes, thus 30^{11}, which is around 18 million billion. On this theme of the superabundant combination of (uninterpretable) elements, see Eco 1962, Chomsky 1995, Moro 2000, De Mauro 2003, and the references cited therein.

8. See also Harris 1951 for a discussion that takes the consequences of distributionalism to the extreme, a subject we'll return to at greater length in the next section.

9. In taking this position, Chomsky explicitly opposed Claude Shannon's so-called "information theory" (Shannon 1948), or at least its application to natural languages. Shannon's idea was that, to explain the regularities in the sequence of words (or morphemes or sounds) of a natural language, perhaps a "finite-state" grammar was sufficient, that is, a system expressible with a Markov chain, a finite-state stochastic system described by the probability of transition from one state to another. In intuitive terms, the idea is that in a Markov chain the probability of an element recurring in a certain position depends entirely and solely on the immediately preceding position.

It's very interesting to see how Chomsky dismantled this claim. Instead of immediately attempting to apply it to a natural language, he constructed a simple artificial language, made up of only two symbols—a and b—and one grammatical rule according to which a given number of adjacent a symbols must always be followed by the same number of b symbols. He then demonstrated that the sentences of this language cannot be generated by a finite-state grammar, and that a natural language contains countless isomorphic cases. For example, in the sentence *aaaaabbbbb* from this artificial language, when we write the third b symbol we know that it is conditioned by the fact that at least three a symbols precede the first b. Also, if it's true that in this case there are exactly four elements between the third a and the third b, it's also true that in a longer sentence the elements between the third a and the third b can be as numerous as desired, as long as we respect the fact that the number of a symbols and the number of following b symbols are identical. So, it's not enough to know what element precedes a certain other element to decide what's likely to happen: what we need to know, so to speak, is the history that precedes that point in the structure or, in more technical terms, it must be admitted that there are nonlocal dependencies. In order to generate all and only the sentences of such a language, it's necessary to move on to a more powerful grammar, which introduces symbols that aren't words in that language (technically called "context-free grammar"). For example, a rule like $Z \rightarrow aZb$ or $Z \rightarrow ab$, read as "rewrite Z as *aZb* or as *ab*," is able to generate this language.

All of this finds an immediate correspondence in natural languages. A classic example is the dependency between two words such as *if* and *then*. When I say *then John gets wet*, I know that previously I must have said the word *if*, as in *If it rains, then John gets wet*. But between *if* and *then* there doesn't have to be a fixed number of words; for example, if I say *If it rains tomorrow, then John will get wet*, the number of intervening words increases to three, and so on, potentially to infinity. So, a finite-state grammar based on Markov chains isn't suitable for natural languages and Shannon was wrong.

It's interesting to note that this system, which grasps the core of the recursive component of natural languages and therefore the ability to produce sentences of infinite length, is currently the center of attention as a model for neurolinguistic experiments, on both humans and animals (on this topic, see Moro 2006b and the references cited therein). It should also be noted that this specific example taken from Chomsky's early work wasn't free from formal criticism (for example, counters in languages must be explicitly excluded). In any case, two other artificial languages considered by Chomsky in those early works—namely, languages where each sentence is made up of a certain sequence of symbols followed by the same sequence or the mirror image of the same sequence—confirm the conclusion flawlessly.

On this topic, in addition to Chomsky 1957 see Chomsky 1956 and, for an overview, Hopcroft, Motwani, and Ullman 2006.

10. In fact, Chomsky's early works ushered in two distinct currents of research. On the one hand, we have the abstract classification of languages in general (both natural and formal) captured by the famous "Chomsky hierarchy" that influenced the development of computer science and artificial intelligence over the following years and that is still in use (on this topic, see Hopcroft, Motwani, and Ullman 2006). On the other hand, we have natural language grammars known as "generative," a term that means

nothing more than 'explicit'—that is, able to assign the structures that generate all and only the sentences of a language without relying on an "intelligent reader" who may unconsciously adopt shortcuts (Chomsky 1995, 162–63n1). A generative grammar of Italian, for example, must explicitly say that the article precedes the noun it refers to, even if this is taken for granted in traditional grammars or better yet, in those written in all languages where the same phenomenon occurs.

11. For an alternative hypothesis that explores the possibility that there are no degrees of freedom and that all syntactic differences are forced by principles, relative to the idiosyncratic morphological properties of a lexicon, see Moro 2006b and the references cited therein.

12. Alternatively, instead of square brackets we can use what are known as "tree diagrams." For example, the expression [A B] is equivalent to a graphic representation where two straight line segments called "branches" connect the two elements A and B, thus:

A B

We can also give a label, such as C, to the conjunction of these elements: in this case, the label of [A B] is represented as a subscript ([$_C$ A B]), while in the tree structure it's the point where the two line segments come together that is labeled C.

A B

In this book, for the sake of graphic compactness, I'll almost always use the square bracket representation, even if I call the structures "trees" from time to time.

13. The hypothesis that linguistic elements are always and only grouped in pairs, obviously starting with single words, other than intuitively being the simplest hypothesis, was and is the subject of fundamental research in generative grammar. See for example the pioneering work of Richard Kayne (1984), where he proposed, among other things, the term "Binary

Branching Principle," which refers to this property; see also Kayne 1994, Chomsky 1995, Moro 2000, and see Chomsky 2008 for a recent version of this principle associated with the basic operation of syntax ("Merge"). The fact that two-dimensional representation (with trees or brackets) is necessary and sufficient to account for all syntactic relations is probably due to the effect of this principle; theoretically, nothing prohibits imagining representations in three or more dimensions.

14. There are, indeed, important exceptions to the ability to build infinitely bracketed structures. The most notable and widely discussed case is that of relative clauses. Let's take the three sentences *Andrea met the angel*, *The angel made the announcement*, and *Francesca greeted Andrea*. I can combine them by bracketing one sentence within the other as a relative clause: [*the angel who* [*Andrea met*] *made the announcement*] and [*Andrea who* [*Francesca greeted*] *met the angel*]. However, if I repeat the process in order to combine all three sentences, I obtain an ungrammatical structure: *[*the angel who* [*Andrea who* [*Francesca greeted*] *met*] *made the announcement*]. There is no unique explanation of this fact on a grammatical basis; indeed, phenomena such as this are often used to introduce extragrammatical linguistic restrictions, attributable to the actual computation mechanisms, often referred to as theories of sequential analysis or "parsing" (on this topic, see Berwick and Niyogi 1999 and the references cited therein).

15. For discussion of the relationship between syntax and music, see Lerdahl and Jackendoff 1983; for the relationship between language and numbers, see Dehaene 1999; for an overview, see Hauser, Chomsky, and Fitch 2002.

16. In the technical literature, the two terms "constituent" and "phrase" are substantially equivalent; here, I've preferred to adopt the latter.

17. Syntactic movement is an example of what is technically called "transformation," a term that justifies the now obsolete label of "transformational-generative grammar" given to generative grammar in Chomsky's early works. In fact, Chomsky borrowed the term "transformation" from his teacher, Zellig Harris (Harris 1951), but used it in a completely different sense:

> For Harris, transformations were systematic relations between sentences. ... Technically, a transformation in this sense is an unordered pair of linguistic structures, taken to be structurally equivalent in a

certain sense. ... [For me] a transformation is not a relation between two sets of sentences ... [; rather,] a transformational rule applies to an abstract representation of this sentence and transforms it into another abstract representation. (Chomsky 1979, 120, 123)

18. Assuming the contrary—namely, that the direct object *which pizza* in the example *Which pizza do they think Frank will cook?* originates as an interrogative and moves into its base position in an affirmative sentence—wouldn't be conceptually contradictory in itself. However, it would be not only counterintuitive but also less elegant in terms of simplicity and plausibility in the psychological arena.

19. It is often noted that the dichotomy between competence and performance is related to the Saussurean one between *langue* (an invariant grammatical system resulting from social sharing) and *parole* (the individual and creative act of language). The fundamental difference lies in the reference to social sharing, which is never to be found in Chomsky's works. (On this point, see Graffi and Scalise 2003.)

20. This is one of the empirical facts that led to hypothesizing "logical form." (The term "logical form" is certainly charged with demanding historical connotations, which created some confusion especially with respect to its meaning in the context of Frege and Russell; in this regard, see Graffi 2001.) Logical form is an abstract representation of the syntactic structure where, as the current theory allows, some elements move in order to attain the configuration in which the logical relationships (domain, variable-binding operators, etc.) are made explicit. In addition to movement of interrogative elements, a movement typical of logical form is "Quantifier Raising," whereby elements like *every* and *some*—assimilated to logical quantifiers—move to the left periphery of the sentence. This movement removes ambiguity in cases such as *Every man seeks a woman*, where there are two possible readings: there is exactly one woman that is being sought by all men, or there is one woman for each man to seek. In the first case, it's assumed that the phrase *a woman* moves to a peripheral position at the beginning of the sentence and that the existential quantifier contained in it takes scope over the rest of the proposition. The notion of logical form, developed beginning with Chomsky's work in the 1970s, was canonized in various texts: for example, for critical surveys, see May 1985, Chierchia and McConnell-Ginet 1990, Longobardi 1991, May and Huang 1991.

21. It's interesting to note that agreement isn't necessarily present in a predicative bond. In fact, alongside sentences like *I consider Mary a good physicist*, compared to **I consider Mary good physicists*, there are striking cases where agreement is not obligatory, as in the Italian *Ritengo gli scacchi la mia passione* 'I consider chess my passion', where *gli scacchi* is masculine plural and *la mia passione* is feminine singular. For an in-depth investigation of the phenomenon of agreement in the presence of predicative NPs, see Moro 1997 and the category of so-called "psych-nouns."

22. It's a common but controversial hypothesis that there can be only one specifier for each phrase (cf. Kayne 1994 and Chomsky 1995; see also Cinque 1996, and see Moro 2000 for a version of phrase structure that uses Kayne's theory and for further critical comments on the nature of specifiers). Obviously, in the case of Italian structures like *la mia foto di un angelo* '(lit.) the my picture of an angel', where *foto*, the "head" of the phrase, is preceded by two words, if we don't adopt the hypothesis that there can be two specifiers, we must hypothesize that more phrases are involved. In effect, this is the direction that research has taken; for a detailed theory, see Giorgi and Longobardi 1991.

23. For the sake of simplicity, we can view the element *'s*, the so-called "possessive," as a case marker, similar to what happens to *he* when it becomes *his*. For a more fully developed theory that assimilates elements of this kind to heads, and more generally for a more complex theory of noun phrases, see Abney 1987 and Giorgi and Longobardi 1991.

24. Applying this rule to the letter, and limiting ourselves to looking at the NP *many stories about Rome*, based on the ungrammaticality of **I've heard many stories Rome* and **I've heard many stories about*, we deduce that *about* and *Rome* each head a phrase (*about* is the head of the PP *about Rome*, and *Rome* is the head of the NP *Rome*, consisting of just the head).

25. The first work to propose the idea of splitting the IP into two separate phrases and to make TP the head of the sentence was Moro 1987, later published in a journal—as Moro 1988. This proposal is in fact generally associated with Jean-Yves Pollock (1989) and, because of extension to other portions of sentence structure, with Adriana Belletti (1990), although the structure suggested on the basis of seminar work by Pollock has been heavily modified and now survives only as the reduction of IP to TP (on this topic, see Chomsky 1995; and see Graffi 2001 for a detailed analysis

of this historical development). It should also be mentioned that, while the version of the split-Infl hypothesis in Moro 1988 already assumed TP as the head of the sentence, the version derived from Pollock 1989 instead assumed that the head of the sentence was a projection of the features of verbal agreement with the subject (technically AgrP, Agreement Phrase) and that TP was in a lower position—a hypothesis that has fallen into disuse.

26. The double TP label is only a notational artifice meaning that the subject (*John*) and the predicate (*borrowed a book*) are part of the same phrase divided into two segments, as if, so to speak, they were living under the same roof. The same artifice is currently used for all phrases.

27. Naturally, even in this case, locality restrictions apply; for example, the head *ne* can't cross the phrasal barrier and hop onto the verb of the main clause, as in **Andrea ne sa che Alberto ha udito molti __ su Roma*. '(lit.) Andrea of-it knows that Albert has heard many __ about Rome'.

28. Caution is required when referring to the notion of predication in linguistics: in this case, we're referring to the relationship between subject and predicate that is expressed by a phrasal structure. Semanticists, especially those who adhere to the neo-Fregean and Montagovian analytical program (so-called "truth-value" semantics), presuppose a predicative relationship that is also relevant to the analysis of a noun phrase in isolation. For example, if I say *a book*, the logical form of this phrase includes a predicative relationship, where *book* is the predicate of a variable x bound by an existential quantifier, which to a first approximation we can think is realized by *a*, as in "$\exists x$: book (x)." This usage has no immediate relevance to the theory of sentences with the verb *to be* because it doesn't distinguish the asymmetry of the two noun phrases that may constitute a sentence of this kind, as in *This is a book*. In fact, it's clear that the head *book* and the phrase *a book* are different kinds of predicates; in particular, *a book* functions as the predicate of *this*, while *book* is the predicate of the variable (on the presence of a predication relationship within a nominal structure, see Chierchia and McConnell-Ginet 1990).

29. Against this hypothesis, see Kayne 1994 and the development of antisymmetry theory, one of the twentieth century's most flourishing and innovative currents of research on syntactic theory. We'll briefly discuss this theory and its link with the verb *to be* in chapter 4 (among the works in this area, see Kayne 2003; and see Cinque 1996 and Moro 2000 for

some critical comments and proposals for the development of antisymmetry theory).

30. To be precise, this is the state of the art regarding, so to speak, the "nuclear" region of the sentence. In fact, the sentence is also equipped with a peripheral structure, where we find for example interrogative-type operators such as the *wh*-elements (essentially, interrogative and relative pronouns and adjectives such as *who, which, what, how, when, where, why*, and so on; the label comes from the morpheme *wh-* that indicates these elements in English) and subordinate conjunctions, such as *if* and *that* for finite sentences and *from* and *to* for infinitive sentences. On this topic, which is also often called the "left periphery," see the classic work by Luigi Rizzi (1997) and the references cited therein. The head around which the left periphery develops is called the "complementizer" or, technically, "C"; the corresponding phrase is therefore called "CP."

To sum up, the sentence is composed of three functional levels, built around independent heads: a core VP where, in the case of verbal predicates, thematic roles are assigned; a TP level where subject and predicate are determined; and a third level, CP, defined as the "left periphery," where subordination and the system of operators are implemented (in some cases, as in German, this level is also active in affirmative sentences). The representation of the CP level has also been refined with the disaggregation of the various syncretic components (in this regard also, see the pioneering work Rizzi 1997) into further functional levels; the result of that current of research in syntax is broadly known as the "cartographic project" (see Cinque 2002, Moro 2003, Rizzi 2004).

31. Generally it's taught that the compound *to be NP* is a "predicate nominative" and its two components are the copula (*to be*), obviously, and the "predicate noun" (the NP). I will also call the NP that follows the copula "predicate nominative," to maintain parity with English terminology.

Chapter 3

1. Logically, I should say "verbal predicates" without a subject; here I'll use the short form "verbs" even if in doing so I mix two different levels, namely, morphology (using the notion of "verb" that contrasts with the notion of "noun") and grammatical functions (using the concept of "subject" that contrasts with the notion of "predicate").

2. The Latin term *accusativum*, like English "accusative," is a mistranslation of the Greek *aitiatikón*. In truth, the correct translation would be *causativo*, from *aitía*, which means 'cause'.

3. It's hard to tell if the class of unaccusatives has a common semantic trait, although a change in status (location, quality, etc.) is usually considered a possible candidate. The thematic role of the subject is peculiar in unaccusative constructions. It's never agent; rather, it's "experiencer," that is, the one who experiences a (new) state (see the fundamental ideas on this topic in Hale and Keyser 2002).

4. It's worth noting that in Italian, unaccusative constructions share many properties with passive ones. Just compare *Sono affondate molte navi* '(lit.) [they] are sunk many ships' and *Sono state affondate molte navi* '(lit.) [they] have been sunk many ships'. In both cases, it is easy to prove that *ne* 'of-them' extraction is grammatical, while cliticization of the entire NP isn't—evidence for the fact that even in the passive, accusative case can't be assigned to the subject when it occupies the canonical object position, the subject position being occupied by *pro*. For this reason, it is sometimes said that unaccusative constructions are "inherent passives."

5. The unaccusative *si* that appears in Italian shouldn't be confused with the impersonal *si* of *Si sta bene* '(lit.) one stays well' or with the reflexive *si* of *Si comprò un clavicordo* '(lit.) [one] oneself bought a clavichord'. Regarding Italian, see Burzio 1986 and Cinque 1988, particularly for discussion of the other uses of *si*.

6. Technically, this type of null subject, which appears in infinitival sentences, is indicated with the abbreviation *PRO*—written in capital letters to distinguish it from the null subject that pairs with finite verbs, *pro*, which is absent in English. So, both Italian and English have *PRO*, but only Italian also has *pro*.

Note that an infinitival null subject must be hypothesized independently to explain other facts: for example, the possibility of an infinitival sentence serving as a subject, as in *PRO to read does one good*, where *PRO* is interpreted as an arbitrary subject; as a counterexample, if the infinitival sentence contains a reflexive pronoun, the latter agrees with *PRO*, as in *PRO loving oneself is the condition for loving one's neighbor*. These data lead to new questions, such as what blocks a sentence in English like **John wants PRO to love themselves* making the coreference between *John* and *PRO* obligatory.

The branch of grammar that studies these phenomena is called "control theory." Regarding the standard version of control theory, see Manzini 1983; for an updated descriptive version, see Carnie 2006.

7. We mustn't be fooled by a fact that could constitute an important obstacle. In Italian, the verb *sembrare* 'to seem' can also mean 'resembles', as in *Giovanni sembra tutto suo padre* '(lit.) John resembles exactly his father; John looks exactly like his father', where *suo* 'his' can clearly refer to *Giovanni*. In this case, the verb *sembrare* 'to seem' acts like a true predicate and *suo padre* 'his father' is a predicate complement, not the predicate of the sentence. The analogue of *sembrare* in English and in many other languages doesn't have this second meaning; in English, for example, this meaning is in fact conveyed by the verb *to resemble*, as in *John resembles his father*. This is also the case if we introduce the verb *to be*, as in *John seems to be his father*, where *his* can't refer to John. This fact about *sembrare* must be taken into account so as not to muddy the data with idiosyncratic interference from Italian. To reinforce this conclusion, note that, while *Giovanni sembra un suo rivale* 'John seems to be his rival' can be paraphrased as *Sembra che Giovanni sia un suo rivale* 'It seems that John is his rival', the sentence *Giovanni assomiglia a un suo rivale* 'John resembles his rival' can in no way be paraphrased as **Assomiglia che Giovanni sia un suo rivale* '*It resembles that John is his rival'.

8. For an analogy with biology, and particularly with the human immune system, see Niels K. Jerne's (1985) acceptance speech upon receiving the Nobel Prize in Physiology or Medicine and the important critical analysis by Massimo Piattelli-Palmarini (1989).

9. Historically, given that the principle requiring that a verb's thematic roles be all and always assigned to the appropriate phrases is called the "Projection Principle" and since the obligatoriness of the expletive with the verb *to be* in Italian and in English can't depend on the latter, beginning at least with Chomsky 1981 a specific principle was introduced, called the "Extended Projection Principle" or EPP, which requires that the subject of a sentence be realized, independently of the thematic roles.

10. In reality, in this case as in the case of the quasi-copula, we're already dealing with a deviation from the notion of unaccusative constructions. In fact, the subject of a sentence with the verb *to be* isn't generated in the position of direct object; rather, it's generated in the subject position of a small clause, although some works (like Williams 1984, Higginbotham

1987) have suggested that the postcopular NP of an existential sentence is generated in object position, as for an intransitive verb. We'll return to these works in the next section.

11. If we recall that (Western) grammar was also canonized in the Hellenistic period, although with compelling contributions by Latin linguists from the last phase of the Roman Empire, such as Aelius Donatus (fourth century AD) and Priscian (fifth to sixth century AD), we understand what and how much weight that period of history carries: this was the era in which scholars refined the models on which, more than two thousand years later, the cultural background of Western civilization is still based.

12. For an analysis of the semantics of utterances in natural languages based on the analysis of formal grammars, and in particular for the comparison between functions and predicates, see Chierchia and McConnell-Ginet 1990 and Chierchia 1997.

13. Note that the sentence might be perceived as grammatical if pronounced with a marked intonation. Regarding this problem, see Moro 2009.

14. Further extraction from an NP in a preverbal position would still be blocked by independent principles, however.

15. In formal terms, it can be assumed that agreement is always mediated by the presence of a (predicate) *pro* in the position of the immediately preverbal NP and that the lexically realized NP is in a higher position. If this is true, it must be true for every verb, unless we allow that *pro* appears only when the verb *essere* 'to be' appears. Inverse copular sentences would then become a crucial clue in the course of children's language acquisition with regard to the presence or absence of *pro* in a language. In English, in fact, agreement with the verb *to be* is always to the left, as in *The cause of the riot is these pictures of the wall*. For this issue and other more technical ones, see the works cited in Moro 1997. Here it's enough to remember that the construction known as "PP preposing," as in *Under the bed was the king*, shouldn't be confused with inverse copular sentences (Hoekstra and Mulder 1990). In the former case, the PP *under the bed* must be moved to a higher position, because if instead of *the king* the subject is *the king and the queen*, the sentence shows agreement to the right, as in *Under the bed were the king and the queen*.

16. The unified theory of copular sentences shows that proper nouns can also function as predicates: in fact, the sentence *I am Andrea* contains a

first person verb and requires us to conclude that *Andrea* is the predicate in this case.

17. This sentence was analyzed exactly the opposite way in *Lectures on Government and Binding* (Chomsky 1981)—in that analysis, *pro* acts as subject and *io* as predicate—proving that a coherent formal apparatus can lead to significant reversals of structural analysis.

18. In this case, even works in the generative mold (Higgins 1979, Ruwet 1975, Longobardi 1985) don't offer a unified theory that simultaneously takes into consideration facts about sentences of the type NP V NP with a semantically full NP, and existential sentences.

19. Technically, the thematic role of *John* in *John breaks his arm* is called "experiencer"; in *John breaks the piggy bank*, it's called "agent."

20. This difference can be understood formally by allowing a head's change of status to depend only on another head. Elements like *there* and *ci* share with heads the fact that they contain neither specifiers nor complements; *cause*, on the other hand, is always accompanied by at least one article. For all these technical issues, see Moro 1997, 2000 and the references cited therein; for the ability to extract from an NP by virtue of the selective properties of V, see Cinque 1990.

21. See Moro 1997 and Hale and Keyser 2002, which fully expand the consequences of this analysis—that is, of existential sentences' expletives as predicative elements—to all unaccusative constructions (not without some difficulty); moreover, they propose that *all* unaccusative constructions contain a small clause and involve raising of a predicative element to preverbal position.

22. There are marginal cases, such as *There's John, Andrew, and Peter*. The "list" effect of these sentences is in fact the attempt to nevertheless save the interpretation in the absence of mechanisms that characterize the existential sentence (splitting of the NP). This is why the interpretation of this type of sentence is called a "list reading" (that is, a way to list a series of entities that are present in a certain space at a certain time).

23. In reality, the left-dislocation structure would be more like *Un libro, Giovanni lo legge* '(lit.) a book, John it reads'. So, we might imagine a further adjustment that would result in the observed linear order: *Giovanni lo legge, un libro* '(lit.) John it reads, a book', without changing the defining properties of this construction analyzed in Cinque 1990.

24. Naturally, in Italian the second interpretation, although not favored, is nonetheless possible as a clitic left-dislocation structure. However, it's crucial to note that this second reading is impossible in English; *There aren't many prime numbers in the secret code* can only mean that the prime numbers in the secret code are few.

25. As noted earlier, when a sentence starts with a subordinating conjunction—either one that introduces finite verbs (*if, that*) or one that introduces infinitives (*of, to*)—the sentence is labeled "CP," where "C" is a functional head that is technically called a "complementizer." The hypothesis that there must be a position higher than TP is motivated independently of subordination cases and serves to provide a position for interrogative or topicalized elements, such as *quale* in *Quale libro leggi?* 'Which book are you reading?' or *un libro* in *Un libro, leggi* 'A book, you read' in Italian, or arguments of a verb in languages such as German (on these topics, see Cinque 1990 and Rizzi 1997, for Italian, and Tomaselli 1990, 2007, for German).

26. Note also that the verb *to seem* can yield inverse constructions, both with a full predicate as in *The cause of the riot seems to be two pictures of the wall* and with *there* as in *There seem to be many solutions*.

27. As usual, I refer the interested reader to Moro 1997. This analysis of *ci* 'there' seems to also adapt well to another set of constructions, those of the type *C'ho un gatto* '(lit.) there [I] have a cat'. If we want to maintain the proposed analysis, we must say that, like the verb *essere* 'to be', the verb *avere* 'to have' can be followed by a small clause, in which the subject is *un gatto* 'a cat' and *ci* 'there' is a propredicative element. Similarly, we can say that when the verb *avere* 'to have' is used as an auxiliary, it selects a small clause; this conjecture is supported by the use of the equivalent of *ci* 'there' in many Veneto dialects, as in *Gh'ho telefonà al Nani* '(lit.) there [I] have telephoned to Nani'. Under this analysis, the verbs *to be* and *to have* would be much more similar than previously thought, lending new credibility to an influential hypothesis often associated with Émile Benveniste (1966).

28. Once again, a sentence from the Gospel of John poses an interesting syntactic problem. I'm talking in this case about the *incipit*. The Greek original reads, *En archê ên ho lógos, kaì ho lógos ên pròs tòn theón, kaì theòs ên ho lógos* '(lit.) in beginning was the reason and the reason was with the God and God was the reason'. Clearly, we're dealing here with a concatenation of copular sentences: one inverse, one canonical, and one,

the last, that can't be identified a priori. Almost all contemporary translations in all languages, including the recent translation by the Italian Episcopal Conference, break the chain by permuting the two NPs of the last copular sentence, writing *and reason was God*. Possibly, the syntactic structure hasn't been adequately evaluated; certainly, the concatenation in John's sentence makes it quite intense, as if it were a sort of syllogism.

Chapter 4

1. In this chapter, I haven't dealt with the topic of pragmatics, the branch of linguistics that deals with the role of context in determining the content of a communicative act in concrete usage situations. This field of research touches on all areas of linguistics, not just on the verb *to be* in particular: new and promising developments are evolving rapidly both in the formal sense (Bianchi 2006) and in the realm of neuropsychology (Bambini 2010).

2. I share with many the Platonic and then the Aristotelian position according to which it is our wonder at the real world around us that drives science. As Noam Chomsky says, "It is important to *learn* to be surprised by simple things" (1988, 43; emphasis mine). On this subject, see the enlightening essay by Marco Bersanelli and Mario Gargantini (2003).

3. Why syntactic movement is triggered has been one of the major empirical problems and research topics since the beginning of generative grammar. Starting with Chomsky 2008, the situation has been completely reversed: syntactic movement is seen as totally free, basically a reiteration of the binary composition mechanism that takes as one of the elements to be combined a copy of a portion of the already formed structure (as we saw in chapter 3). From this new perspective, according to Chomsky, it's instead the *absence* of syntactic movement that needs explaining (see Chomsky 2008). Whatever the validity of this position—which I've argued against elsewhere (for example, in Moro 2000 and in the U.S. edition of 2006b)—it remains to be asked: if movement is nothing but a free iteration of the composition mechanism, why don't we observe many more cases of syntactic movement?

4. The absence of *pro* in languages like English has always been seen as the reason for raising, both in the case of the verb *to be* and in that of the quasi-copula, whether in passive or in unaccusative constructions that

don't allow the element *there*. The alternative to raising is always and only the insertion of a phonologically realized expletive, but we've seen that there are good reasons to reanalyze structures with expletives in the case of the raising of a predicative NP.

5. Regarding the impact of intonation on copular structures, see Moro 2009.

6. Two technical clarifications: (1) This means that a phrase XP is "prominent" in comparison with a phrase YP in a hierarchical representation, if and only if YP is contained in a phrase adjacent to XP (prominence has also been technically known as (asymmetric) "c-command" since Reinhart 1976). (2) The term "antisymmetry" comes from a property of ordering relations. *Weak ordering* is an ordering relation—that is, a set of ordered pairs of elements in a set U—that has the *transitive property* (if x is in relation with y and y with z, then x is in relation with z), is *total* (given two elements of U, x and y, either x is in relation with y, or y with x), and is *antisymmetric* (if x is in relation with y and y with x, then $x = y$). Regarding this notion and the use of the term "antisymmetry" in linguistics, see, among others, Partee, ter Meulen, and Wall 1990.

Dominance isn't the only example of an antisymmetric relation in syntax. Another relationship, which is very simple to grasp, is the precedence displayed by a succession of words (and of morphemes) in a statement. An alternative way to express the empirical and theoretical content of the LCA is therefore to say that the antisymmetric relations of precedence and dominance are actually the same relation: this is like saying that syntax, at least relative to these two phenomena, doesn't contain redundancies. However, it should be noted that, albeit in a different theoretical framework, the dominance relation was considered the primitive notion of syntax (obviously, intrinsically associated with the binary combinatory operation "Merge"; on this topic, see the fundamental work reported in Frank and Vijay-Shanker 2001, and see Frank 2002). Of course, the same considerations about the notion of dominance are also valid if we use parenthesis notation rather than tree representations.

7. One of the main problems is that, if this theory is true, then the parameter determining the basic linear order of the head relative to a complement in a phrase loses its meaning: the head being prominent over the complement, in its basic order it will always precede the complement. It's obvious that when the superficial order is the opposite—as in Japanese, for example—the only option compatible with the LCA is for the complement

to move into a position to the left of the head, as happens in Italian with object clitics relative to the inflected verb. (On Japanese, and in general on the status of the head-complement order parameter, see Moro 2000, Kayne 2003. On the absence of directionality parameters, see Kayne 2010.)

8. Let's take for example the sentence *I think she spoke to John about mice in the bowl of cream just yesterday*. We can move the indirect object *to John*, giving *To whom do I think she spoke __ about mice in the bowl of cream just yesterday?* The indirect object, like any complement, can only be copied in a higher position in the structure. In this sense, there are no languages where movement gives rise to an opposite configuration equivalent to **I think she spoke __ about mice in the bowl of cream just yesterday to whom?*

9. This proposal was originally made in Moro 1997. See Moro 2000, 2009 for detailed discussion.

10. I should say "when the sentence actually becomes present to consciousness," since, as we all know, although no one can explain why, even when we're simply thinking of a sentence or when we're dreaming, we must put words in a linear order.

11. Should this theory prove to be wholly acceptable—which of course can only be decided on the basis of the results of future research—this would be a new point in favor of a "geometric" interpretation of the syntactic principles that govern our communication code and would support the locality theory implemented in Kayne 1984—called "connectedness"—and Pesetsky 1982 and the theory of thematic roles as configurational relations proposed in Hale and Keyser 2002. This situation naturally suggests the following conjecture: that all syntactic-type phenomena can be explained on a geometric basis.

12. In Moro 2000, 2004, I suggest that all and only the predicative bonds are always the result of a symmetric configuration, thus reinterpreting a proposal by Edwin Williams (1980) in the new minimalist theoretical framework. Note that this graphic representation is equivalent to a symmetric one; the choice of one of the two representations is dictated by the fact that the pages of this book are two-dimensional planes.

13. Here we're basically dealing with a violation of what's called the principle of minimality, carried to its fullest consequences in the Relativized Minimality theory originally proposed by Luigi Rizzi (1990). Note

that the same asymmetry persists even in passive sentences like *Queste foto lo sono ritenute* '(lit.) these pictures so are considered'.

14. The fact that there are heads that are base-generated without phonological content isn't an isolated phenomenon. Italian provides an interesting case: the ability to say either *Penso che sia partito* '[I] think that [he] has left' or *Penso sia partito* '[I] think [he] has left', where *che* 'that' isn't expressed but obviously the subordinating function must remain (see Giorgi and Pianesi 1998 for an analysis of the data pertaining to the declarative *che* 'that' in Italian).

15. In this sense, a phrase is no less true than a model of the atom. For example, Niels Bohr's (1913) model, which equated an atom with a miniature solar system where the interactions were due to electrostatic forces rather than to the force of gravity, wasn't true because it was "observable" but because its structure allowed many physical phenomena to be explained. When, due to advances in quantum mechanics, this model was no longer adequate to explain many phenomena, it was replaced by another, very different one, based on Schrödinger's equation. The same can and should happen for linguistic representations like phrases. If we were to argue that an atom is somehow closer to reality than a phrase because it allows quantitative forecasts—which is to say, substantially, measurements in space and time—keep in mind that by using these syntactic models it's possible to modulate the blood flow in the brain (see in this regard Moro 2006b, the references cited therein, and the following commentary in the text); therefore, even this potential disparity falls by the wayside and the epistemological status of a model of an atom or of a phrase cannot be seen as different.

16. This network, which includes Broca's area (BA 44/45), has some interesting properties. A study reported in Tettamanti et al. 2008b has shown that this area isn't necessarily triggered by signs of a linguistic nature; the same activation effect occurs if meaningless graphic symbols are linked together in sequences generated by recursive-type rules. This suggests that syntax is somehow "prior" to all linguistic stimuli in general (for a review of studies on the functions of Broca's area, including its role in musical perception and motor control, see Grodzinsky and Amunts 2006).

17. More accurately, those neurons discovered in the primate brain that are selectively activated both when an action is performed and when an action is seen (or heard, or imagined) to be performed are called "mirror

neurons." Because it's impossible for ethical reasons to directly measure neuronal activity in humans, the hypothesis that they exist in the individuals of our species is based on measuring cortical activity via neuroimaging techniques. The literature in this area is vast, and it often seems as if the effects of mirror neurons have been overstated, particularly with regard to language learning (see Moro 2014a, 2014b; for an illustration of mirror neurons, see Rizzolatti and Sinigaglia 2006). In the works cited relative to negation, and more generally in those relating to the interpretation of action sentences, the hypothesis of mirror neurons in humans isn't essential: what's decisive, and established, is selective activity by a frontal-parietal-temporal system in the left hemisphere involving the *pars opercularis* of Broca's area in the left inferior frontal gyrus (BA 44). For a very controversial criticism of the extension of the existence of mirror neurons in humans, see also Lingnau, Gesierich, and Caramazza 2009.

18. Recall that recursion can be seen either as a simple iteration of an addition process (like simply constructing a list) or as a process whereby a structure of some type is nested within a structure of the same type, somewhat in the manner of geometric structures like the Koch curve that we looked at in chapter 3. It's this second type of recursion that's relevant to the syntax of human language.

19. What one might call an orthogonal position is naturally the one according to which reality is only known through the filter of language, and different languages correspond to different visions. This hypothesis is often identified by the names of its two leading proponents as the "Sapir-Whorf hypothesis." Despite numerous attempts to verify this vision, it definitely seems on the wane, at least since the publication of Berlin and Kay 1969; on this topic, see the critical commentary and references in Piattelli-Palmarini 2008.

20. In the investigation of the representation of words in the brain we're seeing results unimaginable just a few decades ago, both in the individuation of categories of words (for example, the noun-verb distinction; see Perani et al. 1999, and the references cited therein), and for the identification of networks connected to semantic interpretation of nouns and verbs in isolation or within sentences (see, respectively, Tettamanti et al. 2005 and Just et al. 2010).

21. On the traits that distinguish the various types of animal language, including that of humans, see Hockett 1960 and the references cited therein.

22. If we combine the observations that the structure of our language—in the recursive component of syntax—is unique among living species and that this structure is inextricably linked to the neurobiological architecture of the brain, we must infer that this architecture is unique among living species. Whatever conclusion one wishes to draw from this fact, it seems to me that the final deduction of Jacques Monod in his celebrated essay on evolution is certainly not persuasive:

> The ancient covenant is in pieces; man knows at last that he is alone in the universe's unfeeling immensity, out of which he emerged only by chance. His destiny is nowhere spelled out, nor is his duty. The kingdom above or the darkness below: it is for him to choose. (Monod 1971, 180)

Aside from the implausibility of the idea that our existence is a unique case in the universe, one still wonders—at least I do—why confuse uniqueness with solitude? In fact, I would choose the kingdom.

23. It's not clear whether Kayne's (1984) Binary Branching Principle, cited in chapter 3, plays a simplifying role. Certainly, it's been seen by many as a way to exclude (or limit) ambiguous paths in tree structures, but it doesn't seem to me that there's necessarily a reason why tree structures can't have a different (or unlimited) amount of branching.

Bibliography

Abelard, P. 1956. *Dialectica*. Edited by L. M. de Rijk. Assen: Van Gorcum.

Abney, S. 1987. "The English Noun Phrase in Its Sentential Aspect." PhD diss., MIT.

Ackrill, J. L. 1963. *Aristotle's* Categories *and* De Interpretatione. Oxford: Oxford University Press.

Akmajian, A., Demers, R. A., Farmer, A. K., and R. M. Harnish. 1995. *Linguistics: An Introduction to Language and Communication*. 4th ed. Cambridge, MA: MIT Press.

Albano Leoni, F. 2006. "Lo statuto del fonema." In *Il linguaggio: Teorie e storia delle teorie. In onore di Lia Formigari*, edited by S. Gensini and A. Martone, 281–303. Naples: Liguori.

Ambrosoli, F. 1831. *Manuale di letteratura italiana*. Milan: Antonio Fontana.

Anderson, S. R. 2008. "The logical structure of linguistic theory." Presidential Address to the annual meeting of the Linguistic Society of America. Chicago, 5 January 2008. *Language* 84: 795–814.

Arduini, S. 2004. *La ragione retorica*. Rimini: Guaraldi.

Asimov, I. 1972. "Euclid's Fifth." In *The Left Hand of the Electron*, chap. 10. New York: Doubleday.

Atlan, H. 1979. *Entre le cristal e la fumée: Essai sur l'organisation du vivant*. Paris: Éditions du Seuil.

Augustine of Hippo. 2001. *The Confessions*. Translated by Philip Burton. New York: Alfred A. Knopf.

Bambini, V., ed. 2010. "Neuropragmatics: A Foreword." *Italian Journal of Linguistics* 22: 1–20.

Barrie, M. J. M. 2006. "Dynamic Antisymmetry and the Syntax of Noun Incorporation." PhD diss., University of Toronto.

Basso, A., and R. Cubelli. 1999. "Clinical Aspects of Aphasia." In *Handbook of Clinical and Experimental Neuropsychology*, edited by G. Denes and L. Pizzamiglio, 181–193. Hove, UK: Psychology Press.

Becker, M. 2000. "The Development of the Copula in Child English: The Lightness of 'Be'." PhD diss., UCLA.

Belletti, A. 1990. *Generalized Verb Movement*. Turin: Rosenberg & Sellier.

Bellone, E. 1994. *Spazio e tempo nella nuova scienza*. Rome: La Nuova Italia Scientifica.

Benítez Burraco, A. 2009. *Genes y lenguaje*. Barcelona: Editorial Reverté.

Benveniste, É. 1966. "*Etre* et *avoir* dans leurs fonctions linguistiques." In *Problèmes de linguistique générale*, 187–207. Paris: Gallimard.

Berlin, B., and P. Kay. 1969. *Basic Color Terms: Their Universality and Evolution*. Berkeley: University of California Press.

Berman, R., and A. Grosu. 1976. "Aspects of the Copula in Modern Hebrew." In *Studies in Modern Hebrew Syntax and Semantics*, edited by P. Cole, 261–285. Amsterdam: North-Holland.

Bersanelli, M., and M. Gargantini. 2003. *Solo lo stupore conosce: L'avventura della scoperta scientifica*. Milan: Rizzoli.

Bertinetto, P. M. 1986. *Tempo, aspetto e azione del verbo italiano: Il sistema dell'indicativo*. Florence: Accademia della Crusca.

Berwick, R. C. 1997. "'Syntax Facit Saltum': Computation and the Genotype and Phenotype of Language." *Journal of Neurolinguistics* 10: 231–249.

Berwick, R. C., and N. Chomsky. 2008. "'Poverty of the Stimulus' Revisited: Recent Challenges Reconsidered." In *Proceedings of the 30th Annual Conference of the Cognitive Science Society*, edited by B. C. Love, K. McRae, and V. M. Sloutsky, 383. Mahwah, NJ: Erlbaum.

Berwick, R. C., and P. Niyogi. 1999. *Principle-Based Parsing: From Theory to Practice*. Norwood, MA: Kluwer.

Bianchi, C. 2006. *Pragmatica del linguaggio*. Bari: Laterza.

Bloomfield, L. 1933. *Language*. Chicago: University of Chicago Press.

Boncinelli, E. 1999. *Il cervello, la mente e l'anima*. Milan: Mondadori.

Bonomi, A., and A. Zucchi. 2001. *Tempo e linguaggio: Introduzione alla semantica del tempo e dell'aspetto verbale*. Milan: Mondadori.

Bohr, N. 2013. "On the Constitution of Atoms and Molecules." *Philosophical Magazine* 26, 1–24.

Bourbaki, N. 1948. "L'architecture des mathématiques." In *Les grand courants de la pensée mathématique*, edited by F. Le Lionnais, 35–47. Paris: Cahiers du Sud.

Brekle, H. E., ed. 1966. *Grammaire générale et raisonnée ou la Grammaire de Port-Royal, facsimile of the 1676 edition*. Stuttgart: Friedrich Frommann Verlag.

Burzio, L. 1986. *Italian Syntax: A Government and Binding Approach*. Dordrecht: Reidel.

Calvino, I. 1988. *Six Memos for the Next Millennium*. Cambridge, MA: Harvard University Press.

Caplan, D. 1992. *Language: Structure, Processing, and Disorders*. Cambridge, MA: MIT Press.

Cappa, S. 2001. *Cognitive Neurology: An Introduction*. London: Imperial College Press.

Carnie, A. 2006. *Syntax: A Generative Introduction*. 2nd ed. Oxford: Blackwell.

Casati, R., and A. C. Varzi. 1994. *Holes and Other Superficialities*. Cambridge, MA: MIT Press.

Cathcart, T., and D. Klein. 2007. *Plato and a Platypus Walk into a Bar ...: Understanding Philosophy through Jokes*. New York: H. Abrams.

Cavalli-Sforza, L. L. 1996. *Geni, popoli e lingue*. Milan: Adelphi; *Genes, People, and Languages*. New York: Farrar Straus & Giroux.

Chadwick, H. 1981. *Boethius: The Consolations of Music, Logic, Theology, and Philosophy*. Oxford: Oxford University Press.

Changeux, J.-P. 1983. *L'homme neuronal*. Paris: Fayard. (*Neuronal Man: The Biology of Mind*. Translated by L. Garey. New York: Pantheon Books, 1985.)

Chierchia, G. 1997. *Le strutture del linguaggio: Semantica*. Bologna: Il Mulino.

Chierchia, G. 2004. "A Semantics for Unaccusatives and Its Syntactic Consequences." In *The Unaccusativity Puzzle*, edited by A. Alexiadou, E. Anagnostopoulou, and M. Everaert, 22–59. New York: Oxford University Press.

Chierchia, G., and S. McConnell-Ginet. 1990. *Meaning and Grammar*. Cambridge, MA: MIT Press.

Chomsky, N. 1956. "Three Models for the Description of Language." In *I.R.E. Transactions on Information Theory*, 2: 113–124. (Reprinted in *Readings in Mathematical Psychology*, edited by R. D. Luce, R. R. Bush, and E. Galanter, 2: 105–124. New York: Wiley, 1965.)

Chomsky, N. 1957. *Syntactic Structures*. The Hague: Mouton.

Chomsky, N. 1959. "A Review of B. F. Skinner's *Verbal Behavior* (1957)." *Language* 35: 26–58.

Chomsky, N. 1966. *Cartesian Linguistics: A Chapter in the History of Rationalist Thought*. New York: Harper & Row.

Chomsky, N. 1968. "Quine's Empirical Assumptions." *Synthèse* 19: 53–68.

Chomsky, N. 1975. *The Logical Structure of Linguistic Theory*. Chicago: University of Chicago Press.

Chomsky, N. 1977a. *Dialogues avec Mitsou Ronat*. Paris: Flammarion.

Chomsky, N. 1977b. *Essays on Form and Interpretation*. Amsterdam: North Holland.

Chomsky, N. 1979. *Language and Responsibility*. Translated from the French by John Viertel. New York: Pantheon Books.

Chomsky, N. 1981. *Lectures on Government and Binding: The Pisa Lectures*. Dordrecht: Foris.

Chomsky, N. 1986a. *Barriers*. Cambridge, MA: MIT Press.

Chomsky, N. 1986b. *Knowledge of Language: Its Nature, Origin, and Use*. New York: Praeger.

Chomsky, N. 1988. *Language and Problems of Knowledge: The Managua Lectures*. Cambridge, MA: MIT Press.

Chomsky, N. 1995. *The Minimalist Program*. Cambridge, MA: MIT Press.

Chomsky, N. 2004. *The Generative Enterprise Revisited: Discussions with Riny Huybregts, Henk van Riemsdijk, Naoki Fukui and Mihoko Zushi*. Berlin: Mouton de Gruyter.

Chomsky, N. 2008. "On Phases." In *Foundational Issues in Linguistic Theory: Essays in Honor of Jean-Roger Vergnaud*, edited by R. Freidin, D. Michaels, C. P. Otero, and M. L. Zubizarreta, 133–166. Cambridge, MA: MIT Press.

Cinque, G. 1988. "On *Si* Constructions and the Theory of Arb." *Linguistic Inquiry* 19: 521–581.

Cinque, G. 1990. *Types of Ā-Dependencies*. Cambridge, MA: MIT Press.

Cinque, G. 1996. "The Antisymmetric Program: Theoretical and Typological Implications." *Journal of Linguistics* 32: 447–464.

Cinque, G. 2002. *The Cartography of Syntactic Structures*. Vol. 1, *The Structure of DP and IP*. Oxford: Oxford University Press.

Colli, G., trans. 2003. *Organon*. Milan: Adelphi.

Colson, F. H. 1919. "The Analogist and Anomalist Controversy." *The Classical Quarterly* 13: 24–36.

Comrie, B. 1976. *Aspect: An Introduction to the Study of Verbal Aspect and Related Problems*. Cambridge: Cambridge University Press.

Comrie, B. 1997. "The Typology of Predicate Case Marking." In *Essays on Language Function and Language Type: Dedicated to T. Givón*, edited by J. Haiman, J. Bybee, and S. A. Thompson, 39–50. Amsterdam: John Benjamins.

Cooke, H. P., trans. 1938. "On Interpretation." In *Aristotle, I: Categories. On Interpretation. Prior Analytics*, edited by H. P. Cooke and H. Tredennick, 112–179. Cambridge, MA: Harvard University Press.

Corballis, M. 2003. *From Hand to Mouth: The Origins of Language*. Princeton, NJ: Princeton University Press.

Corballis, M. 2007. "Recursion, Language and Starlings." *Cognitive Science* 31: 697–704.

Corballis, M. 2010. "Mirror Neurons and the Evolution of Language." *Brain and Language* 112: 25–35.

Dahl, Ö. 1994. "Aspect." In *The Encyclopaedia of Language and Linguistics*, edited by R. E. Asher and J. M. Y. Simpson, 240–247. Oxford: Pergamon Press.

Darwin, C. 1859. *The Origin of Species by Means of Natural Selection, or the Preservation of Favoured Species in the Struggle for Life*. London: Murray.

Davidson, D. 2005. *Truth and Predication*. Cambridge, MA: Harvard University Press.

De Dominicis, A. 2003. *Fonologia: Modelli e tecniche di rappresentazione*. Rome: Carocci.

Dehaene, S. 1999. *The Number Sense: How the Mind Creates Mathematics*. Oxford: Oxford University Press.

De Mauro, T. 2003. *Linguistica elementare*. New, revised, and expanded ed. Bari-Rome: Laterza.

De Mauro, T., and A. M. Thornton. 1985. "La predicazione: Teoria e applicazione all'italiano." In *Sintassi e morfologia della lingua italiana d'uso: Teorie e applicazioni descrittive*, edited by A. Franchi De Bellis and L. M. Savoia, 487–519. Rome: Bulzoni.

Denes, G. 2009. *Parlare con la testa*. Bologna: Zanichelli.

Di Francesco, M. 1990. *Introduzione a Russell*. Bari-Rome: Laterza.

Di Francesco, M. 2007. "Menti: Varietà di emergentismo." In *Ontologie regionali*, edited by A. Bottani and R. Davies, 123–140. Sesto San Giovanni, Milan: Mimesis.

Dik, S. C. 1987. "Copula Auxiliarization: How and Why?" In *Historical Development of Auxiliaries*, edited by M. Harris and P. Ramat, 53–84. Berlin: Mouton de Gruyter

Donati, C. 2008. *La sintassi: Regole e strutture*. Bologna: Il Mulino.

Doron, E. 1986. "The Pronominal Copula as an Agreement Clitic." In *The Syntax of Pronominal Clitics*, edited by H. Borer, 313–332. Syntax and Semantics 19. New York: Academic Press.

Dowty, D. R., R. E. Wall, and S. Peters. 1981. *Introduction to Montague Semantics*. Dordrecht: Kluwer.

Eco, U. 1962. *Opera aperta*. Milan: Bompiani.

Edelman, J., and G. Tononi. 2000. *A Universe of Consciousness: How Matter Becomes Imagination*. New York: Basic Books.

Emonds, J. 1976. *A Transformational Approach to English Syntax: Root, Structure-Preserving, and Local Transformations*. New York: Academic Press.

Feuer, L. S. 1982, *Einstein and the Generations of Science*. New Brunswick, NJ: Transaction Books.

Forbes, P. B. R. 1933. "Greek Pioneers in Philology and Grammar." *The Classical Review* 47: 105–112.

Franchi, E. 2006. "Patterns of Copula Omission in Italian Child Language." In *The Acquisition of Syntax in Romance Languages*, edited by V. Torrens and L. Escobar, 135–158. Amsterdam: John Benjamins.

Frank, R. 2002. *Phrase Structure Composition and Syntactic Dependencies*. Cambridge, MA: MIT Press.

Frank, R., and K. Vijay-Shanker. 2001. "Primitive C-Command." *Syntax* 4: 164–204.

Frede, E. 1994. "The Stoic Notion of a 'Lekton.' " In *Companions to Ancient Thought*. Vol. 3, *Language*, edited by S. Everson, 109–128. Cambridge: Cambridge University Press.

Friston, K. J. 1997. "Imaging Cognitive Anatomy." *Trends in Cognitive Sciences* 1: 21–27.

Geach, P. 1962. *Reference and Generality*. Ithaca, NY: Cornell University Press.

Giorgi, A., and G. Longobardi. 1991. *The Syntax of Noun Phrases*. Cambridge: Cambridge University Press.

Giorgi, A., and F. Pianesi. 1998. *Tense and Aspect: From Semantics to Morphosyntax*. Oxford: Oxford University Press.

Goldin, O. 1998. "J. L. Ackrill, 'Essays on Plato and Aristotle' (1997)." *Bryn Mawr Classical Review*, April 1st.

Gould, S. J. 1991. "Exaptation: A Crucial Tool for Evolutionary Psychology." *Journal of Social Issues* 47: 43–65.

Gould, S. J. 2002. *The Structure of Evolutionary Theory*. Cambridge, MA: Harvard University Press.

Gould, S. J., and R. C. Lewontin. 1979. "The Spandrel of San Marco and the Panglossian Paradigm: A Critique of the Adaptationist Programme." [Series B] *Proceedings of the Royal Society of London* 205 (1161): 581–598.

Graffi, G. 1980. "Universali di Greenberg e grammatica generativa." *Lingua e Stile* 15: 371–387.

Graffi, G. 1986. "Una nota sui concetti di 'rhema' e 'logos' in Aristotele." *Athenaeum* 74: 91–101.

Graffi, G. 1994. *Le strutture del linguaggio: Sintassi*. Bologna: Il Mulino.

Graffi, G. 2001. *200 Years of Syntax: A Critical Survey*. Amsterdam: John Benjamins.

Graffi, G. 2002. "The Asterisk from Historical to Descriptive and Theoretical Linguistics: An Historical Note." *Historiographica Linguistica* 29: 329–338.

Graffi, G., and S. Scalise. 2003. *Le lingue e il linguaggio: Introduzione alla linguistica*. Bologna: Il Mulino.

Grasserie, R. de La. 1888. "De la conjugaison objective." *Mémoires de la Société de Linguistique de Paris* 5: 268–300.

Greenberg, J. H., ed. 1963. *Universals of Language*. Cambridge, MA: MIT Press.

Grevisse, M. 2007. *Le bon usage*. Edited by André Goosse. 14th ed. Amsterdam: de Boeck.

Grodzinsky, Y., and K. Amunts, eds. 2006. *Broca's Region*. Oxford: Oxford University Press.

Guasti, M. T. 2017. *Language Acquisition: The Growth of Grammar*. 2nd ed. Cambridge, MA: MIT Press.

Guéron, J., and J. Lecarme. 2004. "Introduction." In *Syntax of Time*, edited by J. Guéron and J. Lecarme, 1–25. Cambridge, MA: MIT Press.

Haegeman, L. 1991. *Introduction to Government and Binding Theory*. Oxford: Blackwell.

Hale, K., and S. J. Keyser. 2002. *Prolegomenon to a Theory of Argument Structure*. Cambridge, MA: MIT Press.

Halliday, M. A. K. 1967. "Notes on Transitivity and Theme in English: Parts I and II." *Journal of Linguistics* 3: 37–82; 3: 199–244.

Halliday, M. A. K. 1968. "Notes on Transitivity and Theme in English: Part III." *Journal of Linguistics* 4: 179–215.

Harris, Z. S. 1951. *Methods in Structural Linguistics*. Chicago: University of Chicago Press.

Haspelmath, M., M. Dryer, D. Gil, and B. Comrie, eds. 2008. *The World Atlas of Language Structures Online (WALS)*. Munich: Max Planck Digital Library. http://wals.info.

Hauser, M. D., N. Chomsky, and W. T. Fitch. 2002. "The Faculty of Language: What Is It, Who Has It, and How Did It Evolve?" *Science* 298: 1569–1579.

Higginbotham, J. 1987. "Indefiniteness and Predication." In *The Representation of (In)definiteness*, edited by E. Reuland and A. ter Meulen, 43–70. Cambridge, MA: MIT Press.

Higgins, F. R. 1979. *The Pseudo-Cleft Construction in English*. New York: Garland.

Hirsch, C., and K. Wexler. 2007. "The Development of Inverse Copulas (and Clefts)." Paper presented at the 37th Western Conference on Linguistics. University of California-San Diego, November 2007.

Hirsch, C., and K. Wexler. 2008. "Clefts, Inverse Copulas, and Passives: Understanding Their Delayed Acquisition as Phasal Difficulties." Paper presented at the 3rd Conference on General Approaches to Language Acquisition North America (GALANA). University of Connecticut, September 2008.

Hockett, C. F. 1960. "The Origin of Speech." *Scientific American* 203: 88–96.

Hoekstra, T., and R. Mulder. 1990. "Unergatives as Copular Verbs: Locational and Existential Predication." *The Linguistic Review* 7: 1–79.

Hopcroft, J. E., R. Motwani, and J. D. Ullman. 2006. *Introduction to Automata Theory, Languages, and Computation*. 3rd ed. Reading, MA: Addison-Wesley.

Hornstein, N. 1990. *As Times Goes By: Tense and Universal Grammar*. Cambridge, MA: MIT Press.

Huang, C.-T. J. 1998. *Logical Relations in Chinese and the Theory of Grammar*. New York: Garland.

Hyams, N. 1986. *Language Acquisition and the Theory of Parameters*. Dordrecht: Reidel.

Ishiguro, H. 1990. *Leibniz's Philosophy of Logic and Language*. 2nd ed. Cambridge: Cambridge University Press.

Jakobson, R., and M. Halle. 1956. *Fundamentals of Language*. The Hague: Mouton.

Jakobson, R. 1963. "Implications of Language Universals for Linguistics." In *Universals of Language*, edited by J. H. Greenberg, 208–219. Cambridge, MA: MIT Press.

Jerne, N. 1985. "The Generative Grammar of the Immune System." *Science* 229: 1057–1059.

Jespersen, O. 1905. *Growth and Structure of the English Language*. Leipzig: B. G. Teubner.

Jespersen, O. 1909–1949. *A Modern English Grammar on Historical Principles*. 7 vols. Heidelberg: Carl Winter.

Jespersen, O. 1924. *The Philosophy of Grammar*. London: Allen & Unwin.

Jespersen, O. 1937. *Analytic Syntax*. Copenhagen: Munksgaard. (Republished, Chicago: University of Chicago Press, 1984.)

Joos, M. 1957. "Description of Language Design." In *Readings in Linguistics I*, edited by M. Joos, 349–356. Chicago: University of Chicago Press.

Just, M. A., V. L. Cherkassy, S. Aryal, and T. M. Mitchell. 2010. "A Neurosemantic Theory of Concrete Noun Representation Based on the Underlying Brain Codes." *PLoS ONE* 5(1) 8622: 1–15.

Kanizsa, G. 1955. "Margini quasi-percettivi in campi con stimolazione omogenea." *Rivista di Psicologia* 49: 7–30.

Kant, I. 1787. *Kritik der reinen Vernunft*. (*Critique of Pure Reason*. Translated by Norman Kemp Smith. Toronto: Macmillan, 1929.)

Katz, J. 1990. "Has the Description Theory of Names Been Refuted?" In *Meaning and Method: Essays in Honor of Hilary Putnam*, edited by G. Boolos, 31–61. Cambridge: Cambridge University Press.

Kayne, R. 1984. *Connectedness and Binary Branching*. Dordrecht: Foris.

Kayne, R. 1994. *The Antisymmetry of Syntax*. Cambridge, MA: MIT Press.

Kayne, R. 2003. "Antisymmetry and Japanese." *English Linguistics* 20: 1–40.

Kayne, R. 2010. "Why Are There No Directionality Parameters?" Paper presented at the workshop "Linguistic Variation in *the Minimalist Framework*." Universitat Autònoma de Barcelona, 15 January 2010.

Kenstowicz, M. 1993. *Phonology in Generative Grammar*. Oxford: Oxford University Press.

Kim, J. 1999. "Making Sense of Emergence." *Philosophical Studies* 95: 3–36.

Kneale, W., and M. Kneale. 1962. *The Development of Logic*. Oxford: Clarendon Press.

Koch, H. von. 1904. "Sur une courbe continue sans tangente, obtenue par une construction géométrique élémentaire." *Archiv för Matematik, Astronomi och Fysik* 1: 681–702.

Lasnik, H. 2000. Syntactic Structures *Revisited*. Cambridge, MA: MIT Press.

Leibniz, G. W. 1896. *New Essays Concerning Human Understanding*. Translated by Alfred Gideon Langley. New York: Macmillan.

Lepschy, G. C., ed. 1990. *Storia della linguistica, vol. 1*. Bologna: Il Mulino.

Lepschy, G. C. 2000. *La linguistica del Novecento*. Bologna: Il Mulino.

Lerdahl, F., and R. Jackendoff. 1983. *A Generative Theory of Tonal Music*. Cambridge, MA: MIT Press.

Lesky, A. 1996. *Storia della letteratura greca*. Vol. 3, *L'Ellenismo*. Translated by F. Codino and G. Ugolini. Milan: Il Saggiatore. (Orig. *Geschichte der griechischen Literatur*. Bern: Francke Verlag, 1957–1958.)

Liebowitz, S. J., and S. E. Margolis. 1990. "The Fable of the Keys." *Journal of Law and Economics* 30: 1–26.

Lingnau, A., B. Gesierich, and A. Caramazza. 2009. "Asymmetric fMRI Adaptation Reveals No Evidence for Mirror Neurons in Humans." *Proceedings of the National Academy of Sciences* 106: 9925–9930.

Lokhorst, G. J. C., and T. T. Kaitaro. 2001. "The Originality of Descartes' Theory about the Pineal Gland." *Journal for the History of the Neurosciences* 10: 6–18.

Longobardi, G. 1985. "Su alcune proprietà della sintassi e della forma logica delle frasi copulari." In *Sintassi e morfologia della lingua italiana d'uso: Teorie e applicazioni descrittive*, edited by A. Franchi De Bellis and L. M. Savoia, 211–213. Rome: Bulzoni.

Longobardi, G. 1991. "In Defense of the Correspondence Hypothesis: Island Effects and Parasitic Constructions in LF." In *Logical Structure and Linguistic Structure*, edited by C.-T. J. Huang and R. May, 149–196. Dordrecht: Kluwer.

Longobardi, G. 2003. "Models of Universal Grammar and Linguistic Variation: Problems and Perspectives at the Turn of the Century." In *Modelli recenti in linguistica*, edited by D. Maggi and G. Poli, 135–150. Rome: Il Calamo.

Lorhard, Jacob. 1606. *Ogdoas Scholastica, continens Diagraphen Typicam artium: Grammatices (Latinae, Graecae), Logices, Rhetorices, Astronomices, Ethices, Physices, Metaphysices, seu Ontologiae*. Sangalli: Straub.

Maglo, K. 2003. "The Reception of Newton's Gravitational Theory by Huygens, Varignon, and Maupertuis: How Normal Science May Be Revolutionary." *Perspectives on Science* 11: 135–169.

Mandelbrot, B. 1984. *Les objets fractals: Forme, hasard et dimension.* 2nd ed. Paris: Flammarion.

Manzini, M. R. 1983. "On Control and Control Theory." *Linguistic Inquiry* 15: 421–446.

Manzini, M. R. 1992. *Locality.* Cambridge, MA: MIT Press.

Manzini, M. R., and K. Wexler. 1987. "Binding Theory, Parameters, and Learnability." *Linguistic Inquiry* 18: 413–444.

Marcus, G., and S. Fisher. 2003. "FOXP2 in Focus: What Can Genes Tell Us about Speech and Language?" *Trends in Cognitive Sciences* 7: 257–262.

Martino, G. 2009. *La medicina che rigenera.* Milan: Editrice San Raffaele.

May, R. 1985. *Logical Form.* Cambridge, MA: MIT Press.

May, R., and C.-T. J. Huang. 1991. *Logical Structure and Linguistic Structure.* Dordrecht: Reidel.

Medawar, P. B., and J. S. Medawar. 1983. *Aristotle to Zoos: A Philosophical Dictionary of Biology.* Cambridge, MA: Harvard University Press.

Mehler, J. 1974. "Connaître par désapprentissage." In *L'unité de l'homme.* Vol. 2, *Le cerveau humain,* edited by E. Morin and M. Piattelli-Palmarini, 287–299. Paris: Éditions du Seuil.

Meillet, A. 1934. *Introduction à l'étude comparative des langues indo-européennes.* 7th rev. ed. Paris: Hachette.

Miceli, G. 1996. "Deficit grammaticali nell'afasia." In *Manuale di neuropsicologia,* edited by G. Denes and L. Pizzamiglio, 326–359. 2nd ed. Bologna: Zanichelli.

Momigliano, A. 1963. *The Conflict between Paganism and Christianity in the Fourth Century.* Oxford: Clarendon Press.

Monod, J. 1971. *Chance and Necessity: An Essay on the Natural Philosophy of Modern Biology.* Translated by A. Wainhouse. New York: Vintage.

Montague, R. 1973. "The Proper Treatment of Quantification in English." In *Approaches to Natural Language: Proceedings of the 1970 Stanford*

Workshop on Grammar and Semantics, edited by J. Hintikka, P. Suppes, and J. Moravcsik, 221–242. Dordrecht: Reidel.

Moro, A. 1987. "Tempo e predicazione nella sintassi delle frasi copulari." Tesi di laurea, University of Pavia.

Moro, A. 1988. "Per una teoria unificata delle frasi copulari." *Rivista di Grammatica Generativa* 13: 81–110.

Moro, A. 1996. "'Virtual Conceptual Necessity': La semplificazione della grammatica generativa nei primi anni novanta." *Lingua e Stile* 30: 637–674.

Moro, A. 1997. *The Raising of Predicates: Predicative Noun Phrases and the Theory of Clause Structure*. Cambridge: Cambridge University Press.

Moro, A. 2000. *Dynamic Antisymmetry*. Cambridge, MA: MIT Press.

Moro, A. 2003. "Notes on Vocative Case: A Case Study in Clause Structure." In *Romance Languages and Linguistic Theory*, edited by J. Quer, J. Schroten, P. Sleeman, and E. Verheugd, 251–265. Amsterdam: John Benjamins.

Moro, A. 2004. "Linear Compression as a Trigger for Movement." In *Triggers*, edited by H. van Riemsdijk and A. Breitbarth, 387–429. Berlin: Mouton de Gruyter.

Moro, A. 2006a. "Copular Sentences." In *The Blackwell Companion to Syntax*, edited by M. Everaert, H. van Riemsdijk, and R. Goedemans, 2:1–18. London: Blackwell.

Moro, A. 2006b. *I confini di Babele: Il cervello e il mistero delle lingue impossibili*. Milan: Longanesi. (*The Boundaries of Babel: The Brain and the Enigma of Impossible Languages*. Rev. ed. Cambridge, MA: MIT Press, 2008.)

Moro, A. 2009. "Rethinking Symmetry: A Note on Labelling and the EPP." In *La grammatica tra storia e teoria: Scritti in onore di Giorgio Graffi*, edited by P. Cotticelli Kurras and A. Tomaselli, 129–131. Alessandria: Edizioni dell'Orso.

Moro, A. 2013. *The Equilibrium of Human Syntax: Symmetries in the Brain*. New York: Routledge.

Moro, A. 2014a. "On the Similarity between Syntax and Actions." *Trends in Cognitive Sciences* 18, 109–110.

Moro, A. 2014b. "A Response to Pulvermüller: The Syntax of Actions and Other Metaphors." *Trends in Cognitive Sciences* 18, 221.

Moro, A. 2016. *Impossible Languages*. Cambridge, MA: MIT Press.

Moro, A. In press a. "Copular Sentences." In *The Blackwell Companion to Syntax*, edited by M. Everaert and H. van Riemsdijk. 2nd ed. Oxford: Blackwell.

Moro, A. In press b. "Existential Sentences and Expletive *There*." In *The Blackwell Companion to Syntax*, edited by M. Everaert and H. van Riemsdijk. 2nd ed. Oxford: Blackwell.

Morpurgo Davies, A. 1996. *La linguistica dell'Ottocento*. Bologna: Il Mulino.

Murchie, G. 1999. *The Seven Mysteries of Life*. New York: Mariner Books.

Nespor, M. 1993. *Fonologia*. Bologna: Il Mulino.

Nespor, M., J. Gervain, and J. Mehler. 2005. "What Do We Learn When We Acquire a Language?" In *Organizing Grammar: Studies in Honor of Henk van Riemsdijk*, edited by H. Broekhuis, N. Corver, R. Huybregts, U. Kleinhenz, and J. Koster, 466–473. Berlin: Mouton de Gruyter.

Partee, B. 1986. "Ambiguous Pseudocleft with Unambiguous 'Be.'" In *Proceedings of NELS XVI*, edited by S. Berman, J.-W. Choe, and J. McDonough, 354–366. Amherst: University of Massachusetts, Graduate Linguistic Student Association.

Partee, B., A. ter Meulen, and R. Wall. 1990. *Mathematical Models in Linguistics*. Dordrecht: Kluwer.

Perani, D., and S. F. Cappa. 1996. "I metodi di bioimmagine: Applicazioni in neuropsicologia." In *Manuale di neuropsicologia*, edited by G. Denes and L. Pizzamiglio, 105–135. 2nd ed. Bologna: Zanichelli.

Perani, D., S. F. Cappa, T. Schnur, M. Tettamanti, S. Collina, M. M. Rosa, and F. Fazio. 1999. "The Neural Correlate of Verb and Noun Processing: A PET Study." *Brain* 122: 2337–2344.

Pereltsvaig, A. 2007. *Copular Sentences in Russian: A Theory of Intra-Clausal Relations*. Dordrecht: Springer.

Pérez de Laborda, A. 1980. *Leibniz y Newton*. Vol. 2, *Física, filosofía y teodicea*. Salamanca: Universitad Pontificia de Salamanca. (*Leibniz e Newton*. Translated by M. Gargantini. Milan: Jaca Book, 1986.)

Perlmutter, D. 1978. "Impersonal Passives and the Unaccusative Hypothesis." In *Proceedings of the 4th Annual Meeting of the Berkeley Linguistics Society*, edited by C. Chiarello, H. Thompson, F. Ackerman, O. Gensler, J. Kingston, E. C. Sweeters, A. C. Woodbury, K. Whistler, and J. Jaeger, 157–189. Berkeley: University of California, Berkeley Linguistics Society.

Perrin, J. 1913. *Les atoms*. Paris: Alcan.

Pesetsky, D. 1982. "Paths and Categories." PhD diss., MIT.

Petitto, L. A., S. Holowka, L. Sergio, and D. Ostry. 2001. "Language Rhythms in Babies' Hand Movements." *Nature* 413: 35–36.

Petterlini, A., G. Brianese, and G. Goggi, eds. 2005. *Le parole dell'Essere*. Milan: Mondadori.

Piattelli-Palmarini, M., ed. 1980. *Language and Learning: The Debate between Jean Piaget and Noam Chomsky*. Cambridge, MA: Harvard University Press.

Piattelli-Palmarini, M. 1989. "Evolution, Selection and Cognition: From 'Learning' to Parameter Setting in Biology and the Study of Language." *Cognition* 31: 1–44.

Piattelli-Palmarini, M. 2008. *Le scienze cognitive classiche: Un panorama*. Turin: Einaudi.

Pike, K. 1943. "Taxemes and Immediate Constituents." *Language* 19: 65–82.

Pinborg, J. 1972. *Logik und Semantik im Mittelalter*. Stuttgart: Frommann-Holzboog.

Pollock, J.-Y. 1989. "Verb Movement, Universal Grammar, and the Structure of IP." *Linguistic Inquiry* 20: 365–424.

Quine, W. V. O. 1987. *Quiddities: An Intermittently Philosophical Dictionary*. Cambridge, MA: Harvard University Press.

Quirk, R., and S. Greenbaum. 1973. *A University Grammar of English*. London: Longman.

Reichenbach, H. 1947. *Elements of Symbolic Logic*. New York: Macmillan.

Reinhart, T. 1976. "The Syntactic Domain of Anaphora." PhD diss., MIT.

Renzi, L., G. Salvi, and A. Cardinaletti, eds. 1988/1991/1995. *Grande grammatica italiana di consultazione*. 3 vols. Bologna: Il Mulino.

Ries, J. 1931. *Was ist ein Satz?* Prague: Taussig & Taussig.

Rizzi, L. 1982. *Issues in Italian Syntax*. Dordrecht: Foris.

Rizzi, L. 1985. "Conditions de bonne formation sur les chaînes." *Modèles Linguistiques* 7: 119–59.

Rizzi, L. 1990. *Relativized Minimality*. Cambridge, MA: MIT Press.

Rizzi, L. 1997. "The Fine Structure of the Left Periphery." In *Elements of Grammar: Handbook of Generative Syntax*, edited by L. Haegeman, 281–337. Dordrecht: Kluwer.

Rizzi, L., ed. 2004. *The Cartography of Syntactic Structures*. Vol. 2, *The Structure of IP and CP*. Oxford: Oxford University Press.

Rizzi, L. 2006. "Grammatically-Based Target Inconsistencies in Child Language." In *The Proceedings of the Inaugural Conference on Generative Approaches to Language Acquisition-North America*, edited by K. U. Deen, J. Nomura, B. Schulz, and B. D. Schwartz, 19–49. University of Connecticut Occasional Papers in Linguistics 4. Cambridge, MA: MIT, MIT Working Papers in Linguistics.

Rizzolatti, G., L. Fogassi, and V. Gallese. 2002. "Neurophysiological Mechanisms Underlying the Understanding of Imitation and Action." *Nature Reviews Neuroscience* 2: 661–670.

Rizzolatti, G., and C. Sinigaglia. 2006. *So quel che fai: Il cervello che agisce e i neuroni specchio*. Milan: Cortina.

Robins, R. H. 1967. *A Short History of Linguistics*. London: Longmans, Green.

Rogers, H. 1967. *Theories of Recursive Functions and Effective Computability*. Cambridge, MA: MIT Press.

Ross, J. R. 1986. *Infinite Syntax!* Norwood, NJ: Ablex.

Rothstein, S. 1983. "The Syntactic Form of Predication." PhD diss., MIT.

Russell, B. 1900. *A Critical Exposition of the Philosophy of Leibniz*. Cambridge: Cambridge University Press.

Russell, B. 1919. *Introduction to Mathematical Philosophy*. London: George Allen & Unwin.

Russell, B. 1945. *A History of Western Philosophy*. London: George Allen & Unwin.

Ruwet, N. 1975. "Les phrases copulatives en français." *Recherches linguistiques de Vincennes* 3: 143–191. Reprinted in Ruwet 1982.

Ruwet, N. 1982. *Grammaire des insultes et autres études*. Paris: Éditions du Seuil.

Saussure, F. de. 1879. *Mémoire sur le système primitif des voyelles dans les langues indo-européennes*. Leipzig: Treubner.

Saussure, F. de. 1916. *Cours de linguistique générale*. Paris: Payot. (*Course in General Linguistics*. Translated by Wade Baskin. New York: Philosophical Library, 1959.)

Seidel, E. 1935. *Geschichte und Kritik der wichtigsten Satzdefinitionen*. Jena: Frommann.

Severino, E. 1992. *Oltre il linguaggio*. Milan: Adelphi.

Shannon, C. E. 1948. "A Mathematical Theory of Communication." *Bell System Technical Journal* 27: 379–423, 623–656 (July and October).

Shlonsky, U. 2000. "Subject Positions and Copular Constructions." In *Interface Strategies*, edited by H. Bennis, M. Everaert, and E. Reuland, 325–47. Amsterdam: Royal Netherlands Academy of Arts and Sciences.

Skinner, B. F. 1957. *Verbal Behavior*. New York: Appleton-Century-Crofts.

Steinthal, H. 1863. *Geschichte der Sprachwissenschaft bei den Griechen und Römern mit besonderer Rücksicht auf die Logik*. Berlin: Dümmler.

ter Meulen, A. 1997. *Representing Time in Natural Language*. Cambridge, MA: MIT Press.

Terrace, H. S., L. A. Petitto, R. J. Sanders, and T. G. Bever. 1979. "Can an Ape Create a Sentence?" *Science* 206: 891–902.

Tettamanti, M., G. Buccino, M. C. Saccuman, V. Gallese, M. Danna, P. Scifo, F. Fazio, G. Rizzolatti, S. F. Cappa, and D. Perani. 2005. "Listening to Action-Related Sentences Activates Fronto-Parietal Motor Circuits." *Journal of Cognitive Neuroscience* 17: 273–281.

Tettamanti, M., R. Manenti, P. Della Rosa, A. Falini, D. Perani, S. Cappa, and A. Moro. 2008a. "Negation in the Brain: Modulating Action Representations." *Neuroimage* 43: 358–367.

Tettamanti, M., I. Rotondi, D. Perani, G. Scotti, F. Fazio, S. F. Cappa, and A. Moro. 2008b. "Syntax without Language: Neurobiological Evidence for Cross-Domain Syntactic Computations." *Cortex* 45: 825–838.

Tomaselli, A. 1990. La sintassi del verbo finito nelle lingue germaniche. *Rivista di Grammatica Generativa* Monograph Series 4. Padua: Unipress.

Tomaselli, A. 2007. *Introduzione alla sintassi del tedesco.* Bari: Edizioni B.A. Graphis.

Travis, L. 1984. "Parameters and Effects of Word Order Variation." PhD diss., MIT.

Turing, A. M. 1950. "Computing Machinery and Intelligence." *Mind* 59: 433–460.

Vecchio, S. 1994. *Le parole come segni: Introduzione alla linguistica agostiniana.* Palermo: Edizioni Novecento.

Vendryes, J. 1921. *Le langage, introduction linguistique à l'histoire.* Paris: Albin Michel.

Wallerand, G., ed. 1913. *Les œuvres de Siger de Coutrai (Étude critique et textes inédits).* Louvain: Institut supérieur de philosophie de l'Université.

Wesson, R. 1991. *Beyond Natural Selection.* Cambridge, MA: MIT Press.

Wexler, K. 1993. "The Subset Principle Is an Intensional Principle." In *Knowledge and Language.* Vol. 1, *From Orwell's Problem to Plato's Problem,* edited by E. Reuland and W. Abraham, 217–239. Dordrecht: Kluwer.

Williams, E. 1980. "Predication." *Linguistic Inquiry* 11: 203–238.

Williams, E. 1984. "There-Insertion." *Linguistic Inquiry* 15: 131–153.

Index

Abelard, Peter, 27, 34–36, 64, 167, 191, 233
Absurdity, reduction of, 36
Accordare, 17
Accusative case, 135–136
Ackrill, John, 17–18
Acquisition, language, 88, 221–223, 236–237n7
Affirmation, *to be* in, 25, 29–30, 43
Agrammatism, 220–221
Alexander the Great, 14
Analogists, 15–16
Analytic philosophy, 46
Analytic Syntax, 58
Anomalists, 15–16
Antisymmetry theory, 198–203, 249–250n29, 257n6
Aphasia, 221
Aristarchus of Samothrace, 15
Aristotle, 30, 59, 154, 191, 221, 237n9. *See also* Greek language
affirmation without verb written by, 25
on declarative sentences, 18–20
Jespersen and, 62, 64–65
on *rhêma,* 21–23
spread of analysis of *to be* by, 28–29
as student of Plato, 17
theory of language, 13–14, 42–43
theory of the syllogism, 32–33, 35–36
translations of, 237n8
on truth and falsehood, 19–20, 19–21
on verb *to be,* 17–28
Arnaud, Antoine, 43–44
Arrivarono, 19
Ars grammatica, 10
Aspect, 9–11
Atlan, Henri, 16
Auxiliary verbs, 137
Avoir, 150

Babel, boundaries of, 209
Bacon, Francis, 34
Bacon, Roger, 32, 209–210
Bally, Charles, 70
Behaviorism, 80–81, 83–84
Benveniste, Émile, 56
Bloomfield, Leonard, 80
Boethius, 21, 237n10
Bolyai, János, 156
Bourbaki, Nicolas, 72
Brain, the
  Broca's area in, 208, 259n16
  Kanizsa triangle and, 217–218
  language in, 205–220
  Mendelian linguistics and, 215–216
  mirror neurons in, 210, 259–260n17
  negation in, 212–213
  relationship to syntax, 87, 207–209

Broca's area, 208, 259n16
Buridan's law, 51–52
Burzio, Luigi, 135, 182

Caesar, Julius, 15
Calvino, Italo, 16
Cardinaletti, Anna, 56, 96
Cartesian thought, 38–41, 207
Categories, 17
Cavalli-Sforza, Luigi Luca, 213
Changeaux, Jean-Pierre, 88
Charlemagne, 31
Chierchia, G, 56, 137–138
Chinese language, 105, 150, 167
Chomsky, Noam, 32, 42, 49, 56, 105, 184
  on competence versus performance, 98–99, 247n19
  on deep structure, 100–101
  on distinction between natural languages and formal languages, 118–119
  on endocentricity, 114
  extended projection principle, 252n9
  extragrammatical principle of economy, 200
  on generative grammar, 84, 244–245n10
  on inserting *there* anywhere, 147
  on language acquisition, 221
  on language and laws of nature, 69
  Lectures on Government and Binding, 85, 87–88
  on null subject, 130
  Pisa Lectures, 85–86
  Shannon's information theory and, 243–244n9
  structuralism and, 87
  on subject of sentences, 157
  Syntactic Structures, 83, 117, 209
  theory of language, 83–84, 223–224
  on transformation, 246–247n17
Church, Alonzo, 56
Ci, 27, 64, 146–151, 176, 181, 184, 255n27
  existential sentences and, 185–186
  theory-internal question and, 172–173

Circumstantial expressions, 225
"Cleft," 91–92
Clement XI, 38
Clitic pronouns, 48, 132, 162
Colli, Giorgio, 25
Commutation principle, 76, 78–80
Competence versus performance, 98–99, 247n19
Complexity, reduction of, 88
Comrie, Bernard, 56
Confessions, 9
Control theory, 252n6
Copula, 44, 65. *See also To be* verb
  anomaly of, 121–125
  in Aristotle, 13–28
  in era of great geniuses, 37–44
  losing and acquiring the, 220–232
  quasi-, 129–142, 187–188, 252–253n10
  in syllogisms, 30–36
  unified theory of copular sentences, 161–171
Corballis, 195
Cours de linguistique générale, 70, 71, 75
Crates of Mallus, 15
Cratylus, 16–17
Crick, Francis, 87
Critique of Pure Reason, 28

Darwin, Charles, 223–224
Davidson, Donald, 56
De analogia, 15
Declarative sentences, 18–20
Deep structure, 100–101
De interpretatione, 17, 26
Delbrêl, Madeleine, 127
De lingua latina, 15
Descartes, René, 38–41
Dialectica, 36
Dik, Simon C., 56
Dionysius Thrax, 10
Dirac, Paul A. M., 77–78, 128
Discontinuous constituents, 96
Distributionalism, 80–81, 90
  endocentricity in, 113–114
  exocentric phrases in, 113–114

on grammar emerging naturally from data, 82–83
Doron, Edit, 169–170
Dowty, David, 57

Edelman, Gerald, 206
Einstein, Albert, 39
Elements, The, 155–156
Emonds, Joseph, 101
Endocentricity, 113–114
Euclid, 16, 155
Event time, 11–12
Exaptation, 151–152
Existence, 26–27
Existential sentences, 63–65, 185–186
Exocentric phrases, 113–114
Expletive, predicate, 183–184
Extragrammatical principle of economy, 200

Focalization, 190
Formalism, 93–94, 155
Formal properties of grammar, 195–205
 antisymmetry theory, 198–203
 extragrammatical principle of economy, 200
 human nature and, 196–197
 raising, 201–203
FOXP2, 213–214
Fractals, 112–113
Frege, Gottlob, 34, 45, 46, 53, 54, 62
French language, 56, 82, 167–168
 avoir in, 150
 inverse copular sentences, 167–168
 rational analysis of, 41–42

Garlandus Compotista, 35
Geach, Peter, 51–52, 125
Generative grammar
 Chomsky hierarchy and, 244–245n10
 competence versus performance in, 98–99
 deep structure, 100–101
 discontinuous constituents, 96
 exocentric phrases in, 114
 formalism and, 93–94
 locality restrictions and, 101–106
 noun phrases, 93–95
 origins of, 83–85
 recursion in, 93–95
 structuralism and, 85, 91–92
 syntactic movement and, 97–99, 239–240n19
 theoretical scaffolding in advancement of, 86–87
Genetics and language, 213–216, 229–231
God, 42
Gospel of John, 237–238n11, 255–256n28
Gould, Stephen Jay, 215–216, 218
Graffi, Giorgio, 69, 96, 101, 119
Grammaire générale et raisonnée: Contenant les fondemens de l'art de parler, expliqués d'une manière claire et naturelle, 41, 43–44
Grammar
 deep, 100–101
 distributionalism and, 82–83
 form of, between linearity and hierarchy, 195–205
 generative (*See* Generative grammar)
 as linear concatenation mechanism, 83–84
 non-Euclidean, 152–161
 Port-Royal school and, 37–42
Greek language, 14–15, 237–238n11. *See also* Aristotle
 foundations of civilization laid in, 16
 Gospel of John, 237–238n11, 255–256n28
 linguistic analysis method, 15
 philosophical reflection on, 16–17
Greenbaum, Sidney, 56
Greenberg, Joseph, 119
Grevisse, Maurice, 56
Grosu, A., 169
Growth and Structure of the English Language, 58
Grundgesetze der Aritmetik (Foundations of Arithmetic, The), 53

Hale, Ken, 135
Halle, Morris, 72, 83
Halliday, M. A. K., 56
Hebrew language, 169–170
Higginbotham, James, 177
Higgins, Roger, 125
History of Western Philosophy, 238n15
Huang, C.-T. James, 105
Hungarian language, 3

Identity and *to be,* 46–57
Il Novellino, 193
Imperfect tense, 11
Inflection, 117–118
Information theory, 243–244n9
Interrogative predicate, 168
Inverse copular sentence, 253n15
Italian language, 24–26, 56, 85–86, 129, 198
  accordare in, 17
  arrivarono in, 19
  auxiliary verbs, 137
  ci in, 27, 64, 146–151, 176, 255n27
  clitic pronouns in, 48, 132, 162
  commutation classes in, 80
  complex NP structure not possible in, 110
  dialects, 135
  esistere in, 27
  essere in, 234n1
  existential sentences in, 63
  is and *and* in, 18
  morphemes in, 77
  ne in, 116–117, 122
  noninfinitive subordinate clauses, 139–140
  null-subjects in, 147–148
  phonemes in, 76
  pro in, 165–166
  pronoun inflections in, 59–60
  quasi-copula in, 142
  raising verbs in, 125
  redundancy principle in, 77, 201
  sembrare in, 252n7
  subject/predicate asymmetry in, 164–165
  tempo in, 8
  temproral relationships in, 12
  to be as always necessary in, 3
  unaccusative construction in, 136, 251n4–5
  verb inflection in, 23
  verbs without predicate in, 27
  vowels in, 74, 241n4
  word combinations in, 104

Jakobson, Roman, 72, 83
Japanese language, 120
Jespersen, Otto, 45, 52, 89, 164
  on existential sentences, 64–65
  and the revenge of language, 57–67
  on scientific thought applied to grammar, 58
  verbs without subjects and, 142–143, 149
Joos, Martin, 209
Joy of Believing, The, 127

Kanizsa, Gaetano, 217
Kanizsa triangle, 217–218
Kant, Immanuel, 28, 34
Katz, Jerrold, 56
Kayne, Richard, 170, 199
Keyser, Samuel Jay, 135
Kneale, Martha, 34
Kneale, William, 34
Koch, Helge von, 112–113
Koch curve, 112–113

Language
  acquisition, 88, 221–223, 236–237n7
  in the brain, 205–220
  Chomsky's theory of, 83–84, 223–224
  emergence of human, 222
  genetics and, 213–216, 229–231
  Kanizsa triangle and, 217–218
  Mendelian linguistics, 215–216
  protolanguages, 223
  Sapir-Whorf hypothesis and, 260n19
  unpredictable differing in, 209
Language, 80
"Learning by forgetting," 88

Lectures on Government and Binding, 85, 87–88, 147
Leibniz, Gottfried Wilhelm, 39
Lepschy, Giulio, 85, 119, 157
Lewontin, Richard, 215–216, 218
Lezioni americane, 16
Linearity and hierarchy, form of grammar between, 195–205
Lobachevsky, Nikolai Ivanovich, 156
Locality restrictions, 101–109, 225–226
   to be and, 106–109
Logical form, 101, 238n14, 247n20
Longobardi, Giuseppe, 125, 191
Lorhard, Jacob, 27

Maltese language, 3
Mandelbrot, Benoît, 112
Martianus Capella, 31
McConnell-Ginet, Sally, 56
Medawar, Peter, 214
Mehler, Jacques, 88
Meillet, Antoine, 29, 82
Mémoire sur le système primitif des voyelles dans les langues indo-européennes, 70
Mendelian linguistics, 215–216
Michelson, Albert, 81
Middle Ages, the, 30–36
Mirror neurons, 210, 259–260n17
Modern English Grammar on Historical Principles, A, 57–58
Modistae, 32, 212
Monod, Jacques, 261n22
Montague, Richard, 56–57
Montague grammar, 54, 56–57
Morphemes, 77, 89, 110
Mutatis mutandis, 151–152

Natural language philosophy, 45, 193–195, 209–210
   distinction between formal languages and natural languages, 118–119
   on identity, 46–57
Natural language theory, 84
Ne (pronoun), 122
Negation in the brain, 212–213

Neogrammarians, 239n18
Neuroimaging, 207–208, 260n20
Neuropsychology, 206
New Essays on Human Understanding, 39
Newton, Isaac, 39, 207
Non-Euclidean grammars, 152–161
Noninfinitive subordinate clauses, 139–140
Nouns, 24–25
   Jespersen on distinction between verb and, 60–61
   phrases, 49, 61–62, 93–95
   replaced by clitic pronouns, 48
   type theory and, 54
Null subjects, 130–132, 165–167, 171, 251n6

Open class words, 168
Organon, 25, 30

Parameters, syntactic, 86–87, 120
Partee, Barbara, 56, 57
Pascale, Blaise, 38
Pavlov, Ivan, 80
Pereltsvaig, Asya, 170
Perlmutter, David, 135, 182
Perrin, Jean-Baptiste, 41
Peters, Stanley, 57
Philosophy of Grammar, The, 58, 61
Phonemes, 76, 242–243n6
Phonology, 72, 74–75
Physics, 81–82
Physics Today, 81
Piattelli-Palmarini, Massimo, 16
Pike, Kenneth, 96
Pisa Lectures, 85–86
Plain cleft sentences, 165
Plato, 1, 16–17, 22, 59
Poetics, 17
Port-Royal school, 37–44, 55, 191
   Jespersen and, 62, 65–66
Posterior Analytics, 26, 28
Postulate, subject, 152–161
Predicate(s)
   detection of, 51–52
   expletive, 183–184

Predicate(s) (cont.)
  interrogative, 168
  subject asymmetry, 164–165
  and subjects structure, 21, 24, 29, 59, 157–161, 249n28
  to be as identity, 50–51, 62
  verbal, 157–158, 250n1
Principia Mathematica, 54
Prior Analytics, 32–33
Priscian, 19
Pro (pronoun), 165–166, 256–257n4
Projection principle, 252n9
Pronouns
  clitic, 48, 132, 162
  its, 50–51
  ne, 116–117
  null-subjects, 131
  pro, 165–166
  third person, 59–60
Proof by contradiction, 27
Protolanguages, 223
Pseudocleft sentences, 165
Psyche, human, 39–40

Quasi-copula, 129–142, 187–188, 252–253n10
Quine, Willard Van Orman, 52, 56
Quirk, Randolph, 56

Racine, Jean, 38
Raising verbs, 125, 140–142, 201–203
Recursion, 94–96, 211, 260n18, 261n22
Reduction of complexity, 88
Reduction to absurdity (reductio ad absurdum), 36
Redundancy principle, 76–77, 201
Reference time, 11–12
Referentiality, 51
Reichenbach, Hans, 11–12
Relativized Minimality theory, 257–258n13
Renzi, Lorenzo, 56, 96
Retrieval principle, 76, 77–78
Rhêma, 21–23, 25
Riemsdijk, Henk van, 85
Ries, John, 18

Rizzi, Luigi, 100
  on null subject, 130
Rizzolatti, Giacomo, 210
Ross, John, 105
Rothstein, Susan, 157
Russell, Bertrand, 45, 191, 192, 238–239n15
  distance from linguists, 47
  identity and, 46–57
  Jespersen and, 62, 63
  on pronouns, 48–49
  rebuilding of mathematics (logic) to eliminate paradoxes, 53
  Russell antimony, 53–54
  type theory and, 55
Russian language, 3, 9, 170, 232
Ruwet, Nicolas, 125

Salernitano, Masuccio, 193
Salvi, Giampaolo, 56, 96
Sapir-Whorf hypothesis, 260n19
Saussure, Ferdinand de, 3, 87, 236n6
  interest in linguistics, 69–70
  on signfied/signifier, 75, 209, 241n5
  on structure, 71, 75
Schola Palatina, 31
Scholasticism, 30, 35
Schrödinger, Erwin, 77–78
Sechehaye, Albert, 70
Seidel, Eugen, 18
Sentence(s)
  anomaly of the copula and, 121–125
  behaviorism and, 83–84
  commutation principle in, 76, 78–80
  distributionalism and, 82–83
  existential, 63–65, 185–186
  formalism and, 93–94
  generative grammar and (*See* Generative grammar)
  inflection of, 117–118
  inverse copular, 253n15
  locality restrictions, 101–109
  molecules of words and, 85–120
  new theory of, 115–120, 128
  noninfinitive subordinate clauses, 139–140

Index

nuclear region of, 250n30
pseudocleft versus plain cleft, 165
quasi-copula and, 129–142
recursion and, 94–96
redundancy principle in, 76–77
retrieval principle in, 76, 77–78
revolution in analysis of, 81–85
Saussure on, 69–71
structuralism applied to, 71–76, 85–86, 90–92
syntactic movement and, 97–99
theory of language and, 84–85
unified theory of copular, 161–171, 253–254n16
verbs without subjects, 142–152
Shannon, Claude, 243–244n9
Shlonsky, U., 169
Signifiers/signified, 75, 209, 241n5
Six Memos for the Next Millennium, 16
Skinner, B. F., 83–84
Sophist, 17
Spanish language, 4
Speech time, 11–12
Steinthal, Heymann, 15
Stoics, 9–10, 135
Structuralism
"cleft" examination, 91–92
commutation principle, 76, 78–80
distributionalism and, 80–81, 90
generative grammar and, 85
in phonology, 72, 74–75
redundancy principle, 76–77
retrieval principle, 76, 77–78
Saussure on, 70–71, 75
spread of ideas related to, 71–72
syntactic elements with different positions in structure and same grammatical function, 96
on value of element in relationship to other elements, 72–76
on word flow in sentences, 90–91
word movement in sentences and, 101–103
Subjects
null-, 130–132, 165–167, 171
postulate, 152–161

and predicate asymmetry, 164–165
and predicate structure, 21, 24, 29, 59, 157–161, 249n28
verbs without (*see* Verbs without subjects)
Subphrasal elements, 113–114
"Switching," 79
Syllogisms, copula in, 30–36
Syntactic movement, 97–99, 119, 239–240n19, 246–247n17, 256n3
Syntactic Structures, 83, 117, 209
Syntactic trees, 99–100
Syntax, 85. *See also* Generative grammar
the brain and, 87, 207–209
discontinuous constituents, 96
elementary cell of, 111–112
formalism and, 93–94
parameters and principles, 86–87, 120
recursion, 93–95, 211, 261n22
relationship between the brain and, 87
rescue mechanism, 200

Tarski, Alfred, 56
Téchne grammatiké, 10
Telegraphic speech, 220
Tempo, 8
Tense, 7–13, 24, 237n9
aspect and, 9–11
copula in Aristotle and, 13–28, 65
imperfect, 11
Tettamanti, M., 212
Theaetetus, 16
Theory-internal question, 172
There is, 142–152, 171–192
Time, 9–10
speech, event, and reference, 11–12
To be verb. *See also* Copula
agrammatism and, 220–221
Aristotle's theory on, 17–29
difficulty in analyzing, 2, 8, 13, 66–67, 233–234
as element in linguistic systems, 5
history of schools of thought on, 6–7
as identity predicate, 46–57, 62

To be verb. *See also* Copula (cont.)
  as key term in philosophical thought, 5–6
  lack of equivalent in all languages, 2–3
  as linchpin of syllogism, 34
  locality theory and, 106–109, 225–226
  as necessary in Italian and English, 3
  noun phrases and, 49, 61–62
  as predicate of existence, 26–27, 64–65
  shattering the scaffolding of the sentence, 121–125
  in subject and predicate structure, 21, 24, 29, 59
  as support for verbal inflection, 8
  tense and, 7–28, 65
  in unaccusative constructions, 151–152
  unified theory of copular sentences, 161–171
  variations in different languages, 3–4
  as verb without subject, 142–152
  viewed as a verb, 4
Trubetzkoy, Nikolai Sergeyevich, 72
Truth, 19–21
Turing, Alan, 221–222
200 Years of Syntax, 69
Type theory, 54–55

Unaccusative constructions, 135–138, 151–152, 251n3–5, 256–257n4
Unified theory of copular sentences, 161–171, 253–254n16

Vendryes, Joseph, 29
Verbal aspect, 9–11
Verbal Behavior, 83–84
Verbal inflection, 8, 13
Verbal predicates, 157–158, 250n1
Verbs without subjects, 127–129
  accusative case, 135–136
  dependent clauses, 141
  expression position in space, 137–138
  "non-Euclidean" grammars and subject postulate, 152–161

null-subjects, 130–132
quasi-copula, 129–142
there is, 171–192
to be and *there is*, 142–152
unaccusative constructions, 135–138
unified theory of copular sentences, 161–171
Vowels, 74, 241n4

Wall, Robert, 57
Watson, James, 87
Wexler, Kenneth, 221
Whitehead, Alfred North, 17, 54
Williams, Edwin, 177
Wittgenstein, Ludwig, 46
Word(s)
  combinations, restrictions on, 104
  definition of, 89
  flow in sentence, 90–91
  locality restrictions, 101–106
  open class, 168
World Atlas of Linguistic Structures Online, 3, 4

Zermelo, Ernst, 54

www.ingramcontent.com/pod-product-compliance
Lightning Source LLC
Chambersburg PA
CBHW021347300426
44114CB00012B/1113